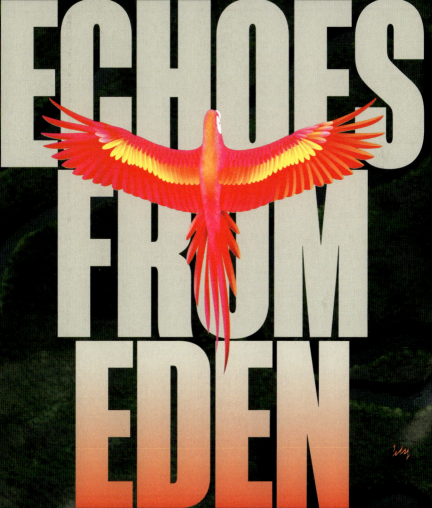

DAX DASILVA
WITH ERIC HENDRIKX

ECHOES FROM EDEN

A DARING VOYAGE TO PROTECT
EARTH'S LAST WILD PLACES

VICTORY BELT PUBLISHING INC.
LAS VEGAS

First published in 2025 by Victory Belt Publishing Inc.

Copyright © 2025 Dax Dasilva

No part of this publication may be reproduced or distributed in any form or by any means, electronic or mechanical, or stored in a database or retrieval system, without prior written permission from the publisher.

ISBN-13: 978-1-628605-69-3

Cover design by Baillat Studio

Interior design and illustrations by Alyanna Alcira, Charisse Reyes, Elita San Juan, and Justin-Aaron Velasco

Author photo by Hector Perez

Back cover photos by Kalaweit (top), Matt Brunette (middle), and Age of Union (bottom)

Printed in Canada
TC 0125

This book is dedicated to the wild animals and untamed places of Eden—whose survival depends not on fate, but on the evolution of human consciousness.

It is also dedicated to Dr. Jane Goodall—a woman I deeply admire, a friend I cherish, and a lifelong warrior for nature whose unwavering dedication continues to inspire us all to act.

All proceeds from this book will be donated to the Jane Goodall Legacy Foundation, ensuring that her extraordinary work carries on for generations to come.

View of the Madre de Dios region in southeastern Peru's Amazon basin.
Credit: Dan Ng

CONTENTS

- 9   FOREWORD: *Jane Goodall*
- 13   PREFACE: *A War in the Woods*

- 19   CHAPTER 1: *Madre de Dios*
- 73   CHAPTER 2: *The Congo Divide*
- 117   CHAPTER 3: *Children of Baille Tourible*
- 147   CHAPTER 4: *The Ghost Fleet of La Rochelle*
- 185   CHAPTER 5: *The Night Watchers of Matura*
- 215   CHAPTER 6: *Where the Wolf Drinks First*
- 243   CHAPTER 7: *The Silence of the Gibbons*
- 277   CHAPTER 8: *Whispers of the Indri*
- 311   CHAPTER 9: *Blessings in Amazonia*

- 347   EPILOGUE
- 351   ACKNOWLEDGMENTS
- 353   AGE OF UNION: *Partnerships and Projects*

Dr. Jane Goodall.
Credit: Richard Ladkani

FOREWORD

JANE GOODALL

Since 1986, I have traveled almost constantly around the globe to raise awareness about the harm we have done and are doing to the environment of our planet. To stress the urgent need for conservation. And to raise funds for the environmental and educational projects of the Jane Goodall Institute.

For years I have worked to improve our relationship with the animals with whom we share, or should share, the planet. And to help people realize that every animal, just like every human, is an individual with a personality and feelings. And that many are, in fact, highly intelligent.

Today we are going through dark times, and my mission has extended to the desperate need to give people hope—for the future of our children and life on Earth.

One of the questions I am asked most often is: Do you honestly believe there is hope for our world? And I answer truthfully that we do have a window of time during which we can start healing the harm we have inflicted on the planet—but that window is closing. If we care about the future of our children, and theirs, and if we care about the health of the natural world, we must get together and take action *now*. Now—before it is too late.

My definition of hope is different from simple optimism—just passively hoping that something will happen. No, for me hope is generated through action. An understanding that every one of us makes an impact on the planet *every* day, and if millions of us undertake even small actions for good—saving water and energy, picking up trash, caring for a sick and homeless dog, sponsoring a disadvantaged child's education—well, the cumulative effect of thousands of ethical actions will improve our world for future generations.

During my travels, I meet a number of remarkable people who are also dedicated to preserving habitats and standing up against the wrongs being inflicted on nature. One such individual is Dax Dasilva, an environmental activist who has prioritized the concept of direct action in conservation. Using methods that he developed as a tech leader and entrepreneur, Dax has helped nonprofit conservation organizations around the world bring communities together to secure the safety of endangered habitats and animals. While we do not come from the same backgrounds and our experiences have been different, Dax and I both feel a strong spiritual connection to the natural world and share a commitment to improving the health and future of our planet. And we both believe that hope is generated through positive actions for good.

It should come as no surprise that I have invited Dax to join the Jane Goodall Legacy Foundation Council for Hope, where he will work in collaboration with other influential individuals from fields of conservation, government, science, business, media, and the arts to make a better world for people, animals, and the environment.

Recently, Dax and I experienced an unforgettable journey to the Amazon Rainforest in Brazil. In the village of Kaarimã, deep in Amazonia, we were welcomed by the Xipaya Indigenous community, where we learned about their urgent need for protection from the destructive impacts of gold mining in their rivers. We received blessings in the forest from their chief, Juma Xipaia—a powerful young woman whom you'll come to know, along with her husband, Hugo, in the pages of this book.

Echoes from Eden tells the story of how Dax first experienced conservation in Canada during a protest against logging. He had an epiphany, realizing it was his duty to help protect the natural world. Soon after that, he founded a successful tech company, yet he never lost sight of the need to protect nature. This book recounts his adventures and the challenges he encountered as he worked to support and empower a number of conservation projects around the world in places where help is most needed. It is a testament to the power of direct action, a blueprint for environmental conservation, and, as well, a deeply personal exploration of spirituality and stewardship of the Earth.

In reading Dax's book, I am reminded of the days when I dreamed of going to Africa, living with wild animals, and writing books about them. The books that inspired me then were *The Voyages of Doctor Dolittle* and *Tarzan of the Apes* (also *The Jungle Book*) and accounts of the adventures of early explorers of "Darkest Africa." *Echoes from Eden* will, I am sure, inspire a desire in many young readers to help protect vital ecosystems and threatened animal species in different parts of the world. And Dax reminds us that each of us has a role to play in safeguarding our planet's future.

It was because of my admiration for Dax that I was honored to be asked to write this foreword for *Echoes from Eden*.

Jane Goodall, PhD, DBE
Founder of the Jane Goodall Institute
UN Messenger of Peace

View of Clayoquot Sound off the west coast of Vancouver Island in the Canadian province of British Columbia. Credit: Dave Hutchinson

Preface

A WAR IN THE WOODS

THE BATTLE FOR CLAYOQUOT SOUND

In the summer of 1993, I stood on the front lines of what would become one of the most significant environmental protests in Canadian history: the War in the Woods at Clayoquot Sound. More than twelve thousand activists—led by Canadian environmentalist Tzeporah Berman—converged on Vancouver Island to oppose the rampant logging of ancient forests, trees that had stood for centuries and sheltered countless species.

I was sixteen years old. My stepbrother, Doug, and I joined the massive blockade where the old-growth forests were being destroyed by loggers. On our drive to the protest, we witnessed miles and miles of moonscape land that had been decimated. Millions of trees had been turned to sawdust, leaving the land dead, a graveyard of what was once a vibrant ecosystem, filled with millions, if not billions, of heartbeats. I felt sick to my stomach. I was young, but I felt rage like few times I've experienced in my life since. Who would do something like this? What about all the animals that lived in the forest? Did they not have a voice in what would become of their home? No, they didn't.

When we reached the heart of Clayoquot Sound, it felt as though the very soul of the forest was alive and fighting alongside us for the trees and the animals. And when I say fight, I mean stand in the path between the land-moving tractors and the forests. We joined blockades made up of local residents, First Nations communities, environmental groups, and fellow activists, all united in a singular purpose: to protect the cathedral of trees, the living, breathing heart of the ecosystem.

The tension was palpable. We stood as human shields, facing down the loggers and their machines—massive chainsaws and bulldozers ready to tear through the forest. But the stakes were far higher than just trees; it was about the billions of heartbeats that existed in those woods, from the towering giants to the smallest of creatures that couldn't fend for themselves.

Nearly nine hundred arrests were made that day—but we won. The loggers were sent packing, and the forests (what remained of them) were saved. I'll never forget what extreme deforestation looks like—it's horrific. Despicable. Unforgivable. I'll never forget what it was like to join thousands of like-minded people fighting for a critical cause. And I'll never forget what it feels like to win a battle for nature; it left a lasting impression on my heart and mind.

Large-scale logging operations withdrew, and the First Nations communities of the Sound gained ownership of 50 percent of the region's logging rights. It wasn't a perfect victory, but it was enough to give the forest a chance to breathe again.

That win has stayed with me my entire life—an indelible reminder of how fragile our ecosystems are and how powerful we can be when we stand together for a cause greater than ourselves. I swore that later in life, once I had the resources, I would come back to conservation and do my part to fight for nature.

At the time, I was living at home with my parents and doing an internship at a small tech startup. Back then, my dream was to win a user interface design award from Steve Jobs. I was working as a Mac support technician, using that experience to lay the foundation for what would become Lightspeed Commerce—a company that would innovate in the retail and hospitality point of sale and payments space.

For the next seventeen years, my life revolved around building Lightspeed. Between 2012 and 2017, we raised over $300 million in venture capital funding. In 2019, we went public on the Toronto Stock Exchange. Today, Lightspeed generates more than a billion dollars in annual revenue, with over three thousand employees globally.

But in 2022, I made the decision to step down as CEO, transitioning to the role of executive chair of the board, where I would guide the company from a strategic level. I wanted to devote more of my time and energy to something even bigger than commerce—our planet.

That's when I founded Age of Union, a nonprofit environmental alliance with an initial $40 million commitment to support urgent conservation projects around the world. Age of Union is my promise to fight for places like Clayoquot Sound. It's the culmination of a lifelong dedication to protecting the Earth's last wild places. The mission is clear: If we can safeguard critical ecosystems for the next fifty years, we can give humanity a chance to recalibrate its relationship with the natural world. But without immediate action, many of the planet's species and ecosystems will vanish forever.

This book is about why we must act *now*. This is the decade of action, and we are at a crossroads where our decisions will shape the future of this planet.

In the chapters ahead, you will join me as I journey to some of the most remote and vulnerable places on Earth. From trekking through the Amazon rainforest with Paul Rosolie and his team of Junglekeepers, replanting forests in Haiti amid perilous social and environmental challenges, sailing with Sea Shepherd off the coast of France to stop illegal dolphin bycatch, and getting stranded on a volcano in Madagascar while viewing a once-lost species of duck—you will meet the changemakers fighting on the front lines of conservation.

This is not just a story of environmental crises. It's a story of hope, an adventure to remote places where local communities are uniting to make a difference, and of the collective power we have to be part of the solution.

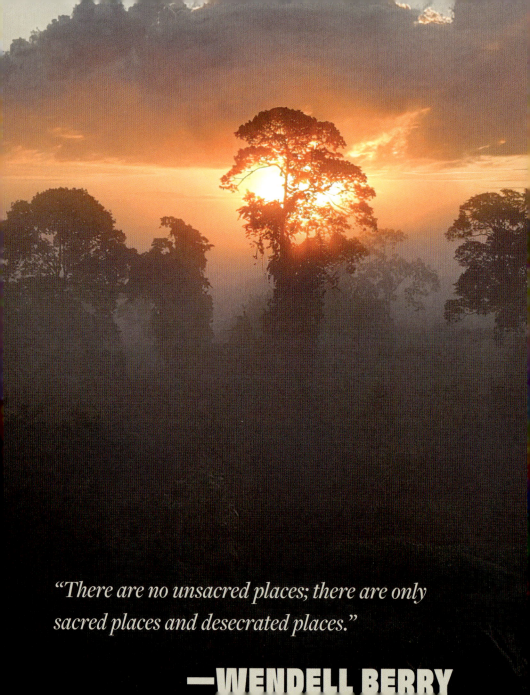

Midair moment, scarlet macaw.
Credit: Paul Rosolie

Chapter 1

MADRE DE DIOS

THE LIFEBLOOD OF THE AMAZON

It felt like flying into the mouth of a god.
 I clutched my seat as the plane bucked again, lurching through furious squalls. Outside, torrents of rain lashed the aircraft, and the sky cracked with static. I squinted into the blur, searching for some signal that all this would end—that the chaos might finally give way to stillness. There was none. Just tempest breath, white light, and the occasional flicker of jungle green, swallowed whole by the storm.

My stomach rolled. The fresh cocktail of tropical vaccines—yellow fever, typhoid, Hep A—coursed through my veins like a chemical itch I couldn't scratch. I was sweating. Nauseous. The recycled air tasted metallic. My tongue stuck to the roof of my mouth.

Miami was only hours behind me, but it felt like another life the moment we crossed into the Southern Hemisphere. I was just a bee in a bottle now—rattled, trapped, at the mercy of some deviant hand. I tightened my belt and stared into the rain-streaked window. Still nothing. Just smear and shadow. Somewhere down there, veiled in vapor and indifference, the Amazon waited—feral, bracing for another trespasser.

The plane slammed down hard at the airstrip in Puerto Maldonado. The wheels screamed. The fuselage shuddered. We didn't land—we dropped. Relief came slow, thick. Like waking from a nightmare with your legs still twitching. I was sick. Sweat-soaked. Dazed. But no longer in the sky.

The place was nearly deserted—residual from the pandemic, and this god-awful storm had likely scared off whoever was left. I crossed the flooded tarmac, ducking rain. Inside, Trevor Frost—our film director—stood, soaked through and pale. The storm had wrung something out of him.

"You survived!" he said, with a half-baked grin. He wasn't joking.

"I wasn't so certain," I replied, still shaking off my own fear.

He stepped closer and placed a hand on my shoulder. "Dax, you've just landed in the most alive and unknowable place on the planet. Welcome to the Amazon. You won't go home the same person."

A truck hauls timber stolen from an ancient Amazonian forest.
Credit: Stephane Thomas

We walked slowly toward baggage claim. Trevor had been down here plenty of times. A National Geographic explorer and filmmaker, he was working on a film about orphaned ocelots—cubs left behind when their mothers were taken by traps or rifles. Lucky for me, he had time to join us, to document our first conservation project.

Two men in Junglekeepers shirts approached us near the carousel. I recognized Juan Julio Durand from a photo in Paul Rosolie's book, *Mother of God*. He was broad-shouldered, with wavy salt-and-pepper hair and a chiseled jawline.

"Hello, friends!" he said, scanning us quickly—boots to backpacks. "Welcome to Peru. This is my colleague, Roy. We'll take you through the jungle. Paul will meet us at the river."

Roy Riquelme smiled. He didn't speak English, but his energy put us instantly at ease.

JJ extended a strong, calloused hand. I shook it. I'd read stories about him. Born in the Ese Eja Indigenous community of Infiero, JJ had grown up barefoot in the jungle, machete in hand, guided by the wisdom of the forest. He knew the medicinal plants, the rhythms and calls of the animals, and the invisible laws of the land. Paul once told me JJ had saved his life using sap from the Sangre de Drago tree—Dragon's Blood—after a life-threatening infection left him bedridden and covered in blisters. Infectious disease specialists had failed—antibiotics, IVs, weeks of treatment, and still the infection only worsened. JJ hadn't. Within days, Paul was on his feet.

"If you're bleeding out, poisoned, or lost in the jungle," Paul had said, "JJ's the guy who'll get you out alive. Or bury you properly." He meant it as a compliment. I was glad JJ was with us.

Standing in a daze, Trevor and I didn't notice our bags had arrived.

"I'm sorry, but we have to leave right away," JJ said. "We're behind schedule, and we need to reach the jungle gate before it closes."

"They close the jungle?" I asked, half-joking.

JJ didn't laugh. "At night, poachers move," he said. "And other things—things that happen in the dark, when no one's watching."

He turned and started walking. "Let's get your bags."

Junglekeepers

I first connected with Paul Rosolie in 2019, after seeing a video that had begun to burn its way across the internet. He stood alone in the smoke of a burning rainforest, ash streaked across his face, tears carving lines through the soot. Behind him, flames tore through the Amazon.

"Everything behind me right now is the forest that I've been working to protect for the last thirteen years," he said, voice cracked and ragged. "It's burning like this every day. And if you think our planet can survive this, you have another think coming."

It wasn't a plea. It was a siren.

Natural fires don't occur in the Amazon. It's simply too wet. You can pour gasoline on the jungle floor and still struggle to start a flame. But every year, after the rains end, people cut the forest, let it dry, and then set it ablaze. For cattle. For farmland. For money.

In 2019, the fires were so widespread that smoke reached as far as São Paulo—2,000 miles away—turning midday skies to black. That year alone, 2.2 million acres went up in smoke. Nearly 400 million metric tons

The Peruvian Amazon, endless and alive.
Credit: Dax Dasilva

of carbon were released into the atmosphere—more than the annual emissions of entire nations.

Paul's video went viral. Joe Rogan shared it. So did CNN, BBC, and Al Jazeera. Millions watched. Donations poured in. But for me, it did something else. It lodged in my mind like a splinter. I couldn't shake it. A direction was set, long before I realized I was following it.

In *Mother of God,* Paul describes Amazonian destruction as "burning down your house to warm a Pop-Tart." Sharp. Absurd. True. But even that doesn't capture the scale. It is more like setting all of Paris on fire to toast a marshmallow.

When it comes to explaining the crisis of the Amazon, everyone has a different story to tell. Scientists track the loss in acres per second. Conservationists warn of vanishing species and collapsing biodiversity. Anthropologists trace the unraveling of Indigenous cultures. Roads cut through ancient forest like scars. And with each new concession, the pages of the world's greatest archive are torn away.

The narratives vary. The angles shift. But they all orbit the same truth: greed, dressed as ambition, leaving extinction in its wake.

Soy to fatten livestock. Palm oil in everything from toothpaste to packaged snacks. Cocoa to sweeten the teeth of wealthier countries. Loggers, miners, and ranchers operating with impunity—bribing officials, torching land, reducing entire ecosystems to ash.

In 2022, the Brazilian Space Agency reported over three thousand active fires by late August. And for what? Flooring. Beef. Fish food. Tires. We aren't just burning trees—we're incinerating medicines not yet discovered, species not yet named, wisdom not yet learned. Carbon sinks become smoke signals, and still we look away.

The urgency isn't just environmental. It's existential. The Amazon produces nearly 20 percent of the world's oxygen—"the lungs of the Earth," it's often called. It is a climate engine, its rainfall patterns reaching far beyond the continent. What happens here doesn't stay here. It moves in the wind. It rides in the clouds. It lands on our plates.

It was this truth—the Amazon's role in the fate of the planet—that shaped Paul Rosolie's life.

Paul didn't grow up in the jungle. He grew up in Brooklyn, buried in adventure books, dreaming of rivers and creatures he'd never seen. While other kids played sports, he imagined rainforests. By nineteen, he was in the Peruvian Amazon—Madre de Dios, the "Mother of God"—with a backpack, a camera, and more heart than plan.

He met JJ Durand, a Peruvian jungle expert, and together they built Tamandua Expeditions and, later, Junglekeepers—a grassroots conservation effort forged in sweat, machete cuts, and mosquito bites.

Paul fell in love with the rainforest. He married it. And when it burned, he burned, too. He had a dangerous hunger—the kind that doesn't flinch in the face of hardship. The kind that builds sanctuaries from nothing. While the rest of the world watched the rainforest vanish through phone screens, Paul chose to vanish into it, piece by piece, until he belonged to it.

During the pandemic, I began hosting live conversations with environmental changemakers—activists, scientists, rangers—all calling in from the front lines of ecological collapse. Paul joined one.

"We're holding the line with duct tape and willpower," he said. A single ranger for every 20,000 acres. "We're outnumbered and exhausted. But if we don't stand our ground, this forest dies—and everything living inside it goes with it."

His words were raw and urgent. He spoke not just about loss, but about love—for a jungle that had given his life meaning and a mission he refused to abandon, even when the odds were brutal.

Junglekeepers had resolve. It had purpose. What it didn't have was funding.

That's when the idea became clear: I would build a nonprofit environmental alliance—Age of Union—to support people like Paul. Not institutions, not theory. Real changemakers. Real forests. Junglekeepers would be our first partner.

In the summer of 2020, I called Paul.

The world was in shambles, and he wasn't spared—broke, mid-divorce, back in New York living with his parents. Junglekeepers was out of money.

Tourism was dead. Any flicker of hope had gone up in smoke.

"I've just set up the new organization," I told him. "I want Junglekeepers to be our first project."

There was silence. Then: "We need everything. Dax, we're getting murdered down there. It might be too far gone."

They'd lost rangers. Forests had been torched. It was open season in the jungle.

But there was still one opportunity: a massive piece of land adjacent to their reserve. The owner—a conservation-minded farmer—had gone broke. The only offers were coming from loggers.

"How big is it?" I asked.

"Twenty-two thousand acres."

"Find out the price."

It was $200,000. Nine bucks an acre.

Let that sink in: For the cost of a Shake Shack burger, you could buy an acre of one of the most biologically rich regions on Earth.

We got the land. Leased it, technically, from the Peruvian government. It became Junglekeepers' fifth concession, bringing their total protected area to over 50,000 acres.

But protecting it was another story. At the time, they had two part-time rangers trying to patrol 30,000 acres. No shelter. No gear. Just a tarp in the rain.

We sent funding for land, a ranger station, boats, tech, salaries, healthcare. Paul and JJ had never drawn a paycheck. Noble, yes. Sustainable, no.

We gave them their first real team. And it changed everything.

Word spread. Locals—many from logging families—began applying to be rangers. Sons and daughters of loggers, raised in the shadow of chainsaws, now stepped forward to become guardians of the forest.

The next step wasn't a choice. It was a responsibility.

If I was going to support changemakers, I had to walk beside them—not just fund their work, but listen to their stories, understand their needs, and see firsthand how we could help.

I booked a flight to the jungle.

The Jungle at Night

An hour outside of Puerto Maldonado, our van sped along a narrow dirt road leading away from the city and toward the jungle's entrance. The farther we got from town, the more our path looked like a forgotten whisper amidst the surrounding wilderness. Wild grasses and untamed flora flirted with the road's edges. I got the feeling we were crossing into another world, one where the rules I knew no longer applied.

Deep ruts plowed by relentless rains sent the back end of the van sliding sideways as we crawled through the muddy terrain.

"Listen," said JJ, locking eyes with me from the driver's seat. "The forest is very beautiful—but it can also be extremely dangerous. Don't touch anything or pick anything up, and don't reach into places you cannot see. There are poisonous insects, toxic plants, venomous snakes— many things you'll regret brushing up against."

He paused, then added casually, "There's an ant here—the bullet ant— that's said to feel like a gunshot when it stings you."

A poison arrow frog used by Indigenous hunters to coat their blowdart tips—an ancient method capable of paralyzing or killing prey with a single strike. Credit: Paul Rosolie

The Schmidt sting pain index—a scale used to rank insect stings—ranks the bullet ant at the very top. Entomologist Justin Schmidt described it as "pure, intense, brilliant pain. Like walking over flaming charcoal with a three-inch nail embedded in your heel."

"Does it actually feel like a gunshot?" I asked.

"It's similar...and it does not feel good." He left it there, and I didn't press for details.

"There's also a poisonous giant centipede," Trevor offered helpfully, "and a wandering spider that can paralyze you."

Add those to the growing list of creatures I was hoping not to encounter.

After ninety minutes of battling the bumpy, slippery road, we reached the jungle gate. Puerto Maldonado may be called the gateway to the Peruvian rainforest, but the real gate sits within a rusted fence on a narrow road that disappears into the forested abyss. JJ hadn't been exaggerating—the gate was being monitored by a local family who locked it up every night at five sharp.

We made it just in time. The gate was still open, and we slipped through. But I hadn't prepared myself for what lay beyond. The forest was thick and dark. It started to rain. Water fell from every direction. Mud pooled in the road's ruts. Vines and branches hung from above or littered the way ahead.

"How long from here?" What I meant was, *Can we even get through this?*

"Usually about an hour to the river," JJ said, squinting through the rain-smeared windshield. "But tonight, my friend, it's going to take a little longer." Roy glanced back with a jeering smile that said it all: *You have no idea what's coming.*

Inside the forest, it was pitch-black. A ghostly mist through the van's headlights. The van fishtailed on every curve. Fallen branches forced us to stop constantly. JJ and Roy would climb out, machetes and axes in hand, clear the path, and then we'd inch forward—until we got stuck.

The back tires spun, spraying wet earth in every direction. JJ and Roy jumped out again, breaking branches and wedging them under the tires.

JJ popped his head back in. "We need more sticks. Go gather as many branches as you can find. We'll pack them under the tires for traction."

Trevor and I leapt out. I couldn't stop thinking about JJ's warning: *Don't touch anything.* And now here I was, knee-deep in the underbrush, reaching blindly into leaves and vines—thinking about bullet ants, paralyzing spiders, and centipedes.

And snakes.

I hadn't told anyone about my fear of snakes. It doesn't matter if they're venomous or harmless—something about the way they move, the cold silence of them, has always unsettled me. Even seeing one behind glass gives me a visceral jolt. And now I was bushwhacking in their living room like an uninvited guest. Every stick I grabbed, I half-expected it to hiss.

We packed branches under the wheels, pushed, got splattered, and cheered when the van finally lurched forward. We scrambled back inside. Then it happened again. And again.

In the back of the van, I thought about what Paul had described in an email as a "quick-and-easy trip through the jungle." Instead, we were in a six-hour mud-wrestling match with a van that was clearly winning. But JJ and Roy weren't discouraged. Disturbingly, they seemed to be enjoying it.

"This is nothing," JJ said. "There have been times when we were stuck in the forest for two or three days."

That wasn't in the email either.

Halfway into our jungle safari, Roy could tell I was starting to lose it. Trevor had probably been through worse, but this was the first time I'd ever felt truly lost—and a little afraid. Roy pulled out a Thermos and poured us two cups of premixed pisco cocktails, made from white brandy and muscat grapes. JJ put on some music.

"Turn it up! Turn it up!" we shouted, drinks sloshing.

Our spirits lifted. We'd get stuck, take a sip, jump out, push, slip in the mud, scramble back in, refill, repeat. Somewhere between the second stuck tire and the third splash of pisco, something shifted. Fear didn't leave me, but it stopped leading the way. We started cheering. Then JJ stopped the van again—but this time, we weren't stuck.

He stepped into the headlights, then returned…with a massive snake.

I scrambled into my seat, grabbing anything I could find nearby to put between me and the serpent thrashing in JJ's hands.

Yellow Amazon tree boa, coiled in silence.
Credit: Gowri Varanashi

"What are you doing?" I yelled.

"Don't worry," JJ said, calm as ever. "It's just a young boa constrictor."

"That's young?" I asked. Apparently, baby snakes in the Amazon qualify as dragons.

"Yes, they get much bigger than this. Move over. He's coming with us."

We never discussed whether snakes would be part of the passenger list. I'd survived a lightning-streaked flight, a blackout jungle crawl, and a van ride from hell—but none of it unnerved me like JJ bringing that boa into the van. It was thick, coiled around his arm, jaw wide open—hissing, spitting, and struggling to get a piece of his flesh.

JJ casually gripped its head, reached under the seat, pulled out a canvas bag, stuffed the snake inside, tied it off, and placed it next to me. The bag writhed.

"He can't get out of there, can he?" I asked.

"If we leave it, the villagers will kill it," he said. "They'll cut it in half."

"Why?" I asked.

"They're afraid," JJ said. "Many of them migrated here from the Andes after the coca crackdown. They didn't grow up around snakes. And here, there are plenty that can kill you."

"And this isn't one of them?" I asked, staring at the pulsing bag.

"No. The poisonous vipers are smaller, with triangle-shaped heads. This one's harmless. Round head. We'll set him free somewhere safe."

I can't say it made me feel better. But I've never been okay with an animal being chopped in half by a machete—even one that just tried to eat my guide. So I leaned back, looked at the twitching bag beside me, and tried to get used to it. I would need to. During the trip, we'd rescue two or three snakes a day.

That night, beneath a twisted cathedral of vines, gripped by the wet breath of the rainforest, I realized the jungle had already claimed me—and it wasn't giving me back. At least, not the same way I'd come.

In the jungle, the river is the road—long tin boats carry the weight.
Credit: Dax Dasilva

Eyes on the Water

The forest finally opened at the river, revealing a sky so thick with stars it seemed unreal. We'd made it to Lucerna—a tiny village where the forest meets the Las Piedras River. The plan was to meet Paul here in daylight and take his boat upriver to the Junglekeepers research center. But it was well past midnight now, and Paul—along with his boat—was long gone.

Lucerna is a town of two identities. By tradition, it's a logging village—trees cut deep in the jungle are floated downriver for processing. Many of the elders are loggers or descendants of them. But recently, a new rhythm had emerged. Ecotourism had crept in, quietly reshaping the local economy. Now, Lucerna hosts biodiversity trails, riverboat tours, and eco-lodges. The elderly loggers move slowly, many broken down by decades of labor. But some of their children have chosen a different path: as conservationists, tour guides, and rangers.

Lucerna also stood at the threshold of something more primal. Past it, cell signals vanished. So did soft assumptions. The jungle beyond didn't run on comfort or convenience—it ran on instinct.

The broader region is just as complex. The headwaters of the Las Piedras River are protected by the Alto Purús National Park. Downstream, the Reserva Territorial Madre de Dios is home to the Mashco-Piro Indigenous people, who have lived in voluntary isolation since the 1800s. Commercial logging still coexists alongside Indigenous territories, Brazil nut concessions, and small mestizo communities like Lucerna and Sabaluyoc. Private conservation groups like Junglekeepers now protect over 100,000 acres of rainforest here. But pressure looms. The controversial Trans-Amazon Highway—completed in 2012—delivered an influx of settlers, miners, and loggers. Ancient forests fell for cedar, ironwood, and makeshift farms.

For most visitors, Lucerna is the final stop. But we were going farther. Paul was waiting at the Junglekeepers research station—somewhere deep downriver. We didn't have a boat. Paul had taken his back to camp.

But JJ, ever resourceful, had that look in his eye. Within minutes, he had commandeered a twelve-foot tin boat with a small outboard motor—banged up, patched with wire, and barely holding together at the seams. It looked like it had ferried ghosts.

"It'll keep the water out," JJ promised.

We loaded up our gear and climbed in. JJ took the rear, steering with one hand and keeping the snake-in-a-bag beside him. It was so dark I couldn't see his face from the front of the boat—but I could feel water around my feet.

"Is there supposed to be this much water in the boat?" I asked.

"Yes," JJ said flatly. "Don't worry."

Nothing ever seemed to bother him—which, I suppose, is an ideal trait in the Amazon.

We zigzagged down the river. Roy sat up front with a flashlight, sweeping the beam across the water, spotlighting large tree branches and trunks felled by the storm and floating downriver. JJ, focused on the beam, steered us to avoid any collisions. I wondered if it was a good time to mention something personal.

"I can't swim," I said.

It wasn't something I advertised. You don't go to the Amazon to confess you're water-adjacent at best. But I figured if I was going to die, they should at least know why.

There was a long pause. "You don't need to swim," JJ said. "We're in a boat."

"Right. But if I *did* need to swim…. I mean, that would be a problem for me."

JJ motioned toward the shimmering beam of the flashlight on the water.

"Trust me, swimming right now isn't a good idea—for anyone. Look."

I followed his arm, pointing out into the dark—and saw two glowing red eyes level with the surface. A black caiman. Then another. And another.

And then it hit me—not all the logs were logs. Some of them watched us. Some of them moved. One drifted past the boat—at least twelve feet long, its armored back rippling like a ridge of knives through the water. I later learned that black caimans can grow to over twenty feet and weigh more than 800 pounds.

JJ's message was clear: If the boat capsized, my inability to swim wouldn't matter. I'd be eaten.

I sat still, tracking the logs ahead like playing a video game on hard mode, waiting for one to smash into the boat and send us flying into dinosaur-infested waters.

As the boat bobbed and creaked, I felt old fears rise like river mist. I've never been good in the water. As a kid, I fell behind in every summer swim class. While the other kids glided through the pool doing butterfly strokes and cannonballs, I clung to the shallow end, pretending I wasn't terrified. Swimming never came naturally. We weren't a beachgoing family. Water was foreign. Deep water was worse. It didn't feel like freedom—it felt like danger.

Every summer, I'd start with hope. *This year, I'll learn to swim.* But it always ended the same: me treading water, head barely above the surface, trying not to drown while everyone else laughed and lapped circles around me. I'd learned to pretend I was fine. That's what fear teaches you—how to mask it with silence.

Now here I was, decades later, in the middle of the Amazon, in a boat full of water, riding through blackness and caimans, with that same childhood dread clutching my chest.

Ahead of us, Roy's flashlight swept across what seemed like an entire tree. JJ grunted and steered hard left to avoid it. The boat banged through the branches, vibrating under our feet. I stayed quiet, gripping the side, counting my fears—snakes in bags, monsters in the water, and a dark, churning river that dared me to fall in.

And yet, above us, stars exploded across the sky—more than I'd ever seen. A thick band of Milky Way light stretched from horizon to horizon. It was breathtaking. A surreal moment of beauty in the middle of chaos.

We moved mostly in silence after that. The hum of the outboard motor was the only constant sound, broken occasionally by JJ and Roy calling to each other in Spanish from opposite ends of the boat. Their voices were calm but alert as they guided us through the wreckage of the swollen river.

We drifted forward, deeper into the jungle, shadows folding over the river like a closing hand. The air was thick and still, broken only by the occasional swirl of water or the slap of something unseen. Crocodiles floated beside us like phantoms. In the stillness, it struck me that this wasn't just a journey to meet Paul. The jungle had its own agenda. It wasn't going to let me pass through untouched. It would find the cracks. And it would press.

Paul

We arrived at the Junglekeepers shore. It was still too dark to see much. Before stepping out of the boat and into the shallow murky water, I asked JJ if there were any caiman around. He smirked and said we were safe. I wondered what JJ considered unsafe, and then hoped I'd never find out.

What I could clearly see was the slope. We were at the base of a muddy incline, with steps made from old tires and sacks of Brazil nuts that led to the top. Hauling our gear up was a slippery game. Going up wasn't great, but each trip down left me wary of becoming river fodder. On our final haul, a man appeared at the crest of the hill—backlit, barefoot, and grinning.

Paul Rosolie looked like he'd just stepped out of the jungle—and in a way, he had. Shirtless, in army green cargo pants, he stood loose-limbed with a bottle in one hand and three dirt-smeared glasses in the other. Curly black hair, ripped abs, scratches across his skin. He moved like someone who belonged to the forest, not someone just passing through. There was a looseness to him—like gravity held him differently out here.

"I was going to make you to drink from the river when you first arrived," he said, handing us each a glass, "but you'll have to wait for morning. If we go down there now, you'll get snatched up by a croc or an anaconda."

I knew it.

Navigating the Madre de Dios with Paul Rosolie.
Credit: Mohsin Kazmi

Chapter 1 | **MADRE DE DIOS**

Meeting Paul in person felt like arriving at the center of a story I'd been chasing for years. We'd shared calls, texts, long emails, and deep conversations, but here—under the stars, soaked in sweat, boots thick with mud—it was real. I admired the hell out of him. I wanted to mark the moment, to say something meaningful. But Paul just splashed pisco into our glasses, raised his, and downed it in one gulp.

"Welcome to the Amazon," he said, wiping his face with the back of his hand.

We followed suit.

Calling him the Tarzan of the Amazon only scratches the surface. Sure, he swings machetes, tracks jaguars, and wrestles anacondas. But the deeper truth is: Paul leads with purpose. He's spent decades giving everything—his time, his body, his peace of mind—to protect the rainforest. He doesn't wear his commitment like a badge—it clings to him like smoke. You feel it in the way he talks about the land, and in the silences he keeps when others would fill the air with noise.

"Come on," said Paul, refilling our glasses. "Let me show you around."

The Junglekeepers research center sat on a raised wooden platform, a few feet above the forest floor. A corrugated metal roof stretched overhead, supported by thick timber posts. There were no walls—just open air and

A curious spider monkey watches from above.
Credit: Stephane Thomas

the scent of earth. A kitchen, a harvest table, a lounge area, and a small library filled the space. Toward the back were bunk rooms and a shower.

We were too wired to sleep. Roy moved quietly around the fire, cooking up some midnight magic. A native of the region, broad-shouldered and grounded, Roy carried the stillness of a man who's spent his life listening to rivers, trees, and smoke. Every herb, root, and protein had purpose—flavor, yes, but also healing, protection, ritual. His meals told stories.

We gathered around, eating, sipping pisco, and sharing stories. At some point, JJ and Roy launched into a heated debate over who really invented pisco—Chile or Peru? I didn't catch every word, but I got the gist. The drink is traditional to both countries, but the Peruvians were adamant—it was theirs.

The night softened. Our bellies warmed us just enough to forget where we were—until Paul broke the spell. He leaned against the table, half-shadowed, eyes unreadable. Swirling the pisco in his glass, he said—almost too casually—"You ever wake up and know something's wrong—before you hear it, before you see it?"

I didn't answer. He wasn't really asking.

"I was five days into a solo trek. Deep jungle. No trail. No backup. Just me, a machete, and my hammock strung between two trees." He paused, eyes fixed on the dark outside the open-air lodge. "Middle of the night, I woke up—dead still. The kind of quiet that doesn't feel empty. A fierce presence. An odor I'd never smelled."

He took a slow sip, then set the glass down.

"Then I heard it. Breathing. Not far off. Deep, guttural breaths, like it was tasting the air off my face. I couldn't see anything, but I could feel its breath. Hot. Slow. Heavy."

He held up his hand, fingers apart. "That close."

I felt my skin tighten.

"I stayed frozen," Paul said. "Not from bravery. From terror. Because I knew what it was. A jaguar. Full-grown. Alpha. I've tracked them for years. When they hunt, they don't make noise. They just decide. Skull or spine. Then it's lights out."

Trevor went quiet. I barely breathed.

"It could've taken me by the neck and disappeared into the dark. No fight. No trace. That's what they do. But it didn't." Paul paused. "It waited. Maybe trying to figure out what I was. Food? Threat? Just another animal that didn't belong."

He leaned forward into the light. "And then, just as quiet as it came—it was gone. Back into the forest like a ghost."

He threw back the last of his pisco, wiped his mouth with the back of his hand, and stood. Trevor let out a low whistle. I couldn't keep my eyes from the empty corner of the room.

"Sleep well," he said, walking off into the dark. "Might not be the only one watching."

In the bunk room, Trevor pointed his flashlight at the ceiling. Dozens of bats clung to the rafters, their glowing eyes staring back at us.

"You ever slept beneath bats?" he asked casually.

I froze in the doorway. Snakes. Crocs. Now bats. Each new creature felt like the jungle testing my resolve.

Something about bats always unsettled me. The way they moved—unpredictable, erratic—like panic with wings. But after the night we'd had, I wasn't sure I had the energy to be afraid of one more thing.

"Oh, no thanks," I said.

"Don't worry, these aren't the bloodsucking kind," he said. "But they will crap all over us unless we scoot them back."

He rolled up a shirt and chucked it at the ceiling. The bats exploded into a frenzy—tiny bodies flapping, shrieking—before settling in a darker corner.

"You've done this a few times," I said, claiming the bunk farthest from them.

"You'll get used to it," he said. "There are far more dangerous animals in the jungle."

"What's the most dangerous?" I asked.

"Humans."

I lay in bed, eyes on the ceiling. The bats barely moved now, but the jungle outside never stopped. Hoots. Howls. Screams in the distance—like New York at night, if taxis had claws.

I thought of Paul's jaguar and stared into the corner, waiting for movement. The bats didn't flinch. Slowly, the sounds gave way to exhaustion. My body sank into the cot.

And eventually, even fear let go of me.

Wildcat

Sunlight beamed into the research center from every direction. Last night's darkness had transformed into a bright emerald morning. The forest looked alive. Branches and vines swayed. Bugs swarmed. Morning dew turned to vapor and drifted along the floorboards. I pulled back the mosquito net and checked the ceiling. The bats were still asleep—and, just as Trevor said, they'd stayed tucked in the corner. Directly beneath them was a big mess of guano.

Paul and Trevor sat with some of the crew and rangers in the kitchen area. I joined them for coffee. That's when I met Harry Turner.

Harry was a young cinematographer working with Trevor on the short film we were making. A former British soldier who had served in Afghanistan, Harry had seen friends and fellow soldiers killed in action. After returning to England, the trauma hit like a shadow—post-traumatic stress disorder and a deep depression that nearly consumed him.

Desperate to find meaning, Harry volunteered at a wildlife sanctuary in the Peruvian jungle. What never left him—what perhaps saved him— was his love for animals. At the sanctuary, he helped raise two orphaned ocelot cubs, teaching them to survive in the wild. In turn, the wild helped heal parts of him that nothing else could touch.

Trevor and his partner, Melissa Lesh, directed and produced a film about Harry and his bond with the ocelots. They called it *Wildcat*. Their early work was stunning, but they needed a co-executive producer to help finish the film. I signed on. Two years later, we reunited in New York at the 44th Annual News & Documentary Emmy Awards, where *Wildcat* won the Emmy for Outstanding Nature Documentary.

Back at the breakfast table, Harry and Trevor were already giggling. I poured a cup of coffee and joined them.

"How were the bats?" Harry asked, blue eyes tearing up with laughter.

That's what they were snickering about.

Trevor raised his arms over his head and flailed around like he was being attacked by invisible winged demons—mimicking my reaction the night before. Harry doubled over.

"Okay, I wasn't *that* freaked out," I said. "But I was freaked by something moving under the bunks."

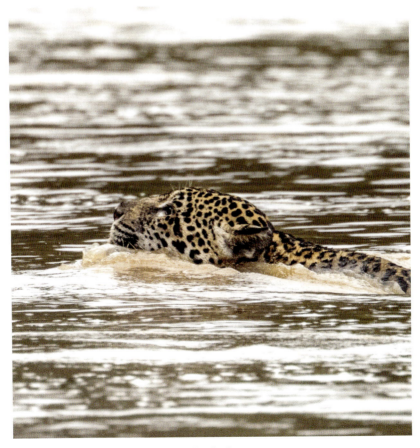

The jaguar, apex predator of the jungle, crossing the river.
Credit: Stephane Thomas

"What was it?" Harry asked.

"I don't know. I didn't want to find out."

"I found jaguar tracks all around the platform this morning," Paul said. "There's been talk in town about a man-eater along the river. He's taken a few people in the last couple of weeks."

If anyone knew about jaguars, it was this group. Paul had tracked dozens. Harry had lived alongside wildcats.

"Do you think it's safe?" I asked. "The bunk rooms don't even have doors."

Harry raised two fingers from each hand like cat ears, snarled, and gave a half-hearted roar. They all burst into laughter.

"That's not funny," I said, flicking at Paul beside me. "Okay, it's a little funny. But were there really tracks?"

"I made up the man-eater part," Paul admitted. "But yeah, there were tracks. Jaguars have been around the center lately. We've caught a few on camera traps. Don't worry. It's unlikely he'll climb into your bunk and eat you."

Leaf frog poised on a slender branch.
Credit: Paul Rosolie

The sound from the night before—the screams in the dark—rushed back to mind.

Then Paul shifted the mood.

"I'm really excited for you, Dax," he said. "Our sponsors rarely come here. Nobody wants to see it firsthand. And there's nothing wrong with writing a check—we need every bit of help we can get. But when you come down here, when you enter the forest and drink from the river—which you'll be doing soon—it shows everyone that you genuinely care. That you're one of us. It tells people here that you want to learn, not just instruct."

That's exactly why I came. I wanted to understand—not from spreadsheets or strategy calls, but from boots-on-mud immersion. I'd spent years in the tech world helping startups grow, build culture, and overcome resource gaps. And I'd quickly realized something: Most conservation nonprofits are startups in spirit. Scrappy, visionary, always one grant or setback away from collapse—but somehow pushing forward, driven by purpose.

We finished our coffee, laughed off the last of the pisco fog, and wiped the sleep from our eyes. I caught Harry glancing up at the rafters.

"You sure they won't fall on us?" I asked.

"They'll only fall on *you*," he said. "The bats remember."

Trevor nearly choked on his coffee. Paul leaned back in his chair, smiling like he'd seen this all before.

"I think the most important thing you can do right now," he said, nodding toward the edge of camp, "is take a walk. Go down those steps. Be alone with the forest. Be still. I'll join you soon."

And with that, I stepped off the platform and faded into the green.

First Steps

I breathed in deeply. Thick air filled my lungs, and I could taste the rich, damp soil. All around me, vibrant hues tussled for my attention. Above me, a leafy kingdom of ancient trees stretched toward the heavens—sentinels of the forest bearing centuries of wisdom. Standing mighty and holding up the canopy with their branches, these hardwood giants were the elders of the rainforest. Paul was right: The feeling was palpable and centering. This was a spiritual walk.

Cascading from the evergreen canopy, the twisting tendrils of strangler figs wound tightly around their host trees. A parasitic nightmare. The fig steals nutrients, water, and sunlight. In time, it envelops the host in a lush embrace, choking the life out of its prey. But it's not all villainy. The strangler fig is a keystone species—its fruit sustains a vast menagerie of animals. Its hollow trunks offer shelter and nesting for bats, birds, and other creatures. And while its eerie aerial roots inspire legends, no tree in the jungle is home to more folklore. Angels and fairies. Spirits and gods. Ghosts and other less-welcome guests.

I took my time, letting my senses adjust as everything slowed down. I felt like I'd been hardwired directly into Mother Nature. The contrast from the tech-driven buzz of my city life to this primordial theater was jarring. Sunbeams pierced the canopy, and a hummingbird appeared like a conjured spell, dancing in midair—its iridescent feathers catching the light and casting little rainbow halos. I'd never seen colors so alive, as if light bent differently near the equator. Or maybe in the jungle, even color evolves to compete.

Paul emerged from the trees, still barefoot and shirtless. "Did you take a moment to really feel your surroundings?" he asked, scanning the forest.

"It's overwhelming," I said. "Almost haunting. But beautiful."

"Well said."

"And everything is…wet," I added, gesturing around. The trees, the leaves, the ground—everything glistened with saturation.

"Exactly," Paul said. "That's why fires don't start naturally in the rainforest. The wood is too wet to burn. If there's a fire here, someone lit it—with gasoline. Even then, it's not easy. That's why we know it's intentional."

He walked over to a strangler fig. "Want to see something cool?"

He knelt by the roots and peered into a hollow. "Yep. She's here."

I crouched beside him and followed his gaze—just in time to spot the legs of a tarantula. I lurched backward and fell on my ass, adding giant hairy spiders to the growing list of things I'd rather not meet face-to-face.

"She's a sweetheart. Lived here a long time," Paul said. "Female tarantulas can live thirty years. That silk mesh around the entrance? That's how you know it's their burrow."

I made a mental note: Avoid holes with silk curtains.

The tarantula sat calmly. Paul, because he's Paul, reached in with a flat hand. She crept out onto his palm—huge, slow, deliberate. She crawled up his forearm, raising one leg at a time, the others clinging gently to his skin.

"She's not dangerous. But there are bigger ones out here. Bird-eaters."

I blinked.

"Yeah," Paul nodded. "Spiders with fangs so big they can kill birds. Even small mammals. I saw one carrying a dead opossum once—size of a dinner plate. When threatened, they'll flip around and eject hairs from their back. Gets in your eyes. Blinds you."

I had officially reached my spider quota.

But watching her delicately wander Paul's arm, it hit me—she wasn't here to scare me. She was here to survive. Just like everything else in this jungle. The armor, the venom, the eerie stillness—it wasn't aggression. It was adaptation. I didn't know if I was getting braver, but I was beginning to understand the rules of this place. And none of them were mine.

Paul lowered his hand. The tarantula, unbothered, turned and walked back into her burrow.

"Okay," he said, wiping his hands on his cargo pants. "This probably shouldn't wait any longer. Come with me."

Jungle Baptism

Paul and I stood at the edge of the Las Piedras. This wide river is the longest tributary of the Madre de Dios River, serving as an important source for countless species of birds and animals, including the jaguar, whose footprints we saw along the shoreline. It's also an important region for Brazil nut harvesting, a major sustainable export. Farther upriver, areas of the Las Piedras are home to some of the last uncontacted tribes on Earth.

"Dax, before we do anything else, you need to drink from the river," Paul said.

"What? Oof," I said, reactively. I knew this moment was coming, and I wasn't looking forward to it.

I'd dodged this moment in every phone call, every planning session. Now there was no more dodging. The baptism was here—and the water looked like something you'd wring out of a rainforest mop.

The water along the river's muddy shoreline looked suspicious. There were bits and pieces of all sorts of things floating past. Upon closer inspection, parades of tiny crablike bugs swam from bit to bit. Also, I thought of the not-so-state-of-the-art plumbing in the communities along the river. I was pretty sure that local public health authorities would advise against my sipping downstream. But there wasn't a health official anywhere in sight—just Paul, waiting for me to test my fate with the buggy water.

"This is important," he said, sensing my reluctance. "Don't overthink it. Scoop it, drink it, become part of it. You see the thunderheads form in the afternoon and you watch the rain fall back into the river. You drink the water, and it flows through your body and hydrates you. Then you sweat, and the water leaves your body and turns back to vapor, returning to the sky. This is a cycle of life."

I appreciated the lesson—I just didn't want the life cycle to end with mine. I was averse, quite certain that I would end up with a waterborne infection or parasite. Nevertheless, I took a deep breath, exhaled, and plunged my hands into the river. I dished up an extra-large helping and drank it down. It was warm and gritty and earthy tasting. *Here's to Giardia*, I thought.

"This is the moment when you stop being an observer," Paul said, giving the speech he probably delivered to every first-time conservationist. "You've come all the way down here, and now you're part of the Amazon's life cycle."

I wasn't sure my stomach would agree, but something shifted. I wasn't just watching the jungle anymore—I was in it. And it was in me.

Despite my dread of bug water, it did feel like a ceremony—thanks mostly to Paul waxing poetic about rainforest evapotranspiration. I still figured I'd be purging by morning, but the symbolism of a jungle baptism wasn't lost on me.

The banks of the Amazon were lush with life, as far as we could see. Birds flew between the trees and overhead. Not far from where we stood, a massive tree trunk floated in shallow water.

"Let's go jump on that," said Paul, like a gleeful child who just discovered a new playground.

"Aren't there caiman in here?" I asked.

"No, they don't come into this area," he said. I scanned the river. I was pretty sure this was the exact spot where we saw glowing eyes in the beams of Roy's flashlight the night before.

"Come on!" he said.

Paul charged into the river and waded to the trunk. He threw one arm over and pulled himself up. I followed him, more cautiously, and climbed atop the slippery log. Paul decided we should take turns trying to balance from one end to the other without falling into the river.

From opposite ends, we tried to pass each other. I don't remember who pushed whom first—it was probably Paul—but we both ended up in the river, laughing our heads off. There is a game that kids in elementary school play called King of the Castle, where the object is to knock everyone else off the structure. This was very much that game. Deep in the Amazon, Paul and I transformed into Tom Sawyer and Huckleberry Finn, performing wrestling matches on a log in the middle of caiman-infested waters. At some point, it stopped mattering who was winning. We were covered in mud, soaked in river water, and howling like lunatics.

Ranger Station

About an hour's boat ride downriver from the research center, Paul, Trevor, Harry, and I pulled up onto the shore. We were still within the boundaries of the first Junglekeepers concession, JK1. It was staggering to see how much forest this group protected—dense, wild, endless.

"Come on," Paul said. "I have something to show you." He headed up a trail into the forest, and I followed.

The trail opened into a clearing—and there stood Dina Tsouluhas, grinning beside a newly built ranger station.

Dina was the reason it existed. As co-founder of Junglekeepers, she had once traveled to Las Piedras from Montréal to lead a yoga retreat and never left. She fell in love with the jungle, then helped build a movement to protect it. Since day one, she's run operations, managed logistics, and led the team's growth—and today, she was welcoming us to the new hub in the rainforest.

"We did it," she said, smiling and sweeping a hand toward the station. "Welcome to the future of Junglekeepers."

"Incredible," I said. "You all built this fast."

"Dina and the crew worked around the clock to get it done before you arrived," Paul added.

"All of this is here because of you, Dax," she said.

That wasn't true. None of it would've happened without the grit, sweat, and tireless belief of Paul, JJ, Roy, Dina, and the Junglekeepers team. If I was part of this, it was only because they made space for people like me to join the mission. I was lucky to be here. And I knew it.

Like the research center, the ranger station was a raised platform on stilts, open to the elements, with a corrugated roof and cabanas on either side for sleeping. But this one had something the last didn't: power.

Inside, rangers worked with handheld GPS devices and laptops at shared tables. "No more tarps or backpacker stoves," Dina said, with a well-earned smirk. A few weeks earlier on a video call, she had described their old field station as a tarp strung between trees. No beds. No toilets. No gear. Just rain and mud and commitment.

Now, thanks to Dina's leadership, the rangers had solar-powered lighting, satellite communication, stovetops, dry storage, and a working kitchen. The new ranger station wasn't just shelter—it was infrastructure that could sustain a team of rangers for long periods of time.

And the tech? That was all Dina, too.

During a trip to Kenya, she'd spent time with the Maasai Wilderness Conservation Trust and learned how their rangers used SMART Mobile, a conservation software built for spatial monitoring. It lets rangers track their routes, log wildlife sightings, and document forest threats in real time—all through GPS, even offline.

When she returned to Peru, Dina implemented SMART across Junglekeepers' eighty square miles of protected rainforest. Now, every patrol becomes data: which animals are seen, where illegal logging might be creeping in, how the ecosystem is shifting over time. The ranger

Visiting JK1, the first Junglekeepers concession.
Credit: Junglekeepers

stations are connected through Wi-Fi and satellite links, turning boots-on-the-ground patrols into a living database of the forest's health.

Dina made that happen. And yet, she never spoke like a founder. She spoke like a team captain. A problem solver. A woman who'd traded city comforts for rainforest resolve—because the cause was worth it.

But tech alone won't save the Amazon. That's why Junglekeepers also does it the old way—face-to-face. JJ and Roy lead the community outreach programs, building trust with local families and Indigenous groups. The truth is, conservation here depends on relationships. Lucerna and the surrounding communities are critical allies. If the land works for the people—if they can farm it, forage it, and thrive alongside it—they'll fight to protect it, too.

That's the vision the whole team is chasing—not just technology and data, but partnership and trust. Because conservation only works if it's built for everyone.

Caiman Wrestling

The sky was brushing pastel watercolors across the canopy as we headed back toward the research center. It felt like every bird in the jungle had launched into flight at once, wheeling through the evening light in search of somewhere to roost. Our long tin boat sliced across the Las Piedras, rippling the surface, carving trails through the reflections. Onshore, sandy banks appeared in intervals, just wide enough for caiman to bask before the jungle tugged its vines and branches back down toward the water.

Speeding upriver was the only true escape from the bugs. The rest of the time—unless you were zipped into a mosquito-netted bunk—was an unending assault of wings, stingers, and things too small to see. By morning

Paul holds a caiman—Amazon fieldwork up close.
Credit: Junglekeepers

I was already itching. By evening, I was crawling back into that net like it was a bunker.

At the start of the trip, I stuck to Trevor's jungle protocol wardrobe: long-sleeve shirt, pants, boots. Every inch of skin covered. But after a few days, I loosened up. Paul rarely wore a shirt. He always looked so at ease in the wild, and I figured I could do the same. I swapped into a tank top and swim trunks.

Big mistake.

By sundown, my legs looked like a connect-the-dots puzzle. Turns out, "no-see-ums" are a very real thing—tiny bloodsuckers that bite without you noticing. The irritation comes from the chemical in the saliva that the bug injects to prevent its victim's blood from clotting and gumming up its microscopic beak, leaving behind painful welts that last for days.

Paul had lived in the Amazon for so long his immune system tolerated the bites. No welts. But I was fresh meat for these micro-monsters. The lower half of my body was a polka-dotted freak show.

And yet it could have been so much worse.

One of our crew even had a botfly larva burrow under her skin. Botflies inject their eggs beneath the flesh of a mammal, where the larva feeds off its host until it's ready to emerge as a full-grown fly—and move on to its next victim. You can't squeeze them out; rupturing the larva can trigger a dangerous anaphylactic reaction. The best option is removal at a medical center. But in the jungle, there is only one option—to outsmart them.

JJ pulled a small piece of meat from his satchel, dangling it over the wound. Sure enough, the larva rose from the wound, grasping at the meat with its teeth. JJ quickly pinched and yanked the parasite with surgical precision. I immediately recommitted to Trevor's dress code.

Later that night, Paul hit me with another curveball. "Get ready," he said. "We're going to catch caimans."

I looked at him like he'd just said we were going to fistfight dragons. "Now? As in, *right now?*"

"It's the best time," he said. Of course it was.

We launched back onto the river under a moonless sky. JJ steered slowly along the edge. With headlamps, we scanned the water's edge for eyes—those telltale twin glints that meant a caiman was watching us back.

"Welcome to nightmare soup," Paul grinned, gesturing at the surface. "You step in here and it gets weird fast. Everything is multiplying rapidly. Long-fanged tarantulas skate across the water, searching for frogs. Insects crawl into your clothes. It's a festival of sex and death."

He told me about a researcher who'd been bitten sixteen times in the thigh by a giant aquatic spider that scurried up her leg—each bite injecting venom until her skin swelled and she lost balance in the river.

Cool. That's just what this night needed.

Caimans, up close, look like creatures the dinosaurs left behind. And rightly so—they've been around for over 250 million years, and they're still here because they've mastered the art of the ambush: snap, spin, and tear.

Paul made the first grab. He leaned over the boat and snatched a juvenile by the back of the head with both hands. It jolted, froze, and then settled—secured in his grip. "This safely paralyzes it," Paul explained. "As long as you don't let go." The heavy scar across his left hand made the warning stick.

We took measurements, logged the data, and released the caiman back into the black water. We repeated the process a few more times—Paul catching, me measuring, JJ taking notes. Then it was my turn to catch.

I aimed for a smaller set of eyes, leaned over, and grabbed tight. The body was firmer than I expected, armored and heavy. I held steady.

"That's a white caiman," Paul said, tapping the ridge between its eyes. "Spectacled caiman. See that bone line? Looks like it's wearing glasses."

"And the black ones don't have that?" I asked.

"Nope. They're bigger. Meaner. And they usually have three dark spots on the jaw."

That night, I learned the differences between species of caiman in the Amazon. The smooth-fronted, and the dwarf caiman, grew to between three and five feet. We were after crocs that would grow much larger.

Paul logged the measurements. Then came the hard part—letting go.

Releasing a crocodile just inches from my fingers was a strange test of trust. The thing hadn't moved much yet, but it was packed with prehistoric rage. I eased its tail into the water, then the legs, then gave it a nudge and yanked my hands back like it was a live wire.

It thrashed and vanished beneath the surface.

"There ya go," Paul said. "You're catching on, Dax. You might make a good croc man yet."

The adrenaline hit, surging through me; fear escaped, and confidence took its place. I was still covered in bug bites, sunburned and soaked—but I felt alive. I wasn't just along for the ride anymore. Over the next few hours, we took turns catching caiman, collecting data, trading roles. My hands stopped shaking. My instincts kicked in. Whatever I'd been before this—city guy, observer, outsider—I was something else now.

The Asháninka

My sleep was intermittent, and morning arrived too quickly. I had grown more comfortable rooming with bats and falling asleep to the jungle's sounds. But my skin was on fire—covered in bites. Whatever protection the mosquito net offered at night was avenged by swarms of insects throughout the day.

JJ handed me a small bottle of a locally made tincture to soothe the burning and itching. It was made from Sangre de Drago—Dragon's Blood—the same tree sap he once used to save Paul from a life-threatening infection. Just a few drops of this stuff are magical. I later learned it's packed with antiviral and antibacterial properties, effective against ulcers, hepatitis, even certain cancers. Its healing potential was staggering—one more reason we should be preserving forests, not clearing them. Each tree here might hold secrets still undiscovered.

We packed the boat with extra gear, prepared to travel farther downriver and stay the night. Paul warned us that this part of the journey could be dangerous. But it wasn't the type of danger we'd faced before—this wasn't about snakes or caimans. This was political. Human. Territorial.

Chapter 1 | **MADRE DE DIOS** 55

During the pandemic, while resources were scarce and eyes were elsewhere, loggers had coerced a group of Asháninka—migrants from the Andes—to burn down a large section of concession JK4. They'd built a settlement camp where the primary forest had once stood. Paul and JJ said we needed to confront them and convince them to leave.

The Asháninka are one of South America's largest Indigenous nations, numbering around seventy thousand across the Upper Amazon. For centuries, they've endured violent displacement—from enslavement during the rubber boom to atrocities during Peru's civil war. More than once, they've been forced from ancestral lands, their immunity shattered by contact, often losing more than half their people to disease.

Their culture is deeply rooted in the rainforest. The Asháninka live in dispersed, semi-nomadic communities. Men hunt tapir, boar, and monkey. Women cultivate yuca, bananas, sweet potatoes, and peppers in rotational gardens. Traditionally, they move as needed—following game, responding to floods or fire, or seeking safer territory.

The group we were approaching had squatted on Junglekeepers land while the rangers were away. But this wasn't a case of ancestral return. These families had been manipulated—coerced by outside forces to settle

Surveying the aftermath—forest reduced to ash.
Credit: Paul Rosolie

on protected land. Paul and JJ suspected loggers were behind it, using the Asháninka as pawns to quietly reopen access to the concession. It was a familiar tactic: Install Indigenous villagers on conservation territory, wait for them to build shelter, and then push for legal reassignment of the land. In the end, the trees fall, the land is cleared, and the tribe receives next to nothing in return.

Trekking to the site was brutal. Every step demanded focus—slick roots and thorned vines turned the rainforest into an obstacle course. With eyes locked on the forest floor, I was constantly untangling myself from vines, slipping on roots and leaves, clawing for grip on inclines, and checking—always checking—that the root I grabbed for wasn't a snake. Bugs swarmed endlessly. Bullet ants, mosquitoes, parasitic flies.

Still, Paul warned me of something worse than bullet ants.

"Bullet ants suck," he said, wiping his forehead as he stepped through vines. "But the sting is nothing compared to what this caterpillar did to me."

While using a leaf to pick up an unknown caterpillar, the leaf bent, dropping the large insect right onto his hand.

"It pierced me with venomous barbs, and I was thrown into a world of electro-shocking pain like nothing I'd ever felt. Whatever that thing did, it messed me up for days."

Canopy dweller: the emerald tree boa.
Credit: Paul Rosolie

What stuck with me was there were creatures that Paul was unaware of, after all this time in the jungle.

As we neared the encampment, the smell hit first—burnt wood, smoke, and wet ash. Then the trail opened into a vast clearing. A war zone. Acres of forest had been razed, reduced to a scorched earth of toppled, blackened trunks. Thick smoke curled from still-smoldering stumps. Nothing green survived.

"This is a graveyard," Paul said, stepping over a fallen log, wiping sweat from his brow. "This was primary forest. Hundreds of years of life—gone." His voice cracked. I could see the hurt in his eyes. Trevor filmed quietly, capturing the devastation.

In the clearing stood makeshift huts and a group of forty or so villagers—men, women, and children. Some bore traditional red and black body paint. Others looked wary, staring at us from under thatched roofs. They'd marked off more trees to burn.

This wasn't just displacement. It was manipulation. There were signs they were receiving outside support: gasoline containers, heavy-duty equipment, steel tools, nylon tarps. Paul and JJ believed the logging industry in Lucerna was behind it—sending Indigenous families to squat and clear Junglekeepers' concessions, hoping to invalidate their protection. If the Asháninka claimed the land long enough, without action to protect the concession, the government might reassign ownership, opening the door to legal logging.

JJ, fluent in both Spanish and the local dialect, stepped forward and initiated a conversation. His tone was calm, respectful. He asked questions. Where had they come from? Who had told them they could settle here?

It was a complicated moment. Ethically murky. These were people with a tragic history of displacement, and yet here they were, possibly being used as pawns to do the loggers' bidding. Everyone loses in that equation—especially the forest.

Their leader, a stout man wearing a beaded robe and a feathered headdress, stepped forward. He said they had been waiting for us. Several in the group were sick. They needed medicine. Then they handed over a gift—a red-tailed boa in a gasoline container, weak, pulled from the fires.

It was dying. It was also symbolic. Outsiders to the region traditionally kill snakes, not being able to decipher between normal snakes and deadly ones, yet here they were offering one they had saved.

Harry crouched beside the boa. The camera hung loose around his neck. His voice faltered as he whispered to the snake, "I'm so sorry, little guy—we'll find you a safe home." For a moment, the burned forest faded. It was just Harry and the snake, two fragile beings in a shattered world.

JJ and Roy chose to stay behind. They would help the Asháninka obtain medicine and try to prevent further burning. Paul, Trevor, Harry, and I left camp with the sick snake and rising anxiety. We didn't know how this would end.

At a small stream, we released the boa to soak. It drank immediately. Paul watched in silence, then began to sob. He wasn't just crying for the snake. He cried for the forest. For everything we had lost. For what may still be lost. I put my hand on his shoulder. There were no words.

Near the river's edge, far from the ashes, we placed the snake in the folds of a kapok tree. It slithered upward, disappearing into the canopy— one quiet life spared. A whisper of hope in a forest gasping for breath.

The Sacred Tree

After leaving the Asháninka camp, Paul, Trevor, Harry, and I set out on the river to visit the newest concession—22,000 acres I helped secure for Junglekeepers. JK5 may have looked like the forests we'd seen in days prior, but after the smoldering ruins of JK4, it held more weight. This was the first of many conservation projects I intended to support. It marked a beginning—one I hoped might bring renewal.

We drifted downriver for hours, the jungle slowly softening around us. Eventually, we reached a quiet crossing where an old tributary met the Las Piedras. Paul pointed out the invisible boundary where JK4 ended and JK5 began.

Just then, four brilliant scarlet macaws soared overhead, screeching as they passed in a flash of red and blue. In Jewish spirituality, the number four is sacred—it represents unity and wholeness. God's name is spelled with four letters. In numerology, the number symbolizes foundation and stability—like the four legs of a chair. Take one away and everything collapses.

I've always paid attention to spiritual signals, and in that moment, those macaws seemed like more than birds. They were a message. After the destruction we had witnessed upstream, this felt like a gift from the jungle itself—a moment of relief, and a reminder: *Keep going. You're on the right path.*

"They look prehistoric, like dinosaurs," I said, watching their colorful wings slice the air.

"In a way, they are," Paul replied, smiling as they glided into the canopy. "They come from the theropods—same lineage as *T. rex* and velociraptors."

He wasn't wrong. The day before, watching them waddle along the clay banks, I'd thought the same thing—tiny jungle raptors.

"Macaws are fantastic, yet so fragile," Paul said, pointing to a cluster on the shoreline. "They spend their lives between the clay banks and the ironwood trees where they breed."

Tree climbing prep: Paul rigging lines on a kapok.
Credit: Dax Dasilva

As we neared the shore, Paul cut the motor and leapt into waist-deep water, guiding the boat onto the sandbar. "They'll only nest in old ironwoods," he said. "If the right hole in the right tree doesn't exist, they won't breed. That's how specific they are. No ironwood? No macaws."

We grabbed our gear and followed Paul along a narrow trail. He explained how there were less than fifty thousand scarlet macaws left in the world. Their habitat was vanishing—and with it, their ability to reproduce.

The ironwood trees in this area were between five and eight hundred years old. Nesting holes only occurred in trees that old, and even then, not every tree would do. Only 17 to 20 percent of the macaw population breeds each year, simply because there aren't enough holes in the forest to go around.

"Per hectare, there are only so many viable nest sites," Paul said. "That's their ecological barrier. It's not food. It's not mates. It's real estate."

We reached a towering kapok tree, a mythic presence among the giants. It stretched upward nearly two hundred feet, at least twelve feet around at its base. Kapoks are known to house life at every level of the rainforest, from insects and bats to monkeys and jaguars. Its bark, resin, and leaves have long been used to treat fever, asthma, kidney disease, even dysentery. Some cultures believe it's a sacred bridge between heaven and Earth—a tree where the souls of the dead climb upward to reach the gods.

This one had been outfitted with ropes and platforms for canopy observation.

Paul and I strapped into harnesses, clipped onto carabiners, and began the climb. Trevor and Harry filmed from below. We passed a series of platforms, each one revealing more of the jungle's vertical expanse—ferns, fungi, orchids, bromeliads, and flashes of wings. With every pull upward, the world fell farther below us.

Near the top of the canopy, Paul paused.

"Half of all rainforest life is up here," he said, looking out over the canopy. "Most science happens down there—on the ground. That's like studying the ocean from the seafloor. The real life? The rare stuff? It's up here, where the sunlight is. Only 3 percent of the sunlight makes it to the rainforest floor."

That urgency—in his words and his world—was why I'd partnered with Junglekeepers.

Not far off, a dark body of water shimmered. "That's where your concession begins," Paul said, pointing toward it. "That's JK5. It stretches from that lagoon to the far side of the horizon."

The sky had cleared. The view was endless. Everything I could see was forest we'd helped protect. It was a surreal, humbling moment.

"What's in the lagoon?" I asked.

"Giant river otters," Paul grinned. "You'll see them up close—we're staying there tonight."

We rappelled back down the tree and hiked toward the water. Even before we arrived, we could hear them—barks, hums, chatter. And then we saw them.

"They're massive," I said.

"They're the largest species of otter in the world," Paul replied.

We crouched behind a strangler fig and watched them swim. On a sandy bank, a mother lifted her cub by the scruff and carried it to the water. Others play-wrestled and periscoped their heads, curious and alert.

"This is a special group," Paul said. "There are a few families here— maybe twenty in each. Giant otters are endangered. Back in the 1950s and '60s, they were trapped for their fur. It almost wiped them out."

They were listed as endangered in 1999. Fewer than five thousand remain.

"And they just eat fish?" I asked.

"Mostly piranha," Paul said. "But they'll also kill caiman. Even small anacondas."

"There are piranhas in this lagoon?"

"Dax, we're in the Amazon," he said, slinging his pack over his shoulder. "You've been swimming in piranha-infested waters since you got here."

It was probably for the best I didn't know that when we were log-wrestling in the river.

"But don't swim with the otters," he added, smirking. "They'll kill you."

We continued past the lagoon to a cluster of small huts once owned by a man named Pepe—an ex-military guy who'd taken conservation into his own hands. His methods weren't as diplomatic. Paul joked that there were probably loggers at the bottom of the lagoon—if anything had made it past the otters and piranhas.

As Pepe aged, he got tired of fighting alone. He trusted Paul and sold the land to Junglekeepers.

We stayed at his place that night. Harry and I dropped our bags inside one of the huts. I went to draw the curtain and nearly grabbed a beady-eyed bat hanging in the folds. I yelped and jumped back.

"Yep," Harry said, eyes locked on it. "That's a vampire."

He grabbed a towel and scooped it out of the hut. "They're a real problem in Peru," he said. "Vampire bats swoop in at night to bite livestock, spreading rabies to the herds."

Later, we sat by the lagoon as Paul and JJ set up fishing poles to catch dinner. JJ, ever resourceful, unsheathed his belt knife, sliced a hardened slab of dead skin from the bottom of his foot, and hooked it to a fishing line.

"There's no better bait," he said, casting it into the dark water with a grin. Within minutes, he pulled out a piranha. Then another.

That night, as the fire crackled and the stars opened above us, grilled piranha became the main course.

Dwarfed by the rainforest—JJ and I beneath a giant.
Credit: Paul Rosolie

More Than a Mission

On my last day in the Amazon, Dina and the rangers surprised us with a celebration at the new ranger station. Roy cooked a feast. Paul poured glasses of pisco. Dina gave a moving speech about what the station meant—not just for Junglekeepers, but for the future of the forest itself. There were toasts, laughter, and tears. Not just from joy, but from the weight of saying goodbye.

Trevor had been right. I wouldn't go home the same. I felt changed—maybe it was the moment I drank from the river, or maybe it was everything that followed. I had become part of the life cycle I came to protect. Funding the project was important, but living in the Amazon with Paul, JJ, Roy, Dina, Trevor, Harry, and the rest of the team gave me something deeper: clarity. I understood how it all worked—how Junglekeepers was protecting land, building trust, growing community, and staying agile in the face of every new threat.

There's something about standing in the jungle that no photo, reel, or drone shot can ever convey. It's not just the magnitude of it—it's the feeling. The current of life you can't quite explain, only absorb. The energy here humbles you. It reminds you that we're guests on this planet, not landlords. That our responsibility isn't just to marvel at what's left of the natural world, but to defend it while we still can.

By the end of my time there, I wasn't the only one changed. I could see it in Paul and the team. There was a renewed sense of optimism. With more resources and support, we all felt it—that we could do more. Yes, there would be more threats: new roads, new settlers, new logging schemes. But for the first time, it felt like we were ready. That the momentum was ours.

The Junglekeepers program became a true success story. Between my first trip and writing this chapter, we expanded protections to over 100,000 acres. With continued funding, Junglekeepers could support a growing ranger team, along with the infrastructure to defend the forest and all who live in it. And perhaps most important: The team was empowered to share their own stories and vision for the future.

Together, we produced *Heart of the Mission,* a short film spotlighting Junglekeepers and our efforts to protect the Las Piedras corridor—one of the most critical and biodiverse wildlife pathways on Earth. This was the first film made in support of Age of Union's conservation work. I believe deeply in the power of storytelling. Not just to raise awareness, but to spark real change.

Junglekeepers also built Alta Sanctuary—the tallest treehouse in the Amazon—named one of *TIME*'s World's Greatest Places. Perched 160 feet above the jungle floor, the tree house offers guests a rare vantage point to witness the rainforest canopy at dawn, to explore the forest with Junglekeepers rangers, and to learn what it means to protect a place that's still wild, still alive.

Leaving Madre de Dios was far easier than arriving. The sky was clear, the river calm, and the road out dry. No vapor ghosts. No fangs. No detours. But that's not what stayed with me.

What stayed was the sense that I had seen the jungle for what it really is—sacred, chaotic, threatened, and alive. What stayed was the memory of the four scarlet macaws over the river, the weight of the boa in my arms, and the sight of a smoldering graveyard where forest used to be. What stayed was the feeling that I wasn't just passing through.

I was part of it now.

Macaws in flight at dawn.
Credit: Moshin Kazmi

United Nations

The United Nations Climate Change Conferences—known as COP, short for *Conference of the Parties*—are annual gatherings where countries commit to voluntary action against human-caused environmental destruction. Each year, a different nation hosts, and delegates share progress reports, update goals, and negotiate global strategies for environmental protection. In December 2022, COP 15, the United Nations Biodiversity Conference, took place in Montréal.

I was invited to speak on a panel at the World Biodiversity Summit, a parallel event to COP 15. Coincidentally, Paul happened to be in New York visiting family. I invited him to join me, and he turned up the next day. It was great to see him—but also strange. No trees, no rivers, no machete—just Paul, in a city, wearing a shirt.

"So *that's* what you look like in a collared shirt," I joked, as we strolled the icy streets of Montréal.

We were there with news.

Paul and I held a joint press conference in the United Nations Press Briefing Room at COP 15. He shared the Junglekeepers story with powerful slides that captured both the urgency and the beauty of the Amazon. Then we made the announcement: Age of Union was pledging $3.5 million to Junglekeepers over the next five years.

The five-year commitment would give Paul, Dina, and the rest of the team the ability to expand conservation efforts—protecting more land, building new ranger infrastructure, growing patrol forces, and creating stronger partnerships with Indigenous communities to help secure legal rights to their ancestral lands. The announcement generated buzz, inspired new financial supporters, and reinforced Junglekeepers' place on the global conservation map.

That night, Paul and I decided to trade the smell of fire and clay for a fancy bar and cocktails. Seeing Paul, Tarzan of the Amazon, in a polished bar with a three-olive martini in hand was almost comical. He looked like a wild animal that had wandered into an art museum.

"How bad are you itching to get back to the jungle?" I asked.

Paul leaned in, the gleam of the wild still in his eyes. "I'm more comfortable with a machete in my hand than a computer mouse," he said, laying his two scarred, callused hands on the table. "In the jungle, these are my tools. I can catch a fish, build a shelter, start a fire, and climb anything."

He looked around the bar—at the polished glassware, the fancy dresses, the glow of phone screens—and then finished his martini in a single gulp. Just like he did with the pisco at the ranger station.

"This life," he said, motioning around us, "the traffic, the tall buildings, the business suits—it's not for me. I prefer the lawless dance of the jungle."

Standing for the wild at the UN Biodiversity Summit, Montréal.
Credit: Age of Union

The Sapling

Junglekeepers' work to halt the damage to JK4 got worse before it got better. The negotiations were difficult. Members of the Junglekeepers team received death threats. The settlers in the encampment kept burning trees, hunting wildlife, and clearing massive tracts of forest with chainsaws and equipment provided by loggers.

We brought in lawyers and spent long, stressful nights trying to devise a plan. Eventually, it paid off. We worked with local authorities to relocate the group from the concession. It took months of effort, but the once-violated land was finally at peace. The hunting stopped. The chainsaws went quiet. No more ancient trees fell.

A year later, we returned to JK4 to assess the damage—to see if reforestation would be necessary or if the land had begun to heal on its own. What we found was nothing short of a miracle. The forest, once scarred by fire and destruction, was teeming with new life. In the absence of human interference, nature had begun its recovery—and fast.

Where the clearings once stood, green secondary forest had returned. Fast-growing trees like cecropia, balsa, and bamboo were thriving, casting shade and laying the groundwork for a full ecosystem to return. Fallen leaves nourished fungi and vines. It was a powerful display of nature's resilience.

Signs of wildlife gave us more reason to hope. Paul found tracks of ocelots, deer, peccaries, and armadillos. There were burrows and signs of tayra—a rare jungle weasel—as well as a fluttering explosion of butterflies, birds, and reptiles. The jungle had begun to mend itself.

Birds and bats had returned, dispersing seeds across the damaged terrain. Deer droppings fertilized the ground and nurtured new saplings. The forest was healing, quietly and persistently—despite everything we humans had done.

We know it will take hundreds of years for the full ecosystem to return—a climax community with towering ironwoods, tangled canopies, and species living in balance. But this regrowth, this young forest, is already a haven for life. It's a living proof-of-concept. With protection and time, the Amazon can bounce back.

One morning, Paul texted me a photo. "Look at this," the message read. The image showed a tiny sapling, barely knee-high, pushing up through the soil.

"It's a baby ironwood," he wrote. "This is why we fight."

I stared at the photo longer than I expected. That small green shoot said everything—resilience, redemption, possibility. In time, it would grow into one of the jungle's giants, sheltering hundreds of species and, if we did our job right, giving macaws a place to raise their young again.

I teared up. I'd seen that forest when it was burning. I'd watched it fall, and then I watched the team rise to protect it. That little sapling was proof that we had helped it stand back up.

I thought of the red-tailed boa we released into the kapok tree. That snake was more than a rescue—it was a promise that not all was lost. I remembered those four macaws that flew over us on the river. At the time, their screeches had sounded like a warning. Now, they echoed like a chorus of hope.

In Amazonian culture, the kapok symbolizes the sacred cycle of life. To me, it became something else, too—a reminder that even the smallest acts, when done with care and purpose, can grow into legacies that outlive us all.

"We are facing an environmental tipping point unprecedented in human history—and our very survival depends on protecting nature."

—LEONARDO DICAPRIO

A rare moment with a young Grauer's gorilla.
Credit: Matt Brunette

Chapter 2

THE CONGO DIVIDE

GRAUER'S GORILLAS AND THE UNSEEN WAR

There might be a million ways to die in the West, but in the Congo, the possibilities are infinite—and the odds were in our favor. I just hoped a plane crash wasn't on the menu as we dropped into the heart of Africa, the engines whining while the pilot adjusted pitch, guiding us lower into the basin. The vibration in the fuselage rose to a higher frequency—metal shuddering in a way I remembered all too well. Another rainforest, another descent through cloud and turbulence, and that same quiet calculation in the back of my mind: *What am I doing here?*

Below us, the forest opened up: vast, green, and unknowable.

The Congo was a place of political instability, armed militias, and diseases you wouldn't wish on your worst enemy. I'd been warned. Dismissed the Canadian government advisories and headed into the Democratic Republic of the Congo (DRC) during a time of severe military strife.

My stomach turned. Too many flights and too little rest. Beside me, Dr. Kerry Bowman sat calmly, arms crossed, as if we were landing in Palm Springs instead of a region steeped in volatility. His colleague Matt Brunette was clicking away on a laptop, running through the itinerary again.

Dr. Bowman has a PhD in bioethics, a fellowship in cultural psychiatry, and a master's degree in social work. He founded the Forest Health Alliance, an organization that operates and oversees projects in the Eastern DRC that are designed to reflect local cultures, as well as economic and political realities. But what he is mostly interested in are eastern lowland gorillas, known as the Grauer's gorilla. Dr. Bowman has spent a large part of his life battling the extinction of the Grauer's gorilla, in which he has worked with local organizations to develop a habitat corridor to promote gene flow and reduce deforestation. We had plans to trek into the forest to visit a troop of gorillas that Dr. Bowman had been studying for decades.

I stared out the window.

"Dax, you know this was your idea, right?" he said, glancing over, grinning. Of course he was.

"Yeah," I sighed. "Thanks for the reminder."

"Just making sure. In case the thrill of dodging militias and malaria hasn't quite set in."

Dr. Bowman had been to the DRC over thirty times. He'd survived rebel ambushes, been held at gunpoint, escaped the country—only to come right back. Fear wasn't a factor anymore. For him, this was routine. For me, it was a calculated leap into the unknown. Nine government advisories hadn't exactly painted a comforting picture. A border closure

On the front lines of ethics and ecology—Dr. Kerry Bowman.
Credit: Matt Brunette

could detour us from getting into the DRC or prevent us from getting out.

I tugged at my seatbelt. "You're really not concerned?"

I already knew the answer. Dr. Bowman had a habit of describing things—harrowing situations that would terrify most people—as "no big deal."

He smirked, the corners of his mouth twitching. "Excited for malaria, kidnappings, and maybe a little Ebola? Or was it the rebels that sold you on the vacation package?"

He said it breezily, like he wasn't listing actual threats.

"You're not helping."

"You're here. That's what counts. Most people wouldn't step foot in Congo right now—especially not during a pandemic."

He wasn't wrong. But it was easy for him to joke—he'd spent decades doing this. I was still trying to catch my breath. The Congo Basin sprawled out below us like the last wild pulse of Earth. We'd just come from the Amazon; this was the second largest rainforest in the world, absorbing nearly 5 percent of global carbon emissions. And like the Amazon, it was being eaten alive by deforestation, slash-and-burn farming, charcoal kilns, and mining for the metals powering our phones.

I exhaled. "Alright, here's the plan," I muttered, mostly to myself. "If the border closes, we need contingencies. No mission ever goes according to plan, but I'm not putting the crew at risk."

We were bringing a small team to document several programs we'd begun funding—reforestation, agriculture, microcredit initiatives. In the Congo, like most places, conservation is never just about saving trees or gorillas. It's about poverty. It's about survival.

The crew included director of photography Marc Lamy and filmmaker Ray Klonsky, along with local cinematographer Mathieu Roy. Mathieu wasn't just a shooter—he was our fixer. Without someone like him, you don't move safely or effectively in the DRC.

Dr. Bowman turned from the window. "You and I get it. But the guys out there with AKs and chainsaws? They don't."

It was a joke. Sort of. But it landed like a brick in my gut. There was something about this place—something ancient and wounded—that pressed on the soul. A forest alive with creatures on the brink, and we were here to protect them. But between intention and impact lay a brutal, tangled road.

The plane touched down hard—rubber screamed against tarmac—and we were in Kigali, Rwanda. The closest major airport with reliable access. Flying into the DRC directly meant navigating a maze of sketchy visas and security risks. Kigali, by comparison, was smooth. Clean. Stable. Just a few hours by road to the Congolese border. The go-to jumping-off point for journalists, aid workers, and conservationists alike.

Soldiers flanked the runway. Casual, but armed. A reminder: This wasn't a nature documentary. This was a live zone.

"Welcome to Congo," Dr. Bowman muttered with a grin.

I rolled my eyes. "You're impossible."

He shrugged. "You wouldn't have me any other way."

He was right. In places like this, you don't want someone who panics at the first checkpoint or second-guesses every move. You want calm. You want instinct. Dr. Bowman had both—and a kind of practiced detachment that let him read a room, or a jungle, before the rest of us knew we were in it.

Inside, guards stood at every door, their stares trained and alert. The weight of it settled fast. I wasn't strolling anywhere. Marc had tested positive for COVID just before departure, which meant I was hauling a mountain of gear solo. We'd meet Ray and Mathieu at the hotel.

News broke: The North Kivu border had just closed due to a rebel attack. We were headed to South Kivu—but if that border shut, we could be trapped inside the DRC.

"That's not a big deal," said Dr. Bowman. "In all my years coming here, I've only been held at gunpoint once."

Matt appeared behind us. "Twice, actually."

"Right, twice. But the second time was right outside the hotel we're staying at in Kivu." He smiled. "We'll be fine. Ready?"

The hotel we are staying at?

I hesitated. Then nodded. "Yeah. I'm ready."

"Good," he said. "Because the real adventure starts now."

We piled into a waiting vehicle, the streets already chaos—motors buzzing, horns blaring, people everywhere. My stomach churned with a familiar cocktail of nerves and adrenaline.

"Matt's got logistics covered," Dr. Bowman said, turning around. "And our hotel has the best gin and tonic in Kigali."

That was his superpower: making everything sound easy.

We pulled into Hotel Chez Lando, a redbrick oasis in the Remera district, just off the airport road. With its arched windows and manicured gardens, it looked like peace. But beneath its beauty was a scar. In 1994, the Rwandan genocide erupted. The hotel's founder, Landoald Ndasingwa, his wife, kids, and mother were abducted and executed. The hotel was nearly destroyed. His sister, Anne-Marie Kantengwa, rebuilt it in their honor.

The air was thick and fragrant, buzzing with cicadas and the scent of damp earth. The nervous tension was fading, replaced by something else: resolve.

Dinner on the terrace was lit by the fading gold of the Kigali sunset. Bougainvillea and jasmine framed the garden. Long-tailed starlings darted and whistled around us, a living chorus. A waiter brought steaming bowls of isombe—cassava leaf stew with eggplant and tomatoes.

"I've been reading about Rwanda," I said. "It's wild how a country this small has become a tech hub, while the DRC—ten times the size—keeps unraveling."

"Rwanda has vision," Dr. Bowman said. "Congo has resources, but no infrastructure. It bleeds for the benefit of others."

"Cobalt, coltan, tin, gold," Matt added. "In every phone, every electric car. Yet the profits never stay here."

Dr. Bowman leaned in. "And a lot of that mining is illegal. Controlled by warlords, fueled by child labor. The minerals are smuggled out, processed in Rwanda, labeled 'clean.' Then they're shipped to the world."

I nodded. "Tech giants, governments, middlemen…"

"And warlords," he finished. "As long as there's demand, the conflict never stops. Rwanda profits. But Congo?" He paused. "Congo keeps bleeding."

Silence fell between us.

I stared into my glass, the ice circling slowly. Conservation here wasn't just about saving gorillas or planting trees. Not in a place like this, where everything was tangled: politics, war, survival.

South Kivu

I woke early. Morning light reached across the bougainvillea and tangled green outside my window, golden and soft. The air was thick but cool—night still lingering in the folds of dawn. After days of back-to-back flights and dragging a mountain of gear through airports, I finally felt human again. A few hours of sleep had reset something in me. We were nearly through the hardest part of the journey. Soon, Ray and Mathieu would arrive, and we would continue to the DRC.

Later that morning, we boarded a RwandAir Dash 8 turboprop bound for Kamembe. Just a short hop southwest, hugging the edge of Rwanda. From the sky, Lake Kivu spread out below us, deep and blue, glinting in the sun like polished stone.

"Beautiful," I murmured, staring down.

Dr. Bowman gave a slow nod, arms crossed. "Yeah. Also, one of the deadliest lakes on Earth."

I turned to him. "How's that?"

Dominique Bikaba—forest guardian, community leader.
Credit: Matt Brunette

"Methane," he said. "A gas pocket trapped deep under the surface. If it ever ruptures—boom. Suffocation for miles."

"Like Lake Nyos?" I asked.

He nodded. "Cameroon. Killed seventeen hundred in a single night."

I looked back at the water. It no longer looked serene.

"And the history here," he added, quieter now. "During the genocide, thousands of bodies were dumped. Some say the lake turned red."

Silence. I kept my eyes on the surface, but all I could think about was what lay beneath.

When we landed, soldiers were scattered along the runway—rifles slung casually, but nothing about their presence felt casual. As we stepped into the heat, security split our group from the other passengers, directing us toward a gated lot. It was quiet. Their eyes tracked us too carefully.

Then another group arrived, this one hauling our luggage. Their movements felt rehearsed—too precise. Voices in Kinyarwanda clipped the air, sharp and fast. I couldn't follow the exchange, but I felt the tension.

I looked to Dr. Bowman. He was watching, calm but alert. His jaw had set.

Then came the sound of engines.

A convoy of white Toyota Land Cruisers pulled into the lot. Clean. Official. Military or government—hard to say. The lead door opened, and a broad-shouldered man stepped out. Mirrored aviators. Khakis. Sleeves rolled. His dark skin shone with sweat. He walked straight toward us, toward Bowman. No greeting. No expression.

I braced.

Then Dr. Bowman broke the silence. "You got something to say, let's hear it."

A pause. Then a smile. The stranger clapped a hand on Bowman's shoulder and laughed.

"Brother, I've missed you."

The tension shattered.

It was Dominique Bikaba. Our contact. Our conservation partner. The man we had come to meet. He turned to me, his grin wide.

"Welcome! It's a beautiful day in Congo!"

The fear I'd been carrying evaporated. Dominique wasn't just a familiar face—he was the one you wanted on your side here. Charismatic. Grounded. Respected. The guards relaxed the moment he laughed, trading words with him like old friends. We shook hands. I could feel the relief in my own grip.

Dominique carried weight. The kind that settles things, even in tense spaces. Within minutes, he had the entire scene smoothed over. He wasn't just connected—he was trusted.

"Let's move," he said, turning toward the convoy. "We've got to reach the border before it closes."

Apparently, even jungles have curfews.

He gave me a knowing smile. "You're in for something extraordinary. The gorillas are waiting." There was something in the way he said it—like they really were. As if the forest knew we were coming.

We loaded the Land Cruisers. Bowman leaned back and nodded toward Dominique. "Told you—Dom's the guy you want out here." And I believed him. In Bowman's world, "we've been through a lot together" wasn't small talk.

Dominique chuckled, starting the engine. "Back in the day, your good doctor smuggled cash sewn into his shirt collars. Just to get us what we needed."

I turned to Bowman. "That true?"

He smirked. "I'd still do it. This place requires creativity."

Dominique's eyes caught mine in the mirror. "Dax, Dr. Bowman's been here so many times, we might consider him part Congolese." Not far from the truth.

Dominique was the reason we were here. The founder of Strong Roots, he'd spent decades working with local and Indigenous communities, fighting to protect both forest and future. What began with gorillas had grown into a fight for land rights, sustainable economies, and the creation of massive wildlife corridors.

"In 2013," he said, "we pressured the government to recognize Indigenous and local management of traditional lands. That law is everything."

This trip was about making that law real. We were helping communities define their ancestral territories—mapping them and registering them. If successful, these land titles would shield hundreds of thousands of hectares from corporate exploitation. They would protect not only gorillas, but the people who had lived alongside them for generations.

And we weren't just here to work. We were here to document.

And we were filming it all—capturing Dominique's fight. The challenges. The victories. The raw truth of conservation in a place where nothing comes easy. A story the world needed to hear.

The road opened ahead of us, Lake Kivu glittering at our side as the sky began to burn gold. The hills rolled in waves, green and terraced, each slope carved by hand into neat rows of red soil. Farmers moved through the fields, slow and steady, their tools flashing in the light. Banana trees leaned into the breeze, their broad leaves flicking sunbeams across the hills. Children waved from the roadside, running barefoot beside our convoy, kicking up clouds of dust that drifted through the windows and settled on our skin, our lips, the backs of our throats.

A young boy paddles along the shores of Lake Kivu.
Credit: Matt Brunette

Dominique talked easily, stories rolling off his tongue—of forests, of family, of years navigating bureaucracy and broken promises. But beneath every word was something deeper. He wasn't just protecting land. He was protecting home.

"When I was a child, we lived in the forest," Dominique said. "I remember those peaceful days. But colonialism tore that bond apart. They pushed our people out of the jungle and into the cities. Now, when our people return to the forest, they no longer know how to coexist. They only know how to take from it."

His voice was low, even, as if the story had been told too many times to need embellishment. "That's what we're trying to do—reconnect people to the land. Not just to protect it, but to belong to it again."

We reached the Rusizi River crossing into South Kivu. The immigration building gleamed—new construction, clearly backed by international funds.

"This is new," Bowman said. "World Bank, probably."

Once again, Dominique took the lead. His charm smoothed the way like water over stone. Visas, vaccination records—all reviewed without incident. Minutes later, we were back in the convoy, crossing into the DRC.

Bowman glanced at me. "Welcome to the real Africa."

The contrast was immediate. Paved roads gave way to red dust. The polished infrastructure fell behind us. But the spirit here—louder, brighter—rushed in to fill the space. We passed rusted rooftops, crowded street stalls, and women balancing woven baskets on their heads like practiced art.

We drove through Bukavu, the capital city of South Kivu, stacked along the southern rim of Lake Kivu. The streets were alive. Vendors shouted over the hum of motorcycles. Women moved through the chaos draped in brilliant hues. Colonial facades crumbled beside tin shacks. Old and new. Chaotic and electric. This place had survived—and kept its color.

We arrived at the Orchids' Safari Club Hotel, perched above the lake, its terraces crowded with white Land Rovers. Clearly, it was a base for NGOs and diplomats. Not the place to forget where you parked.

Inside, we were briefed on growing conflict in North Kivu. The border remained closed. And though we were considered safe, we were warned: Don't wander after dark.

Matt reminded us of one of Bowman's past visits—held at gunpoint outside this very hotel.

"Calm as ever," Matt said. "He saw them coming. Ducked into the bushes. Hid fifteen grand in cash under the weeds—money for Strong Roots. They searched him, found nothing. Let him go."

Bowman shrugged. "It wasn't a big deal."

That phrase again. As if danger was just part of the job description.

Later, on the veranda, gin and tonics had just hit the table when Dr. Bowman offered something else.

"In the Congo," he said, "you never know what's coming. But the real danger? Not taking risks. That's what gets you nowhere—which is far worse than any danger, if you ask me."

After dinner, we followed a stone path down to the lake. The light was softening, the air cooling. Ripples danced along the water's surface.

A black-headed heron stepped through the shallows, neck arched. A boy in a dugout canoe paddled silently, cutting through the water like a memory. We watched in silence as his silhouette drifted into dusk.

Then came another boat—three soldiers, rifles slung, eyes sharp. Patrolling the invisible line between two nations in conflict. The tension returned, silent and spectral, like a ghost skimming just beyond the edge of vision—there, then gone.

The soldiers drifted into the haze. Above us, the moon lifted over the hills, its pale light spilling across the lake. Lake Kivu mirrored it perfectly—shifting, watching, waiting.

"Lake Kivu is a changeling," Bowman said. "It never looks the same twice."

Seedlings

I rose early, my circadian rhythm scrambled but overridden by anticipation—the kind of restless energy that pulls you out of bed before dawn with a purpose that feels half dream, half calling. I should've been tired, but I wasn't. The idea of seeing gorillas in the wild—my first time—burned through the haze of jet lag like sun through mist. Our mission in the Congo Basin was wide-ranging, but at its core, it involved protecting the great apes.

It's strange to think how recently the world even knew they existed. For centuries, gorillas were myth—half-man, half-monster. Traders whispered about them. Villagers feared them. European naturalists dismissed them as fantasy. And even once they were proven real, the old stories lingered. Feral giants. Forest brutes. What they were, in truth, was something else entirely. Gorillas, despite their hulking size and fangs and impossible strength, are quiet beings. Gentle foragers. Attentive parents. They move through the forest like old spirits—grounded, deliberate, ancient.

Dust, heat, and a flat—on the road with our team.
Credit: Matt Brunette

And today, with proper guides and a bit of luck, I would meet them in their home.

From my balcony, the sky dissolved from early-morning indigo to a soft, gathering blue. The lake shimmered with a hush. Pink clouds hung low and violet, their undersides kissed with gold. A tropical boubou hooted across the water, answered a moment later by the metallic rasp of its mate. Below me, lantanas spilled wild over a stone wall—riotous color and foul scent, something between sour citrus and cat piss. And yet their leaves, I'd been told, were medicine for ulcers, fevers, and malaria. That contradiction stayed with me. Here, the cure lived beside the disease. Often in the same breath.

We rolled northwest in a dusty convoy, bound for Kahuzi-Biega. The road wound upward through the mountainous Kabare and Kidumbi territories, narrow and crumbling, shouldered by volcanic rock and the kind of wild beauty that asked for no forgiveness. Along the way, villages came and went—echoes of colonial-era Bukavu shrunk into narrow, crooked shops and tin-roofed stalls clinging to the hillsides.

But what I noticed most were the children. They were everywhere. Running barefoot through open fields. Laughing in clusters. Clinging to their mothers' skirts. Their joy cracked open the morning air in bursts of color and sound. By far, they outnumbered the adults I could see.

Then I thought of the statistics I'd read. The DRC: 100 million people, climbing toward 170 million by the year 2030. Six births per woman on average. Four percent population growth. And I looked at those kids, waving like they knew us, like we'd promised them something. The question came uninvited: How does conservation hold its ground against the rising tide of human need?

The road narrowed. The village pressed close. People turned from storefronts. They waved.

"Mufasa! Mufasa!" The name rose with the dust, called out from doorways, market stalls, the mouths of kids keeping pace with our wheels. It didn't feel like a name so much as a summoning. Dominique leaned out the window, beaming, calling back to the children, one hand raised in greeting. It felt less like we were arriving and more like he was returning.

"It's what they call me," he said, still waving.

Dr. Bowman explained it. "It means 'king' in Swahili. Dominique is Congolese-born, raised by a Batwa nursemaid. He's the bridge that connects them all."

The Batwa had been the forest's original stewards. Small in stature, but immense in knowledge and tradition, they lived within the rhythm of the canopy, never above it. But they'd been scattered, pushed out by the same tides of violence and greed that had driven the gorillas to the edge. Their songs were fading. Their stories, barely kept alive. Dominique still knew them. He carried the memory. And more than that—the obligation.

He shouted again, laughing now, waving at a group of children sprinting to keep up with the convoy. Their laughter chased us down the road. The dust hung behind like a ribbon.

Future forests start in these hands.
Credit: Matt Brunette

The name still echoed in the distance.

Mufasa.

Then came the jolt—a sound too familiar to mistake. The thud of rubber surrendering to stone. A blowout. Dominique eased us over, and the dust curled around the truck like breath. Within minutes, villagers appeared—no hesitation, no need for instruction. They set to work on the tire, pulling down a spare from the roof like they'd done it a hundred times. Maybe they had.

I stepped out and walked ahead with Dominique. He pointed to the horizon, where green rolled thick and wide across the hills.

"There, Dax," he said. "That's our reforestation project. That's where the forest returns."

From a distance, it looked eternal. But I'd seen the satellite photos—the deforested scars. What I saw now was resurrection.

"You planted all that?"

"Two and a half million trees," he said. "Where there was nothing."

He didn't say more. He didn't need to.

We drove on, the next stop a Strong Roots seedling nursery tucked beneath the shade of banana trees. Here, the reforestation began not in boardrooms or headlines, but in soil and hands. Women moved through rows of saplings with the quiet dignity of those who know exactly what they're doing. The place smelled of damp earth and ash, and it hummed—not with noise, but with purpose.

Dominique walked slowly, speaking low. "They've taken back what no one thought could be returned. This isn't about planting. It's about reclaiming. These women can provide food for their families, with a surplus to earn."

Nearby, a woman knelt beside a child, guiding her hands into the dirt. The girl didn't ask questions. She pressed the soil as though it had asked something of her.

We spent the afternoon walking those rows, listening more than talking. Children ran between the women, hauling water, lifting saplings, laughing when the wind caught the shade cloth and lifted it like a wave. They weren't growing up around conservation. They were growing up inside it.

By noon, we reached the Kahuzi-Biega Environmental School—another Strong Roots–funded program. Classes spilled outside, where children sat with notebooks balanced on knees. Nearly a hundred students were present, their chatter rising like birdsong through the heat. For many—especially the Batwa children—this was more than an education. It was the one place they'd eat a full meal that day.

They studied math and reading, but also birdsong, tree names, the healing power of plants. They were learning the language of the forest—its creatures, its cycles, its wisdom. A foundation not just for education, but for belonging.

Before we left, the children stood and sang for us. They danced, voices high and bright, spilling into the valley like a prayer. It was pure joy—unfiltered, radiant. My heart swelled. A quiet send-off into the forest.

The sun climbed higher, sharp and unforgiving. The road turned rough again, winding uphill over the rocky terrain—only one place left to go.

Dr. Bowman leaned in. "You know what's next?"

I didn't answer. Just nodded.

Somewhere ahead, in that cathedral of green, the gorillas were waiting.

Children singing and dancing at the Strong Roots School.
Credit: Matt Brunette

Bonne Année

The air seemed impossibly thick as we approached Kahuzi-Biega National Park, named for the forest's two dormant volcanoes. Spanning more than 600,000 hectares, the park was a sprawling wilderness of staggering biodiversity. Within its vast, breathing maze lived leopards, forest elephants, antelope, and chimpanzees. But perhaps most urgently, it remained one of the last refuges for the eastern lowland gorilla—Grauer's gorilla, classified as critically endangered. Fewer than 250 were believed to inhabit this forest. And Dr. Bowman and Dominique had spent much of their lives fighting to protect them.

Rangers met us at the entry station—local Congolese and Batwa, among them our guide, Lambert. His reputation preceded him: a Batwa whose connection with the gorillas ran so deep it felt almost ancestral. Lambert remembers a time when the forest was home, sharing space and resources with the wild. Coexisting. He spoke quietly but with purpose, delivering the safety briefing and the rule that hung over everything: ten meters minimum. Even habituated gorillas, used to humans, deserved respect and caution.

Into the jungle—tracking signs of gorillas.
Credit: Matt Brunette

As soon as we stepped into the forest, Lambert moved like a shadow, silent, effortless—his body in tune with the jungle in a way that suggested he was less a guide and more an extension of it. Dominique was the same. I watched the way they moved, the quiet certainty in their steps, the way their hands brushed past branches without hesitation. Two men born of these woods. Two men who carried its secrets.

My story was another. I got caught up in vines, tangled in roots. I tried to match their grace, but my mind was racing ahead, scanning every tree, every flicker of movement in the canopy. But the struggle ahead didn't matter—every fiber of me was wired for that first glimpse.

This was why I had come: Grauer's gorillas.

Time has shown that this forest was no fortress. Not anymore. Once, the gorillas numbered in the tens of thousands. By the 1990s, their population was estimated at twenty thousand. Now, less than four thousand remain. And the forces that had driven them to the brink were still closing in. Habitat loss. Poaching. Disease. War. The conflict in the region had taken its toll—not only in killings, but in everything war leaves behind. When fighting sweeps through, conservation collapses. Rangers are forced to flee. Roads are cut through untouched forest. Militia roam in search of profit. Some kill out of fear. Others, just to kill.

Bonne Année watches from the treetops.
Credit: Age of Union

I thought of how these gorillas existed in the minds of the Batwa—not just as animals, but as something more. Kin. Spirits. Ancestors. The forest was a world woven with meaning, where gorillas are the embodiment of ancestral spirits. In animist traditions, they are symbols of strength, of coexistence, of the fragile balance between the human and the wild. But reverence alone had never been enough to protect them.

I moved forward, my breath shallow, feeling the weight of it all. The land. The legends. The precariousness of what I was about to witness.

We hiked deeper into the forest. With a machete in one hand, Lambert cut through vines and branches, and with the other, he sifted through leaves, touching the forest like it might respond. It often did.

Dominique walked beside me. "This forest raised me," he said. "I know every tree, every plant. It gives without asking. Water from its roots. Food from its heart." He paused. "When I'm here, I feel my ancestors. They are in the wind."

I thought of Paul Rosolie in the Amazon, drinking from the river and becoming part of the cycle.

The wild begins with a mother's care.
Credit: Matt Brunette

Dominique bent to pick a small yellow fruit that had fallen from above. It looked like a small pineapple. "Monkey fruit," he said, handing it to me. "Sweet and sour." I bit into it, the flavor sharp and alive. He reached for a vine. "This is for stomach pain. And inflammation." I tried it—peppery, with a citrus edge. "Also, an aphrodisiac," he added with a grin. Perfect, I thought. Just what we need. Horny gorillas.

Then Lambert stopped.

He pointed to a slow swirl of tiny flies above a patch of underbrush. "They feed on gorilla dung," he whispered. "We're close."

I smelled it before I saw it—a mound of pale-yellow poop with a strong grassy odor. The pungent scent of the gorillas hung in the air. My pulse quickened.

Lambert raised his hand.

We froze.

A rustle, heavy and deliberate.

He pointed upward. "There is the big boss."

I followed his gaze and saw what at first looked like a trick of the light, then resolved into something immense, perched high among the branches.

Bonne Année. A silverback unlike anything I had imagined. Nearly five hundred pounds, his body impossibly broad, his presence overwhelming. He moved with slow, effortless strength, snapping down entire limbs with one arm. He stripped bark from branches with his teeth, eyes half-lidded, uninterested.

"Born New Year's Day, 2003," whispered Dr. Bowman, startling me with a hand on my shoulder. "That's how he got the name."

Bonne Année paid us no attention, as though our presence didn't warrant acknowledgment.

Then came another rustle. Two young gorillas exploded from the foliage—twins, I was told—engaged in a wild, tumbling game of tag. One beat his chest, then dashed up a tree. The other flipped, scrambling after him. They chased each other like children set loose at recess. And above it all, the silverback watched.

"Incredible," I whispered to myself.

Bonne Année was the leader of a troop of fourteen. His status gave him authority over the group—where to move, when to rest, how to respond to threats. And though we were clearly intruders, he allowed us to remain.

Lambert grunted softly, a low, guttural sound. Bonne Année responded in kind. It was not mimicry. It was recognition. An exchange between beings who had known each other for years.

"We are in his domain," he said. "If we walk as part of the forest, the big boss feels that."

Still, I asked, "How do you know he won't see us as a threat?"

Lambert glanced at me. "We respect him," he said. "He will show us the same."

Then Bonne Année moved.

Descending hand over hand with terrifying grace, he dropped to the ground with a thud that seemed to rearrange the forest. And he came toward us.

I stood still, every nerve firing. His shoulders rolled forward, dense with muscle. I could hear his breath—deep and steady, like the engine of the world itself. Ten meters closed quickly.

He stopped.

Everything around me held its breath.

Then, without warning, he charged.

The forest exploded. Branches cracked. Leaves erupted. My body didn't react. I was frozen, heart galloping, limbs immobile.

He veered at the last second. Passed me in a rush of heat and sound. My breath flew from my chest.

It wasn't an attack. It was a message. A reminder of whose world this was.

He returned to his bamboo, peeled it, chewed. Unbothered. At ease.

I exhaled, my pulse slamming against my ribs. The others stood wide-eyed, unmoving. Matt finally spoke: "Jesus Christ."

"That was definitely some Old Testament energy," I said.

Bonne Année didn't look back. He had said what he needed to say. He reached for a bamboo shoot, ripped it clean, and began chewing, as if nothing had happened.

For hours, we watched the troop. The mothers were gentle and watchful. The young ones tumbled through the underbrush, always returning to the center of the group. And the silverback, still and present, held it all together with nothing more than his presence.

It was easy to forget they were wild. In their movements was something we knew—something inherited. A mother smoothing the back of her baby. The young collapsing into a pile of limbs after play. Bonds made visible in touch.

I hadn't just seen gorillas. I had witnessed a dream fulfilled—something I'd carried for years, now alive in front of me in all its raw, breathing brilliance. To stand among them, not in a zoo or on a screen, but here—in their forest, on their terms—was more than I'd hoped for.

And with that awe came clarity.

What we were doing here—securing land titles, building corridors, protecting what remained—was no longer just urgent. It was essential. Without this land, there is no future for the gorillas. No future for the people who know this forest best. No future for any of us who still believe in the sacredness of wild places.

On the way out, I turned to Dr. Bowman. "I thought I'd be afraid," I said. "But I wasn't. It felt like…he understood. Like we had an agreement. Don't challenge me, and I won't challenge you. Maybe that was naïve."

Dr. Bowman nodded. "You stayed calm. Most don't. But gorillas aren't violent—that was dominant behavior, but not an attack."

I looked back once more into the trees. They had swallowed the troop already.

Dominique spoke as we walked. "The first time I saw a gorilla, I was a boy. Eight, maybe. Near my grandmother's house. He was massive, with regal posture—like a king. When I saw his eyes looking back at me, with the wisdom of the forest, it changed the way I see animals entirely. I've never forgotten that moment."

And now, having stood in their presence, I understood what Dominique had carried all along. Bonne Année had seen right through us. And it was clear—we were the ones still learning how to belong.

The Batwa

It had already been a full day, but we had one more stop to make. We were heading to a Batwa village just outside the forest—a place where the first people of the Congo now lived in exile from their ancestral home. When the Kahuzi-Biega Forest was declared a national park in the 1970s, the Batwa were evicted without compensation or resettlement. Forced from the forest that had sustained them for generations, they were left to survive on its outskirts—on land that was foreign, with no trees to hunt under, no medicinal plants to gather, no spiritual connection to root them. They were never given the chance to fully acclimate, and in many ways, they never would.

Our convoy passed through a stretch of rolling hills draped in tea plantations. Laborers moved through the fields, their figures bending and shifting in rhythm with the green.

"They won't hire the Batwa," Dr. Bowman said. "They're viewed as unreliable—too deeply rooted in the forest to conform to plantation work."

The Batwa village.
Credit: Age of Union

Dominique exhaled slowly. "The Batwa have been pushed to the margins of a world they once shaped. Now, they're conservation refugees—exiled by the very protections meant to preserve the forest." His voice carried something weighty. Personal.

The Batwa had always seemed mythical to me—maybe because their bond with the land ran so deep it felt like they carried the breath of the forest inside them. They were the original inhabitants of the Congo Basin, a semi-nomadic hunter-gatherer people whose small stature led outsiders to label them "pygmies"—a term that shrinks their dignity, reducing them to spectacle. But their history stretches back millennia. They weren't just part of the forest—they were born of it.

The first thing I noticed when we arrived were the children. They came running barefoot across the dirt, voices rising in chorus—"Mufasa!

Batwa women prepare to perform a ceremonial dance.
Credit: Matt Brunette

Mufasa!"—as they surrounded Dominique. Some grabbed his hands. Others danced around him, cheering. The village itself was a patchwork of worn-out huts, walls stitched together from scrap wood, tarps, and rusted tin. Smoke rose from small cooking fires. And noticeably—painfully—there were almost no elders.

"The average life expectancy here is twenty-eight years," Dr. Bowman said, his voice heavy. "And four out of ten children won't make it to age five."

I felt that number settle in my chest like a stone.

Dominique swept his arms toward the village. "You have to understand—the Batwa are the forest's first children. Their spirits are woven into the soil, their stories carved into the bark of the oldest trees. And yet they are forgotten—like fallen leaves swept away by the wind of progress."

I looked around. Poverty was everywhere, a dark shadow that loomed over the Batwa. The kind that made your stomach clench and your mind struggle. Children with distended bellies, skin riddled with scabies. Mothers with hollow eyes worn thin by generations of exhaustion.

Dr. Bowman had been coming here for three decades. Most of the people he once knew were gone—claimed by disease, hunger, or that slow death delivered by hopelessness.

Dominique greeted the village women—matriarchs of a lost world. They spoke in firm, rhythmic phrases, their voices carrying both pain and persistence. In a dim building that passed as a clinic, the sick lay on the dirt floor, coughing and wheezing. A fever had swept through the village. Several were already gone. Among the ill was Dominique's childhood caretaker.

I saw something shift in him when he knelt at her side—a crack in his usual composure. There was no hospital here. No medicine. No clean water. Just the thinnest hope that the sickness might move on.

Outside, the villagers gathered for a town hall meeting. The women spoke with conviction—about microcredit programs, fuel-efficient stoves, and organic charcoal recipes. They had heard about the reforestation co-op and wanted in. Their ideas were brilliant—born from urgency, shaped by survival. But here, hope was a delicate thing. Before they could build a future, they had to outlast the present.

We listened. Not just to respond, but to understand—to find more ways to support them. The land Dominique had secured for the Batwa was a start, but it wasn't enough.

As we prepared to leave, the Batwa formed a tight circle around us. Then came the blessing dance.

The sound of the drums, the flutes, the rhythmic chant of their voices—it wasn't just music. This was memory. Power. Their movements were fluid, almost supernatural, like the spirits of the forest were guiding their limbs. Dust rose from the stamping of bare feet, swirled into the last rays of sun.

"They believe they're changelings," Dr. Bowman said. "That in this trance, they become something else."

Then one of them was in front of me. A woman, her skin slick with sweat, breath rapid. Her arms spun around me like a storm, hands open, framing my face. Her eyes met mine—wide, unblinking, piercing. She stepped closer, her hands trembling, hovering just beyond my skin.

Then—she blew.

A full, deliberate breath, hot and thick with something I couldn't name. It hit me like a pulse. My breath caught. The world blinked. For a moment, I felt the space between us collapse—folding inward into something ancient, something electric.

Her fingers shook violently in the air, vibrating with an unseen force. And then she was gone. Vanished into the dance, her body folding seamlessly into the others as if she'd never been there at all.

Dominique stood apart, watching. I wondered if he saw himself in them—half in this world, half in the one they had lost. Before we left, he returned to see his former caretaker one more time. It might be the last.

As we walked back to the trucks, I couldn't shake the feeling that, like the Batwa, the forest itself was on the edge of vanishing.

Saving one meant saving the other.

We left the village under a sky of fading embers, the voices still humming in my chest. The drive back was quiet. Headlights cut through the darkness like threads through fabric. No one spoke much. It felt like we were leaving one world for another—one that somehow felt less real.

Chapter 2 | **THE CONGO DIVIDE** 99

I glanced at Dominique. He stared out the window, his thoughts drifting somewhere between past and future. Between what had been lost and what might still be saved.

I felt a friction inside me—the thrill of witnessing wild gorillas, the heartbreak of seeing the Batwa's condition. The tension between beauty and loss. But that dissonance was why I had come. That ache to do something. To help. My mind raced with ideas. We needed to do more.

By the time we reached The Orchids, night had settled deep over Bukavu. I collapsed onto my bed, my body sore, my mind spiraling. But it wasn't fatigue that kept me awake.

It was her breath. That woman's stare. That exhale. As if something—or someone—was reaching through her. Speaking to me.

I didn't know if I had dreamed it. But it clung to me.

And sometime in the night, the sickness began.

Joy and curiosity in a Congolese village.
Credit: Matt Brunette

Fever Dream

For two days, The Orchids turned into a field hospital.

It started with Ray. Then Matthieu. By mid-morning, half the crew had gone down. Fevers, sweating, stomach cramps, delusions. Something viral—most likely food or water-borne. We'd taken every recommended vaccination before entering the Congo, but risk travels with you here. The Congo had its own rules.

We remained at the hotel. I watched from the sidelines, waiting for the sickness to take me, too. Somehow, it didn't. Dr. Bowman and Matt were also spared. The others spent forty-eight hours in a blur of fever and groans.

And then—slowly—it broke. Color began returning to faces. Eyes opened with some clarity. Energy crawled back in. It was like watching the dead come back to life.

When the worst had passed, a few of us left The Orchids and headed for Bukavu to visit Dominique at home. The drive snaked along the shoreline of Lake Kivu, calm as glass in the morning light. A deceptive kind of peace. I watched the ripples brushing the rocks and thought about how quickly the land here could turn against you.

Bukavu was kinetic. The streets pulsed with traffic and footfall, alive with the sounds of bustling markets, honking vehicles, and the rhythms of city life unfolding in real time. Trucks jostled through tight corridors. Motorbikes darted between them like sparks. Street vendors called out over the clamor. Women in bright patterned dresses balanced baskets on their heads with effortless grace.

It was a city that thrived on energy and ambition, despite its poverty. Movement, architecture, expression—this city had its own signature heartbeat. As Dr. Bowman explained, Bukavu had once been known as the "Switzerland of Congo." The colonial-era Art Deco buildings hinted at that more prosperous past. But this was now a city of survival. Its people hustled to carve out a living, day by day.

At Dominique's home, his wife, Yvette, was cooking breakfast over an open flame while their six children got ready for school. The yard overlooked a hillside view of the city. It was beautiful. But Dominique was still thinking about his Batwa nursemaid and our tour of the jungle.

"I miss life in the forest," he said, gesturing toward a photo of his grandmother on the wall. "It's dusty here, and there's always noise. In the forest, there was peace. Life was simpler."

Under his grandmother's care, Dominique had learned the rhythms of the forest and the depth of his family's connection to it. But war changed everything. His family was stripped from their home by armed men and forced to flee. His mother was shot—twice. She survived, but nothing was ever the same.

"The colonists believed conservation meant removing people from the forest," he said. "That's when the Batwa—and my own community—were expelled. My grandmother didn't understand why. But she raised her boys to be ready. To do something about it."

After walking his children to school, we stopped at the Strong Roots office. Dominique laid out the next steps of the project: We were heading south to Burhinyi, where tribal chiefs would participate in a community mapping process to help define the wildlife corridor. The vision was to connect Kahuzi-Biega National Park with the Itombwe Nature Reserve—more than half a million hectares under protection, co-managed by the people—Indigenous communities and Congolese—who had always lived there.

"This is the first time communities in South Kivu are being given the authority to govern their ancestral forests," Dominique said. "We have to get this right."

Before the mapping process, we had one important stop to make: a visit to the Queen of Burhinyi. We were seeking her support for the wildlife corridor project—a crucial endorsement from a figure of deep cultural and political influence. The king, known for his unwavering stance on gorilla protection, was away on parliamentary duty. Today, it was the queen who would represent the kingdom.

Inside the royal residence lobby, we waited—Dominique, Dr. Bowman, our crew, and local dignitaries. Hand-carved masks lined the walls. Colorful murals told stories of lineage, land, and tradition. The room held the stillness of ceremony.

The queen entered quietly. Her presence commanded attention without asking for it. She wore a deep maroon dress and intricate beads around her wrists and neck and moved with a regal grace. Her beauty was ageless—not just in the symmetry of her features, but in the way she carried herself, as if she had long since outgrown the need for ornamentation to announce her power.

She didn't speak much. Her approval wasn't given through grand declarations, but through gesture and the occasional nod. She listened as Dominique laid out the vision for the corridor. Dr. Bowman added a few words on the benefits to both people and wildlife. When the queen finally spoke, her voice was calm, but her words carried weight.

"The king's heart is with the forest," she said in French, her translator echoing her words. "But the forest is not just a resource. It is our past. Our spirit. It is where our people belong. If you are to protect it, you must protect those who live with it—both people and animals. You must understand this."

That was all. But it was enough. With a subtle nod, she gave her blessing. The king would hear of it when he returned. There were no signatures, no ceremony—just a quiet shift in tone that signaled permission had been granted.

Before leaving the room, the queen turned and offered us a final salutation. "I hope you will return before the end of your journey," she said, with a faint smile. "You are always welcome in Burhinyi."

Colored Chalk

Not far from the royal residence, we reached the Burhinyi village hall, where the community had prepared a meal—fufu, meat stew, and fresh fruit. The scent of slow-cooked spices filled the open-air space, smoke curling up from the communal fire. Sitting down to eat together wasn't just hospitality—it was solidarity. A bond formed over shared plates, a way of breaking down barriers before the real work began.

The villagers ate with the kind of patience that spoke of deep tradition. Meals weren't rushed. They were a ritual, a conversation, a reaffirmation of connection. A social understanding of the greater good we could accomplish together.

Dominique explained the challenges ahead. "The land holds its own truth, older than any of us—there are no defined borders," he said. "The villagers know where their forests begin and end. But putting that on paper? That's another story. Every place has its own memory—this tree, that stone, a bend in the river.

Dr. Bowman added, "If the government sends in cartographers, it creates conflict. We need a participatory process for the results to be honored. The people here have to draw their land—literally."

Capturing the process of participatory land mapping.
Credit: Age of Union

The method was brilliant in its simplicity. Chiefs and elders gathered around the floor with sticks of colored chalk. They began to sketch: forests, rivers, footpaths, sacred groves. Lines appeared. Arguments followed—two villages claiming the same stretch of forest, the same rock, a shared water source. But a chief-appointed referee settled disputes, and slowly, consensus emerged.

These maps were step one. The government required fixed boundaries before community forests could be legally recognized. The chalk lines were copied to paper. The next section drawn. Later, GPS teams would ground-truth every mark, producing scaled maps for submission with the land title applications.

I was mesmerized by the colorful lines on the concrete floor slowly forming some semblance of villages, forests, and landmarks.

"This is how we prevent future conflict," Dominique said. "If you hand them a map, they'll reject it. But if they draw it together, they'll defend it. They'll own it."

With the day's maps finalized, we headed down into the valley toward a cluster of old Norwegian missionary bungalows—our base for the night. The skies had turned violet. Clouds stretched like torn silk across the horizon. There was peace and beauty as the Congo folded into itself, settling into its nocturnal rhythm.

Inside, the bungalows told another story. The walls were streaked with a viscous black ooze, dripping like something left behind after a crime. The air was wet and sour with mildew. Everything seemed to move, tiny things scattering into cracks as the light shifted.

The room was stripped to essentials: two warped cots and, in the corner, a makeshift washroom—two mismatched plastic buckets on the floor.

Matt leaned in the doorway, smirking. "One's the sink. The other's the toilet."

I said nothing.

In the corner, something shifted. A millipede emerged from the wall—long, segmented, surreal. I watched it crawl like a hallucination across the floor.

That was it. Sleep was out of the question.

Night fell hard and absolute. Outside, the forest came alive—the distant hoots of colobus monkeys, the low insect hum, a single high-pitched shriek that cut too close.

Inside, we did the only thing we could do: We drank.

Dr. Bowman, Matt, and I sat around a tiny, rickety table, a lone candle flickering between us, passing a bottle of whiskey back and forth, trading stories, laughing in that tired, delirious way that comes when you're half-drunk and slightly horrified by your surroundings. The walls around us breathed with life—things crawling, shifting in the dark—but we, or at least I, pretended not to notice.

Matt looked around and said, "If this place had Yelp reviews, I'd give it one star for atmosphere, five for realism."

Dr. Bowman stared into the flame, grinning, and said quietly, "Feels like the jungle's just waiting for us to fall asleep."

I took another sip.

We waited for morning. The soft gold that would cut through the damp. Until then, we drank and talked—three men in the jungle, doing their best not to look too hard at the walls.

Rabbits

A staple food across much of western and central Africa is fufu—a starchy, doughlike side dish made from cassava, yams, or plantains. In the Democratic Republic of Congo, it's almost always cassava. The process is labor-intensive: The root is peeled, boiled, and then pounded smooth in large wooden mortars. Women work tirelessly, pounding the root into submission and shaping it into small balls to serve alongside rich stews of meat, fish, or vegetables. Eaten by hand, fufu is used to scoop up the sauce.

It fills bellies. It's not miraculous, but it's dependable—carbohydrates, fiber, potassium, a daily constant in a region where families survive on what little they can grow.

At the Strong Roots agricultural cooperative in the Burhinyi valley, we were invited to a garden meal. Fufu, mildly sour and doughy, was served with a thick vegetable stew.

The garden was alive with color and movement—women tilling beds of bitekuteku, cassava, and sweet potato. Farther back, tomatoes, onions, eggplant, and amaranth. Along the edges, rows of corn, bananas, and sugarcane. It was lush, productive.

"These gardens are yielding a surplus for the first time," Dominique said, beaming. "They feed families—and now we're selling at market."

The women greeted us with broad smiles, vibrant in patterned dresses and headscarves, proud to show what they'd harvested. This was more than food—it was agency. They weren't just feeding their households; they were entering an economy. But beneath the surface of this success was a persistent obstacle: fertilizer. The land, cultivated season after season, was growing tired. Each harvest pulled more minerals and nutrients from the soil, leaving it weaker and less productive. Yields had begun to suffer. The only solution was to purchase fertilizer from a small village miles away—a half-day journey on foot, and a costly one. It was a time-and-money equation that never added up in the women's favor. But Dominique had been working on a different kind of solution.

The night before, he had left to coordinate the delivery of our gift. Now Dominique arrived with two hundred rabbits. A soft, wriggling strategy. Their droppings would replace expensive fertilizer, eliminating long treks and high costs. More nutrient-rich soil meant stronger crops. More food. More sales.

The women's excitement was immediate. When we opened the crates, a wave of laughter and surprise passed through the group. Eyes widened as the rabbits were lifted out one by one. Some women had never seen one in real life. They giggled, stroked the fur, held the rabbits close. A few were unsure at first, but instinct settled in quickly—they crouched low, whispering, letting their hands adjust to the softness.

Then—chaos.

A blur of white fur shot between my legs. One rabbit made a break for it, bolting into the garden. Then another. A flash of brown and gray. The women shrieked, then burst into laughter as the first rebels claimed their new home.

I turned to Dr. Bowman, grinning. "Let's just hope they don't start multiplying like—well, you know."

He smirked as another rabbit slipped from someone's grip, landing with a soft thud before being scooped back up.

"Well," he said, "if they do, we'll call it a population boom for sustainability. These little guys are doing their part to enrich the land."

He clapped me on the shoulder. "Who knows—maybe the rabbits will teach us something about thriving in hard conditions."

The rabbits were more than livestock—they were a shift in possibility. Manure became fertilizer. Fertilizer became nutrient-dense crops. Crops became income. Income meant school fees, medicine, savings. The ripple effect was tangible.

And with richer soil came a deeper reward—less pressure to cut forest. Fewer trees felled. Fewer gorilla habitats lost. More forest left standing. It was all connected. A cycle not of depletion, but renewal. Soil, crops, forest, people.

A rabbit. A harvest. A future.

After the delivery, we were invited to walk the sacred forest. The film crew documented as the chieftains continued identifying landmark trees and rock formations for the mapping. Anastasie Bahati, Strong Roots's head of community forestry, joined us with a wide smile. Women were rarely allowed on these paths, but today, the king had granted her special permission.

"This is an honor," she said, her voice soft, her eyes gleaming. "It's rare that I'm permitted to walk this ground."

The walk, described casually as a brief one, became a four-hour climb. We cut through thick jungle, sidestepped vines that curled like rope traps, ducked beneath low branches slick with rain. By the time we reached the sacred forest, sweat soaked through our clothes. But the struggle faded.

Here, the forest changed.

It was quieter. Cooler. The light softened. The trees stood like sentinels, massive and unmoving, their bark slick with moss, their branches braided high into a natural cathedral. The air felt heavier—not oppressive, but charged. Ancient.

"This forest is our history," Dominique said. "Every tree, every vine has a spirit. A memory."

His voice was low, almost reverent. He didn't speak like someone explaining something. He spoke like someone returning.

I looked around. Something in the canopy whispered. Not words, but presence. The feeling that we were being watched—but not by animals. By time itself. By the ones who had walked here long before us.

"This isn't just about saving land, is it?" I asked. "It's about preserving the soul of it."

Dominique smiled. "You're beginning to see."

A small delivery, a big step—rabbits for sustainable farming.
Credit: Dax Dasilva

One of the chieftains led us to a towering lombi tree. Its buttress roots fanned out like wings.

"This tree," he said, laying a hand gently on the bark, "represents the nineteen kings of our kingdom."

His tone wasn't ceremonial. It was sacred. You could feel it. The tree wasn't a metaphor—it was lineage. The kind that still lived in the leaves.

Farther on, we found a cave—shallow and dark, with a blackened fire ring and a bed of dried grass. A chieftain explained that this place had offered shelter to travelers for generations. He spoke as if the forest itself had memory. As if it remembered who had slept there.

The film crew—Marc, Ray, Matthieu—stayed behind in the village, living under tarps, documenting the geotagging of sacred landmarks. They'd be there for up to two weeks, walking with the chieftains and tribal leaders, recording what could not be written.

Dominique, Dr. Bowman, and I needed to return to Bukavu before dark. As Dr. Bowman often reminded us, driving after sunset in the Congo wasn't safe. The sun here didn't set; it dropped. One minute it was day. The next, darkness fell like a curtain.

Escape from the Congo

Back at The Orchids' Safari Club, morning came quickly. Birdsong filled the air. On the veranda, a charm of finches flitted between tables. One bold waxbill landed near mine, pecking for crumbs—its vivid red beak and belly flashing in the soft light of dawn.

It was our last morning in the Congo. What began in calm dissolved quickly into unease.

News spread fast: A rebel militia had taken the town of Bunagana on the DRC-Rwanda border. The violence, once distant, was creeping south.

Toward us. Toward the border we needed to cross. Whispers ran through the hotel: The border might close at any moment. If it did, we'd be trapped.

The Orchids, once a haven, bristled with tension. Trucks of soldiers rolled past the hotel, armed and ready for whatever came next. We didn't need anyone to tell us what was happening—the urgency in the air was potent.

"Looks like our easy ride home just got complicated," Dr. Bowman muttered.

Confirmation came quickly. The border was closing.

Dominique was already moving, gathering us in the lobby. His voice was calm but commanding.

"We have to go—now. There will be a rush for the border, and only a few will get through."

We scrambled. Bags stuffed, gear half-zipped. The lazy rhythm of morning vanished, replaced by sharp, frantic movement. The realization sank in: We could be caught in the middle of a militia–military standoff. I thought of the gunfire in the north when we first arrived. That had felt distant. This didn't.

The Land Cruiser tore down the dirt road, bouncing over ruts in the road as if the ground itself aimed to swallow us. My heart was pounding in time with the wheels as they slid around each gravel-strewn curve.

The scene at the crossing was nothing like the quiet, almost ceremonial passage from days before. Soldiers now lined the road. Military trucks blocked the way. The once-sleepy checkpoint had hardened—grim faces, rifles ready.

As we pulled up, a guard stepped forward, rifle slung, eyes scanning the vehicle. Cold. Measured.

Dominique jumped out, moving quickly toward the officers. I couldn't hear him, but his delivery seemed firm and serious. Papers passed between hands. The guard didn't flinch. No small talk. No smiles. We stayed in the truck, still. Waiting.

Minutes stretched. Around us, soldiers shifted, adjusting grips, scanning the crowd. No one said anything.

"This doesn't look good," Matt whispered.

"Let's hope Dominique works his magic," I said.

Dr. Bowman stayed silent. Not hearing him say, "This is no big deal," somehow made things more unsettling.

Then Dominique turned and gave the smallest nod. We were through.

And more: We'd be escorted by a military truck all the way to the airport.

Relief flooded in—but didn't erase the tension. We weren't in the clear yet. The road still seemed uncertain. The window still appeared narrow.

Two soldiers rode ahead in a truck, leading the way. We followed fast, the road curling through the hills toward Kamembe. It felt like we were chasing the last seconds of a closing door. All I could see was the back of their truck—and dust.

When we reached the tarmac and boarded the small turboprop back to Kigali, something in my chest finally let go. As the engines roared and we lifted into the sky, I turned to the window. The Congo receded beneath the clouds. Roads vanished into trees. Rivers wound into the jungle. Forest, endless and dark, swallowed the land whole.

Nothing about this place would fade quickly. This place had marked me.

We had come to work, to witness the conservation efforts in motion—but the DRC had revealed something much deeper. Its fragility. Its resilience. The unyielding spirit of its people.

As we soared toward safer ground, I realized I wasn't really leaving. The Congo had a way of holding on to you, of threading itself into your bones. Of reshaping your idea of what's possible—and what's at stake.

Now I understood what Dominique meant when he said Dr. Bowman was half-Congolese.

And I knew, deep down, that I'd be back.

Some places you leave. Others never let you go.

The Corridor

In September 2023, we premiered *The Corridor* at the Paradise Theatre during the Toronto International Film Festival. The documentary follows Dominique's journey—from a Congolese boy with Batwa roots to a determined advocate for both people and nature—as he leads a mission to secure twenty-one interconnected land titles across the eastern Congo. More than protecting gorilla habitat, the initiative empowers local communities and safeguards the Congo Basin Rainforest—the planet's "second lung"—ensuring its survival for future generations.

Just a few months later, another victory arrived. A total of 226,541 hectares of previously unprotected land had been secured—marking the first thirteen concessions of the Kahuzi–Itombwe Community Forest Corridor. And by the time of writing this book, that number had grown. Over a million hectares of land were now protected under community-managed forest titles.

What we had set out to do—create a wildlife corridor, protect endangered species, and support the people who live among them—had become reality.

These land titles were the first of their kind. More than a legal document, they were a promise: that the people who called these forests home would have the power to protect them, and that the wildlife—gorillas like Bonne Année and so many others—would have a future.

The corridor connects two of the most important conservation areas in the DRC, giving species like the eastern lowland gorilla the space they need to move, to feed, and to survive. For the communities, it meant less conflict, clearer boundaries, and a new way forward—villages managing the forest in cooperation rather than competition, free from foreign extraction or occupation.

And it was only beginning.

Dominique and his team at Strong Roots continued filing applications for additional land titles. The program was catching fire—chieftains from neighboring territories began attending meetings to learn how they could join. With support for biological surveys, reforestation, and forest-friendly livelihoods, we worked side by side with the people of the eastern Congo, knowing real change could only rise from the ground up.

Back in Montréal, I joined Dominique, Matt, and Dr. Bowman on a video call to mark the milestone. Years of fieldwork, diplomacy, setbacks, and breakthroughs had led to this moment.

It wasn't often that conservation felt like a win. Too often it felt like pushing against an unrelenting tide. But tonight, we let ourselves exhale.

On screen, Dominique wore a quiet smile. "A new Congo is not just a hope," he said. "It's a seed we water with our work. A tree we must tend—so the future can shelter beneath its branches."

The fight wasn't over—it never would be. But for once, we weren't just fighting.

We were winning.

Mufasa! Mufasa!

"By overthrowing me, you have only defeated the trunk of the tree of freedom; it will grow back because its roots are deep, numerous and vivacious."

—TOUSSAINT LOUVERTURE

Baille Tourible in the remote highlands of Haiti's Central Plateau.
Credit: Josue Azor

Climbing the hills in layers, Port-au-Prince's homes tell stories of survival, struggle, and community. Credit: La Corivo

Chapter 3

CHILDREN OF BAILLE TOURIBLE

PLANTING HOPE IN A HAITI TORN BY VIOLENCE

On Monday, January 22, 2024, I stepped onto the tarmac at Toussaint Louverture International Airport in Port-au-Prince, Haiti. I was en route to Baille Tourible, a remote, vulnerable stretch of the Central Plateau, to see the early stages of our reforestation and agroforestry project. In the thick of the pandemic, Age of Union had partnered with KANPE, a foundation supporting underserved rural communities, to plant new forests in a region where the soil was weary, the people resilient, and hope scarce.

Two armed members of CORE's reconnaissance team met me at the gate and escorted me through the airport. Originally formed after the 2010 earthquake, CORE—co-founded by actor Sean Penn and humanitarian leader Ann Young Lee—has grown into a global response organization tackling everything from natural disasters to conflict, public health crises, food insecurity, and climate change. In Haiti, it's all of the above.

My only baggage was a small roller. I'd been advised to pack light and stay mobile. I was guided through a private corridor to a desk for immigration control. Other than my passport, which was kept secure, my real name was nowhere—no itinerary, no hotel register, no paperwork. For the next three days, I would travel under a pseudonym: Simba Njeri, listed as a Canadian consultant to CORE. The real Simba, a member of the team, wasn't in-country. But his name was unlikely to draw attention. Or kidnappers.

We moved quickly through the terminal. One escort went ahead to check the scene while the other stayed close. The airport throbbed with tension—alive with movement, but taut. At the curb, four armored vehicles rolled up. Doors flew open. Soldiers stepped out. One gestured sharply—get in. I crossed the sidewalk, grabbed my bag, and jumped in as the door slammed shut. The convoy started up and sped down the road.

Inside was Ann Young Lee.

"Welcome to Haiti," she said. "This is Felix sitting shotgun—it's not a pun, and he carries a lot more than a 12-gauge." The man in the passenger seat nodded once, eyes locked forward. "Felix will be your personal security while you're here," she said. "He doesn't leave your side."

"Thanks," I said, still catching my breath. "Nice to meet you, Felix."

He turned briefly. Military cap. Aviators. Broad-shouldered and alert. He offered a tight grin before a transmission came through his satellite phone.

Inside the bulletproof vehicles, we were *safer*—but not safe. Gangs in Port-au-Prince often staged fake car accidents or roadblocks to inspect vehicles, hunting for targets. Stuck in traffic, you're a sitting duck.

A bustling Haitian marketplace.
Credit: McIninch

Felix and the driver stayed on comms with the scouts up ahead. They reported closures, detours, and potential threats. As we tore through a narrow corridor between shanties, I heard gunfire pop, close enough to feel it. Kidnappings near the airport were common—it was the perfect place to snatch fresh arrivals.

CORE's team was experienced, but not immune. Ann had recently negotiated the release of two kidnapped team members. The only headline I caught at the airport was the abduction of several nuns. They were taken from a bus—sisters using public transport, grabbed in broad daylight like easy prey.

Since the assassination of President Jovenel Moïse, Haiti has been locked in chaos. On July 7, 2021, at around 1 a.m., twenty-eight foreign mercenaries—most of them Colombian—surrounded the president's residence, disabled the guards, and stormed the bedroom. Moïse was beaten, shot a dozen times, and left to die. First Lady Martine Moïse was shot multiple times but survived. Their daughter hid in a bathroom and escaped physically unharmed, but forever traumatized.

Since then, gang violence has escalated to historic levels. The UN estimates gangs now control nearly 80 percent of Port-au-Prince. One of Haiti's most notorious gang leaders, Jimmy "Barbecue" Cherizier, seeks to topple the government. His G9 federation, armed beyond the government's reach, has joined forces with rival gangs under a pact called *Viv Ansanm*—"Living Together"—to overthrow the state. The truce kept gangs from fighting each other, but the citizens bore the cost: spiraling violence, death, and daily fear.

We sped through dense neighborhoods. A sharp, pungent odor filled the truck.

"What's that smell?" I asked.

Felix turned to me, stoic. "Dead people," he said. "If the families don't claim the bodies or don't pay, there's no burial. They stay in the streets and rot."

We banked hard through side streets, over loose gravel, past packs of feral dogs. Villagers barely flinched. The crowds parted like water as our motorcade pressed through. But all eyes tracked us. On these streets, the game was always live. Lookouts on corners, phones in hand, fed intel to gang operatives who set blockades ahead. Our scouts called them out. New routes were carved mid-drive.

Gunfire echoed in the distance. My hands were shaking. I was scared. In Haiti, I wasn't a celebrity or a politician—just another foreigner. But that was enough. Without a stable government or a functioning police force, gangs kidnapped over a thousand people a year.

In 2021, the 400 Mawozo gang abducted seventeen missionaries in Croix-des-Bouquets, demanding $17 million. Two and a half years later, only two had been released. The gang makes around $70,000 a week from kidnapping and extortion. The profits fund warehouses, weapons, operations—and political movements.

So, what does any of this have to do with trees? What's the connection between gang kidnappings, political unrest, and environmental conservation?

It's everything.

A stripped, resourceless environment breeds desperation. And desperation breeds violence—what Haitians call *mizè*. It means misery. It's not just poverty; it's suffering with no end in sight.

To understand an environment, you must first understand the people within it—their history, their struggle, and their stake in the land. Haiti is among the most deforested nations in the world. Less than 1 percent of its original forests remain. The question is not just how this happened, but why. And how we help reverse it.

Haiti's story is rooted in ransom.

After gaining independence from France in 1804, the country was surrounded by French warships. Haiti's president was forced to accept France's terms. For the next century, Haiti became the only country in history where former slaves paid reparations to their enslavers.

Even before that, the French had cleared much of the land for sugarcane plantations. After 1804, they demanded Haiti repay them for the labor they no longer owned—plundering forests for mahogany and hardwoods. The "independence debt" was extortion, nothing less.

By the 1920s, over 60 percent of Haiti remained forested. But during the 1930s and '40s, deforestation accelerated, spurred by population pressure, anti-Vodou campaigns that destroyed sacred groves, and shortsighted development projects. One Haitian-American initiative bulldozed forests to plant rubber trees for World War II, only to fail when the war ended before the trees matured.

Now, the forests are nearly gone. Of Haiti's fifty largest mountains, forty-two have lost all primary forest. Amphibians, reptiles, and mammals are vanishing. Biodiversity is collapsing. The entirety of the nation is approaching environmental free fall.

I came to Haiti not to witness despair, but to study what might rise from it.

In the world of environmental conservation, Haiti is the endgame—the living case study of what happens when every natural system breaks. While nations like Brazil, Russia, and Indonesia face massive deforestation, Haiti shows us what comes next: drought, heat, hurricane, and famine. And beneath it all, *mizè*.

And yet I believed this could be a place where something powerful begins again.

Artists for Peace and Justice

I was first introduced to Haiti's challenges through Artists for Peace and Justice (APJ), a nonprofit working hand-in-hand with local communities to create real opportunities—education, jobs, stability. APJ built and funded the first free secondary school in Port-au-Prince, a school that's seen thousands of students graduate over the last fifteen years. Today, it supports more than 1,400 kids annually and provides jobs for 180 teachers and staff.

For years, I'd attended the annual APJ gala in Toronto, led by Natasha Koifman—founder of the North American public relations agency NKPR, which I'd worked with for over a decade through Lightspeed and Age of Union. Natasha also serves as Chair of the Board for Artists for Peace and Justice in both Canada and the U.S. Under her leadership, the gala had raised over $35 million, funding everything from teacher salaries and uniforms to technology and infrastructure. It was real progress. You could feel it.

Natasha had been to Haiti many times. She'd walked the school grounds, navigated the neighborhoods, and felt the pulse of the place. She'd been caught in gunfire—trapped between gangs and police. She knew exactly how fast things could unravel. In the days before my trip, she urged me not to go. There was no dramatizing it—just calm, grounded concern. She understood the risk better than anyone.

And I heard her. But I also knew I had to go. Like the DRC, this wasn't a story you could understand from a distance. You had to breathe the same air. Walk the same dirt. Look people in the eye. Only then could you begin to understand what needed to be done.

Supporting APJ deepened my perspective on what advocacy could look like. Education is where it often starts, but if the environment around a school is collapsing, there's no real future for its graduates. I began thinking more seriously about how we might help restore the land itself. That path, almost serendipitously, came through music.

Back in 2010, Régine Chassagne—co-founder of the Canadian rock band Arcade Fire—launched an organization called KANPE. Born in Montréal to Haitian immigrants, Régine wanted to support the most disadvantaged communities in her family's homeland. KANPE, which means "to stand up" in Haitian Creole, was built around six pillars: health, agroforestry, education, leadership, entrepreneurship, and infrastructure. Their mission is to move communities toward autonomy by supporting their own vision of progress.

When it came time to choose a location, KANPE selected Baille Tourible, an isolated mountain village in the Central Plateau. Eleven thousand people lived there, without running water or electricity. It was one of the poorest regions in Haiti, and yet, over the past decade, KANPE had helped transform it—introducing health clinics, education, and innovative agroforestry programs. A new generation was rising—much of it led by women—committed to continuing the work.

At the heart of Baille Tourible is its marching band, created by Régine and the local youth. Eighty young musicians, the pride of the village. It's more than music. It's a heartbeat. It's confidence. It's identity. A generation in step with its future.

I reached out to Régine with an idea: a large-scale reforestation initiative. We would fund the production of twenty-five thousand fruit and forest seedlings each year, planting them along the barren mountain slopes. The program would employ hundreds of locals to cultivate the seedlings, reinforce the terrain with stonework to prevent erosion, and plant forests that would not only hold the soil, but rebuild the future.

Reforestation in Haiti isn't symbolic—it's survival. With tree cover, crops grow better. Storms lose their bite. The economy breathes. The land begins to hold again.

In 2021, Age of Union funded and launched the program. But this trip would be my first time seeing it in person. The program had been in place for nearly two years without a single visit from outsiders. Since before the pandemic in 2020, no foreigner had set foot in Baille Tourible.

I would be the first. And I couldn't wait to walk those hills, meet the people, the children, and see what hope looked like when planted in the ground.

School of Hope and Sunshine

We stopped at a small school on the outskirts of Port-au-Prince. CORE had founded the School of Hope and Sunshine in 2015 to educate children from families living in a sprawling displacement camp—over sixty thousand people still without homes since the 2010 earthquake. Ann wanted to check in on the students and staff and show me the school.

Stepping into a classroom felt like a cold plunge, jolting me out of the tension that had followed us from the airport and through the streets. The anxiety drained from my body. In its place, a swelling warmth. The students were studying, smiling, learning, sharing. They raised their hands, read from notebooks, and leaned into their lessons with a focus and pride I'd never seen anywhere else. As if the chaos outside the schoolyard didn't exist.

Most of their families still sleep in tents—crowded grounds stitched together from whatever materials aid organizations can spare. But the children arrived immaculately dressed, the girls in plaid blouses and navy skirts, bows tied in their hair, the boys in tucked-in shirts and polished shoes. Where sewing machines or laundromats failed them, dignity filled the gaps.

One girl came up to me, smiling brightly. She asked if I was a teacher. Ann explained that I was a visitor. I asked the girl what she wanted to be when she grew up.

"My dream is to be a businesswoman," she said. "To have my own company." Then she paused and added, "And to help others."

My heart cracked wide open.

Ann turned to me. "That's the goal," she said. "We're educating minds—but also nurturing citizens. These children are the future, and we prepare them for it."

I thought of the camps. The violence. The parents doing everything they could to get their children to school each day. It was overwhelming. But here in the classroom, and out in the courtyard where a student band played jazz on brass and wind instruments, there was joy. There was hope. It was stunning.

That night, the convoy took us to the Karibe Hotel in Juvenat. It looked like a sanctuary: colonial-style architecture wrapped in tree-lined gardens, stone fountains, and cafe terraces bathed in golden light. The lobby glowed with marble floors and stained-glass suns. But beneath the hospitality was a fortress.

The United Nations ran operations from inside the hotel. CORE's security teams occupied much of the rest. I checked in as Simba Njeri and took a room across from Felix. An hour later, we gathered in a secured room for the team debriefing, surrounded by military personnel with sidearms and assault rifles at their hips. Even within these walls, the rules were clear: Never share your name. Never go out alone. Never leave without the team.

Recon updates came hourly, and routes would change on the fly. Some trips would require helicopters to bypass high-risk areas. Every move was calculated. Even at the Karibe, we were never truly safe.

I tried to shake the nerves, but they lingered. The day's tension clung to me—roadblocks, armed men, the stench of death in the streets. Visiting the school had been a reprieve, a glimpse into what Haiti could become. But the danger was real. And it haunted every step.

That night, twilight draped the hotel garden in indigo. We gathered for dinner at La Brasserie. It was our first meal of the day. Creole fusion cuisine—crawfish étouffée, jambalaya, chicken Creole—danced with spice and fire. The food was extraordinary. But it was the music that changed everything.

Jazz floated through the courtyard. Dancers appeared—women in traditional dress moving like flames. The PAPJAZZ festival had returned for the first time since the pandemic. Artists had flown in from sixteen countries to perform forty-two concerts across Port-au-Prince. A celebration of Haitian culture—surviving, still alive.

I watched the crowd sway on nearby balconies. I joined them. I let the night take me.

Under the stars, entranced by music and the scent of charcoal and cinnamon, something in me softened. Light flickered in the garden pools. Notes curled into the tropical dark.

Later, back in the hallways, Felix walked me to my room. He said just one thing before turning in: "Stay inside. Lock the door. Open for me only."

I already had that plan.

I lay in bed, let the music carry me, and drifted into the first peaceful sleep I'd had in days.

The Central Plateau

At first light, we loaded up the convoy and headed for the helipad. We drove through a hot zone known for gang activity, winding through alleys and makeshift roads until we reached the fortified compound of Digicel, Haiti's largest cellular provider. Getting there wasn't easy, but once inside, we were safer. Digicel executives are prime targets—gangs know they can extort national corporations for big money.

The helipad sat atop a tall satellite tower inside the compound. Ann, Felix, and I climbed the stairs, received our briefing, and boarded the helicopter. Within minutes, we were airborne, cutting across the sky toward the Central Plateau.

Flying over Haiti, the scars of deforestation were painfully clear. We soared above mountain ranges that once held hardwood forests but now were stripped to dry shrubs and parched soil. So little of Haiti's natural forest remains.

The damage began under French colonization—slaves forced to clear forests for coffee plantations. After the revolution, the new Haitian government was still paying France reparations. Not in gold, but in timber. Mahogany forests fell by the acre to compensate France for lost "property." Independence came with an ax.

Even after colonialism ended, land was unequally distributed. Most Haitians were left with the marginal slopes—land too fragile for farming. Then came Hurricane Hazel in 1954, which drowned forests. Then population growth. Then the charcoal boom. The hillsides collapsed under the weight of survival. With no infrastructure to support alternatives, the forests became fuel. Haiti's story is a fierce warning—what happens when trees are reduced to a resource and a nation is left to scrape life from eroded soil.

Only 1 percent of Haiti's forests remain. The rest—taken.
Credit: Dax Dasilva

We landed in a field behind a stone wall. Locals gathered nearby to see who had arrived. "They're curious," Ann said. "Visitors are extremely uncommon."

Inside a small police station adjacent to the landing zone, the KANPE team met us with off-road trucks. No more bulletproof SUVs—just rugged vehicles built for the terrain.

Felix and I climbed into a truck. With us were Fritz and Archange, two local project leaders. Fritz shared updates as we bounced through mountain trails. Our reforestation plan was originally focused on planting trees, but hunger doesn't wait for forests to grow. So the program had expanded: fruit trees and subsistence gardens to feed the families while they restored the land.

The road was brutal—worse than anything I'd seen in the DRC. We climbed over rocks and ruts for hours. Mountains that once held dense mahogany forests were now stripped bare—some couldn't even hold soil. Just endless, skeletal slopes. Then we stopped.

Fritz stepped out and gestured to a mountainside wrapped in stone terraces.

"In the eighties, we lost all our pigs to swine flu," he said. "And at the same time, coffee prices collapsed on the global market. Haiti's two major

A Haitian woman washes clothes in the stream.
Credit: Josue Azor

exports disappeared. With no income, people turned to the forests—for wood to sell, charcoal to burn, and land to farm. That stripped the mountains. And the farming drained what was left of the soil."

He paused, letting the story settle. Then he nodded toward the hillside.

"This mountain was rebuilt by hand. Seventy-six locals spent three months stacking rock, holding the soil. Now the trees are in. In the rainy season, they'll take root."

I stood there in silence, floored—not by the devastation, but by the scale of the effort. The care. The labor. The quiet force of will.

"And this is just one?" I asked.

Fritz smiled. "We're doing fifty."

Fifty mountainsides.

The weight of it hit me. This was the reforestation program we'd funded through Age of Union—but standing here, it didn't feel like ownership. It felt like reverence. This was their work. Their pride. We had helped ignite the spark, but they had carried the flame.

"This project gives us the power to return what was taken," Fritz said. "It's a promise. That our children will grow up with trees."

I nodded, still taking it in. It wouldn't bring back all the forests Haiti had lost. It wouldn't stop climate change. But it would restore something here. Something living. And that mattered.

Sometimes impact is measured in global hectares. Other times, it's measured in a single hillside, rebuilt stone by stone by people who never gave up.

The Central Plateau is one of the most isolated places in Haiti. Nearly everyone here is a subsistence farmer. Some walk six hours to reach the nearest clinic or market. The disappearance of the trees brought more than just erosion. It brought hunger. Vulnerability. Collapse.

And yet here, on this terraced slope, something was growing again.

Not just trees.

But possibility.

The Baille Tourible Marching Band

"Dax, we are close. Can you hear it?" Fritz asked.

We'd just entered Baille Tourible, beneath a rising canopy of trees, when I heard the unmistakable pulse of a marching band. The music floated across a small stream, bright brass and sharp percussion echoing off the hills. Twenty-five students in school uniforms were assembled, horns gleaming, snare drums popping, bass drums booming. On either side of the band, villagers gathered—parents, elders, children—all in their best dress. And above them, stretched between two trees, a massive banner read:

Welcome Mr. Dax Dasilva. Thank you, Age of Union.

My stomach dropped.

After everything we'd done to avoid using real names, seeing mine suspended in bold letters across the village square felt like a punch—actually, Felix gave me a look like he wanted to punch me. And although

Baille Tourible's vibrant marching band.
Credit: Dax Dasilva

this wasn't my doing, I did find some comfort in geography—it would take hours by rock-strewn roads and a helicopter to get this message to Port-au-Prince. The risk felt distant. And honestly, in that moment, I didn't care. The music, the joy—it drowned out the worry.

Myrlande Jean, KANPE's program lead for Haiti, handed me a locally woven hat and a bouquet of fresh greens and wildflowers. "It's tradition," she said with a warm smile.

It was a parade in my honor. And I was honored.

The band took formation. More than a hundred children followed—grouped by shirt color like living ribbons of white, orange, yellow, blue, and green. The girls danced to the rhythm, twirling their Karabella dresses, bright headwraps bouncing in unison. The boys clapped along, breaking into spontaneous bursts of movement. The path through the village was alive with music and motion.

Two small girls skipped ahead, arms extended, spinning freely.

As we arrived at the heart of the village, the band gathered in front of the school and played one final, thunderous piece. The whole village clapped and swayed. Children grinned. Drums rolled. And in the middle of it all, I stood with tears in my eyes, utterly undone.

Young women dancing in colorful dresses.
Credit: Dax Dasilva

"This school is not just a place for learning," Fritz told me. "It's where they learn about the forest by using their hands—they help to produce the seedlings that we are planting on the mountains."

A young student stepped forward. In Creole, she spoke with power and poise. She talked about growing up without trees, about her dream of helping reforest the mountains, of planting something she could never climb but her children might.

Then the children sang. And for a moment, the entire village became a chorus of hope.

Afterward, we walked. Fritz led us through the landscape, showing me the projects in motion. We met entrepreneurial women who'd received microloans to launch their own planting efforts. We toured school

The KANPE team—partners in progress.
Credit: Dax Dasilva

gardens, small-scale coffee plots, and the local health clinic. There was a pulse of progress everywhere we turned—local seed banks distributing trees, model forests mixing fruit and hardwood, children planting what they'd learned to grow.

We paused near a tree where a Hispaniolan trogon—Haiti's national bird—sat cooing in the branches. Metallic green feathers, gray chest, blood-red belly, white-barred tail. Fritz explained that the Hispaniolan trogon is a cavity-nester, often using holes dug out by the Hispaniolan woodpecker. The trogon is a forest-dependent species, and the biggest threat it faces is rampant habitat loss caused by tree clearing.

Nearby, a tree held another surprise: a candy cane snail. Its multicolored shell glistened like porcelain. Fritz leaned in. "They only live here," he said. "Only on this one species of logwood. They're protected by law, but poachers still take them." The shell was stunning, like jewelry—it's what they were poached for. "Another reason we are replanting forests," he said, raising a hand toward the trees. "We need resources, but so do the wondrous animals of Haiti." I watched the snail slowly maneuver along the branch.

Then Fritz pointed to a wiry tree growing nearby. "Moringa," he said. "The miracle tree."

Native to India but thriving in Haiti's climate, moringa had become a nutritional lifeline. The leaves are dried and ground into a fine emerald-green powder, a superfood powerhouse. Gram for gram, moringa boasts more protein and calcium than milk or yogurt, more potassium than bananas, more vitamin C than oranges, and more iron than spinach. In a country grappling with malnutrition, this is more than a plant. It's a lifeline. For some children, it means the difference between hunger and health.

"Everything here is connected," Fritz said. "The trees, the soil, the people. If one breaks, the rest falls."

He was right. I'd heard it from farmer after farmer—the drought was killing their crops, and the drought, they believed, came from the forests being stripped away. And they weren't wrong. Science confirms it: Over 40 percent of rainfall on land comes from forests. The trees breathe water into the sky. Cut them down, and the rain stops coming.

That's when the cycle begins. No trees, no water. No water, no crops. No food, no jobs. No jobs, no hope. And in that vacuum, desperation breeds violence.

Haiti's environmental crisis is more than erosion or desertification—it's a pressure cooker. A deforested mountain leads to a hungry child. A hungry child grows up in a system with no opportunities. And that's where gangs find recruits.

Reforestation is not just about trees. It's about justice.

As the afternoon waned, we began the brutal journey back—hours of stone, sweat, and silence. We made it to Mirebalais just after dark, arriving at the Wozo Plaza Hotel. A modest cluster of bungalows surrounded a small pool. It was charming in daylight, but I didn't feel safe. The doors didn't lock. Felix stayed across from me. I ordered two rums at dinner, praying for sleep. But it didn't come easy.

The lights wouldn't shut off in my room. I passed out for a few hours, then woke to the sound of dogs fighting, barking, and howling. Every burst of noise felt like a warning. I was certain someone was approaching. But no one came.

At dawn, I stepped outside.

The Wozo Plaza was beautiful in the daylight. Flowers in bloom. Palm trees rustling. For a moment, I wondered if I had dreamt the night before.

Felix emerged from his bungalow, looking equally wrecked.

"How did you sleep?" I asked.

"No sleep," he replied.

"The dogs?"

"The dogs."

We climbed back into the truck and headed for Mirebalais, where the helicopter was waiting. The ride back to Port-au-Prince felt both lighter and heavier. I had witnessed something rare in Baille Tourible—not just hardship, but resolve. Not just poverty, but dignity.

Back at the Karibe, Felix and I walked the long hallway in silence. At our doors, he turned to me.

"Stay inside, lock the door," I said, feeling I could read his mind.

He twisted a cheek at me, turned his back, and went inside.

Security detail every minute of the trip.
Credit: Dax Dasilva

An Unexpected Encounter

We left early. The rotor blades of the United Nations Mi-8AMT helicopter were already cutting the morning air as we boarded. It was a beast of a machine—military troop seating for thirty-seven, an external hydraulic sling system capable of lifting four metric tons mid-flight, built for everything from rescue ops to medical evacuation. I strapped into a canvas seat alongside Ann, Felix, and a few CORE team members and felt the thud of liftoff in my bones.

We banked south toward Nippes, a coastal region edged in mangrove forest. From the air, Haiti's environmental wounds revealed themselves plainly. These mangroves had once teemed with life—birds thick in the canopy, fish swirling below. But over the past four decades, the Cahouane mangroves had been cut, picked, and stripped. Charcoal production. Overfishing. Poaching. By 2015, the birds had all but vanished, the fish stocks were gutted, and the trees snared and felled.

Recently, that tide had started to turn. UNEP-backed programs were restoring biodiversity. Birds had returned. Crustaceans were spawning again. Mangroves—essential buffers against storm surges, carbon sinks twice as dense as rainforests—were growing back. In Haiti, these coastal ecosystems were survival. Food for migrating birds. Honey for locals. A hedge against the changing climate.

CORE's work here centered on building sustainable livelihoods in agroforestry, cashew processing, aquaculture, beekeeping, and sustainable fishing. The program had equipped groups of fishermen with long-range boats, allowing them to reach deeper waters and easing the strain on overfished mangrove zones.

In a dusty clearing inland, we gathered with a group of local farmers. Their concerns were immediate and universal: water. How to capture it. How to store it. How to keep crops alive when the rains didn't come. The conversation wasn't abstract—it was rooted in experience, in trial and error, in survival. Every seed planted depended on the clouds. Every harvest depended on infrastructure that, here, didn't exist yet.

The sun bore down like punishment. Eventually, we returned to the helicopter to wait for a supply run before takeoff. We found what little relief we could under a sprawling tree, the rotor blades silent above us, the heat clinging like a wet shroud. The air was still but not calm. It felt loaded. I scanned the tree line. I felt exposed. I wanted to leave.

Then they appeared.

A dozen men were moving fast across the field—armed, serious, unsmiling. Our security lead trailed behind them, no longer in charge. The knot in my chest cinched tighter with each step they took. It was, without question, the most afraid I'd ever felt.

The man leading the soldiers was Jean Ernest Muscadin.

Once appointed Commissioner of Government for Miragoâne, Muscadin had since gone rogue, commanding his own militia, operating beyond the control of the Haitian National Police. I'd heard his name whispered like folklore. Six months earlier, his men had captured and executed Yzope Georges, a notorious gang enforcer, as he traveled to a ritual site meant to render him bulletproof.

Muscadin was brutal. Zero tolerance for gangs. He was feared, yes—but also revered. People said he was the only reason southern Haiti was still relatively safe. His men enacted justice on the spot. In a country spinning off its axis, many saw him as the last line. For the gangs, the south was a dead zone. For the people, it was still home.

Under the tree, he stepped in close to get a look at us. Lean frame. Coiled intensity. A gaze that measured your worth before you spoke a word. He offered greetings—his familiarity with the UN and CORE teams was known—but he was certainly interested in anything transpiring on his turf.

"Who is this?" he asked, lifting his rifle as casually as a schoolteacher pointing at a chalkboard.

I felt every molecule of sweat rise to the surface.

"This is Simba," Ann said, cool and clear. "He's part of our CORE team from Canada."

Headed south to the coastal regions via this Mi-8AMT helicopter.
Credit: Dax Dasilva

He stared at me longer than I would have liked. Something in his eyes suggested that he didn't buy it. That he was deciding if I was useful or not.

"And her?" he said, nodding toward Dalia beside me.

"That's Dalia," Ann said.

"Where are you from?" he asked.

"Palestine," Dalia replied.

A grin bloomed across his face. "I love Palestine," he said. "You have no state. No land. I love Palestine."

Dalia stayed silent.

Then, without fanfare, Muscadin and his soldiers turned and left. I stayed still beneath the tree, letting the adrenaline bleed out, watching the dust rise from their boots, half-expecting them to turn back.

It wasn't until the pilot waved us toward the chopper that the knot in my chest started to loosen. Even then, I kept glancing back at the tree line, waiting for the next test to come.

As the rotors whipped up dust and lifted us skyward, I exhaled for the first time in what felt like an hour. I don't know if we were ever truly in danger, but being face-to-face with a man who administered justice at the barrel of a gun—pointed at my chest—had etched its way into me.

Back in Port-au-Prince, our convoy took a detour. We pulled up to what looked like a quiet suburban home. Inside, it was something else—a guarded compound, and the home of Maryse Pénette-Kedar.

A diplomat, a former Secretary of State for Tourism, and a consultant to Royal Caribbean, Maryse had helped negotiate Haiti's entry into the Lomé Convention. But she was more than titles. She was a legend in education, in culture, in grace.

"Maryse supports many artists here," Ann told me as we stood before an enormous painting in the foyer. "She has one daughter, but it's said she's mother to all Haitian youth."

And then Maryse entered. Her smile could thaw steel. She moved with the serenity of someone who had carried generations.

"I do consider them my own," she said, taking my hand. "I've built a family of children from all walks of life. I only hope I've enriched their lives as much as they've enriched mine."

That night, we shared dinner at her harvest table. Students, artists, young leaders. I shared updates from Baille Tourible—about the marching band, the women's microcredit groups, the reforestation.

"Dax," she said, eyes shining, "these Haitian-led initiatives—these model schools, these small businesses—are what keep me believing that, against all odds, Haiti will rise. We are in the battle for our future. And you came. Thank you for standing up for the children."

That night at the Karibe, with our touring done, Ann, Dalia, and I leaned into one last breath of Haiti—the Jazz Fest still pulsing in the courtyard. From the terrace, we watched dancers spin beneath string lights, their bodies moving in rhythm with the brass and drums. The city's weight lifted in a peaceful evening embrace.

It didn't last.

Farmers gather to discuss assistance for drought-affected farms.
Credit: Dax Dasilva

Chapter 3 | **CHILDREN OF BAILLE TOURIBLE**

No Safe Passage

I woke in the dark to a knock at my door. Quiet, deliberate. I crept to the peephole. Felix.

"There has been a change to your departure," he said. "We need to leave now."

He walked me to CORE's secured room, where the mood was brittle. Scouts had flagged G9 gang activity rising fast across Port-au-Prince—Cherizier's mercenaries were setting up mass blockades to choke off movement. A convoy to the airport would paint a target on our backs.

We'd go small. The driver, Felix, Dalia, and me. One truck. No entourage. Felix would navigate us through whatever cracks remained.

I packed quickly. We slipped out the back of the Karibe, through a rear gate into the streets. One of CORE's trucks idled down the block. Dalia was already inside, silhouetted by the dash lights.

"Hi," I muttered, sliding in. My nerves hummed.

"This doesn't feel great," she said, voice low.

"I trust Felix," I offered, though I wasn't sure who I was trying to convince.

Felix had his comms live, scouts feeding him updates as we twisted through backroads and alleys, every turn narrowing the world. The city still slept but felt awake. Waiting. We slipped through side streets, the tires eating the road, until we hit a dead end. Our driver shifted hard, reversed, pivoted back out into the unknown.

Silence inside the cab. We needed to stay small. Invisible.

Then the road rose beneath us, cresting into a narrow ridge. The headlights picked up a shape ahead, then more. Armed men. A line across the road. Rifles slung, some masked, some bare-faced, all eyes on us.

We pulled up to the blockade. Gunshots cracked in the distance.

"What's happening?" Dalia whispered.

"I don't know, but let's stay calm," I said, my every nerve lit like a fuse.

Felix stepped out and walked into the light. Words were exchanged, low and steady. One man, bareheaded, rested a hand on Felix's shoulder. Felix did the same. Then he turned and climbed back into the truck.

Our driver threw it in reverse, pivoted fast, and we tore down a narrow road in new direction.

"Is everything okay?" I asked.

Felix nodded. "I know them."

He didn't say more. Didn't need to.

The horizon softened, dawn spreading pink and pale gold across the city. Markets stirred to life—vendors unrolling tarps, setting out fruit, arranging fish on ice. Amid the blockade and the gangs, life continued. It hit me hard—this ordinary day unfolding under siege, resilience born from necessity.

We reached the airport without another stop. Felix led us through a rear gate into a guarded diplomatic salon. Safe. Or as safe as it got.

Dalia and I boarded the plane. Ninety minutes later, the captain welcomed us to Miami. But part of me stayed on those streets—stuck between fear and the stubborn hope that I'd seen in the morning market.

An Overrun Nation

Just days after we escaped Haiti, Port-au-Prince was gripped by a fresh wave of coordinated gang attacks. Police stations were torched. Thousands of inmates were freed from the capital's largest prisons. It was a direct challenge to the interim government and a response to the signing of the Kenyan-led U.N. mission—a force brought in to stem the tide of violence that had drowned the city for years.

Cherizier and his allied gangs left their mark on the streets: burnt-out vehicles, hollowed police stations, a city on edge. Flights stopped. The main port fell under gang control. Supplies dried up. Half the country—five million Haitians—was left stranded, waiting in the dark, without food or medicine.

I thought of Ann. Of Fritz, Felix, Maryse. I thought of the children of Baille Tourible and the forests we were trying to plant. Hope is fragile in places like this, where the soil is thin and the storms come hard.

The Kenyan-led U.N. mission is there now, a patchwork of officers from Jamaica, Guatemala, El Salvador, and Kenya, fighting to hold a line that's been broken too many times. They're outgunned, but not out of the fight. Armored trucks rumble through the streets, while behind the scenes, global funding hangs in the balance. Waivers, freezes, shipments of gear—it all feels as precarious as the soil in the Central Plateau, eroded but still holding on.

There are no easy victories here. The gangs still rule much of Port-au-Prince. Nearly a million Haitians fled their homes in the last year alone, the violence tripling from the year before. The government is a patchwork, the parliament empty, the presidency vacant. Haiti survives in the cracks, in the spaces where community organizers, farmers, teachers, and volunteers refuse to give up.

This is what happens when ecosystems collapse, when desperation replaces opportunity. Haiti's story is the end point of what happens when the land is stripped bare and the people are left to fend for themselves. It's a warning shot for Brazil, for Indonesia, for the Congo Basin—what happens when the forests fall and there's nothing left to hold the soil, or the society, together.

Haiti was once a tropical jewel. Now it's a nation standing on the last thread of international aid, teetering between hope and despair. But that thread hasn't snapped.

I saw it in the farmers, in the women building microbusinesses, in the marching band of Baille Tourible, playing their hearts out under a banner of gratitude. The spirit of Haiti isn't gone. It endures.

With sustained support, with investment in the land and its people, the soil can hold. The forests can return. The country can stand—not on crutches, but on its own.

The path back will be hard. But it's there.

Haiti's spirit beats on—loud as the drums of Baille Tourible, steady as the hands planting trees on stripped mountainsides. Even in ruin, there is resilience. Even in darkness, there's a way forward.

"The answer to an impossible problem is to find the impossible solution. And that solution can be found through passion, courage, and imagination."

—CAPTAIN PAUL WATSON

A pod of spinner dolphins dances through Red Sea waters.
Credit: Will Allen

FRANCE

PERTHUIS BRETON

La Rochelle

PERTUIS D'ANTIOCHE

FRANCE

A final flick of the tail—grace vanishing into the deep.
Credit: Sea Shepherd Global

Chapter 4

THE GHOST FLEET OF LA ROCHELLE

SEA SHEPHERD'S FIGHT TO SAVE EUROPE'S DOLPHINS

Remember Captain Ahab? The peg-legged sailor in Melville's *Moby-Dick*, eyes wild with obsession, steering his ship and crew into ruin in pursuit of the great white whale. Spoiler alert: Ahab isn't the hero—he's the villain. A madman willing to burn the world for a shot at vengeance.

History has never lacked for Ahabs. The real ones traded wooden legs for steel hulls and mechanized harpoons, but the obsession is the same: slaughtering whales, blind to the wreckage they leave behind.

But here's another kind of captain. One who has spent his life standing between harpoons and the gentle giants of the sea. A man who's sacrificed nearly everything—his home, his freedom, even his country—to ensure the whales survive.

Captain Paul Watson. Founder of Sea Shepherd, the marine conservation group feared by whalers and poachers across the globe. For nearly half a century, Sea Shepherd's black-flagged ships have cut through the world's oceans, intercepting illegal hunts, tearing down drift nets, and giving no quarter to those who threaten marine life.

Depending on who you ask, Paul is either a menace or a guardian. To me? He's the reason whales still exist.

Fifty years ago, saving whales seemed impossible. Paul didn't blink. "The answer to an impossible problem," he said, "is to find the impossible solution." Passion, courage, imagination—that was his compass. And it led him straight into battle.

Since then, he has helped drive a harpoon through the heart of global whaling. Ninety percent of it gone. Legal whaling in international waters? Nearly extinct. But none of those victories came from behind a desk. His battlefield has always been the open ocean, face-to-face with the ships that kill.

He's been called a lot of things along the way. Hero. Pirate. Eco-terrorist. That last one—courtesy of governments and corporations—always felt a little rich. Because if you've watched him lead a Sea Shepherd campaign, you know: It's a battle. Nonviolent, but aggressive. Ship against ship. Strategy against greed. And if that makes him a pirate, then maybe the world needs more pirates.

Most people know Captain Paul from *Whale Wars*, where he's seen risking life and limb. Antarctic waters, freezing and hostile. Chasing whaling ships, months at sea, ramming steel hulls broadside—all to send poachers home empty-handed. His defiance forced the world to look, forced policies to change, gave the whales a fighting chance. But the fight isn't over. As Paul says: "If the ocean dies, we all die."

That kind of resistance doesn't come without consequences. Since 2010, he's been a wanted man, targeted by an INTERPOL Red Notice at the request of Japan. The charges: "Breaking into a Vessel, Damage to Property, Forcible Obstruction of Business, and Injury." Costa Rica filed one, too, for interfering with illegal shark finners. Canada, his homeland, arrested him for protesting brutal seal hunts. His passport revoked. Exile permanent. It might've buried another man. But Paul kept going.

He couldn't set foot in Canada, but the U.S. offered safe harbor. Former Secretary of State John Kerry called the charges "bogus." INTERPOL Red Notices are for war criminals and cartel bosses. Paul Watson's crime? Conspiracy to trespass. No one injured. No property damaged. The star witness later recanted, admitting the charges were a fabrication—a vendetta against the man who'd stopped Japan's whaling fleet cold.

And yet, the warrant stayed.

During the writing of this book, Captain Paul sat in a Danish prison cell in Greenland for five long months, a gray winter stretching endlessly beyond the frosted windows, waiting for a decision that could end everything: extradition to Japan, and surely prison. He'd boarded a ship, thinking the Red Notice lifted, to stop a fin whale hunt near Greenland. Instead, he was the one stopped—caught in a carefully laid trap.

For a man who's faced down harpoons at sea, being caught on land felt like irony made flesh.

The prison days were a grind. But Paul is not a man who falters. He spent them mapping strategy, watching the sea from a small window, reminding himself why the fight mattered. Just before Christmas, the decision came: release. Another chapter of resilience written into the logbook.

Even now, into his seventies, Paul sails. He leaves his wife and young son behind and steps once more into the breach—outnumbered, yes, but never outmatched. Not in will, not in persistence. His work hasn't just earned enemies. It's earned respect. In 2024, the Perfect World Foundation named him Conservationist of the Year, honoring a life lived on the front lines.

And yet, there was another turn. In 2022, after decades with Sea Shepherd, Paul severed ties. The organization he founded in 1977 had grown, changed. Leadership disputes made it impossible to continue. But retreat isn't in his blood. He founded the Captain Paul Watson Foundation, a leaner operation, co-created with tech entrepreneur Omar Todd. No bloated bureaucracy. Just action. Paul holds no formal role—he isn't on the payroll. He serves as its heart, its compass, volunteering his time to steer the mission forward.

Paul's story is still being written. He's a man who belongs on the front lines, where the stakes are highest and the odds are uncertain. His fight for the oceans isn't a cause—it's his life. His purpose. Like the waves he's spent decades defending, Paul Watson keeps coming back. Unstoppable. Undeterred. Ready for whatever comes next.

Plymouth

I traveled to Plymouth, Vermont, to see Captain Paul Watson. Paul and I share the same urgency for environmental activism—the same belief that action speaks louder than intention. I'd long held him in high reverence, not just for the battles he's fought, but for the sacrifices he's made. Over the years, we'd become close friends. There's a gravity to Paul, a pull like the tide. You sit with him, and the world feels sharper, the stakes higher.

Plymouth is the kind of town you imagine when you think of New England. Fewer than 650 residents, a scattering of Victorian homes and weathered farmhouses, fields edged with stone walls. The birthplace of Calvin Coolidge. It draws the occasional tourist, but mostly it hums quietly to itself, stitched together by a small community of biologists, scientists, and Paul's Sea Shepherd comrades. Amid this patchwork of meadows and winding roads, Captain Paul lived quietly with his wife and their two boys.

His white hair caught the Vermont sun, a bright shock against the green hills. There was warmth in his smile, but you could see the restlessness underneath, the coiled energy of a man built for rougher waters. Years of being landlocked had left him too big for this small town. After a warm hug, we sat down, and without ceremony, he launched into it.

"Did I ever tell you about the first time I looked into the eye of a whale?" His voice, even in a quiet room, carried the charge of open seas.

I smiled. "Please, share it." I'd heard the story before, but hearing it from the man himself—whose life had so often been wagered on the water—was something else entirely.

"In 1975, when I started with Greenpeace," he began, the words settling into their rhythm, "we thought we could save whales by placing ourselves between them and the harpoons. This was all inspired by Gandhi's nonviolent resistance. We believed the same tactics could work in environmental activism. And to some extent, they did," he began, his eyes lighting up with the memory. "Until I found myself in a small inflatable Zodiac, bouncing around in the rough Antarctic waters. Bearing down on

Chapter 4 | **THE GHOST FLEET OF LA ROCHELLE**

us, a 150-foot Soviet whaling ship with its harpoon cannon aimed right at us—attempting to block a pod of eight sperm whales."

As the story goes, the whaling vessel had targeted a large female that was with her calf. Paul's team steered their Zodiac between the killers and the whale, holding their line as the Soviet captain stood at the flybridge, hands gesturing throat-slash warnings from behind the harpoon gun. The harpoon fired. An explosion cracked the sky. The steel missile roared past Paul's raft and drove deep into the mother whale.

"She screamed," Paul said, his voice catching, tears welling in eyes hardened by decades of battle. "It sounded like a woman screaming. She rolled onto her side, and the sea turned red."

Then the bull whale turned. The largest male in the pod peeled away, circling back toward the Soviet ship, diving deep before breaching in a fury, attacking. Another harpoon fired, catching him in the head, knocking him backward into the bloodied water. But he rose again, breaching one final time—not toward the whalers, but toward Paul.

The bull loomed over the Zodiac, casting a shadow that must have felt like the ocean itself bearing down. And then—a pause. Instead of crushing the tiny raft, the whale hovered, his gaze locked with Paul's.

"I'll never forget that look," Paul whispered, his voice softer now. "There was understanding in his eyes... and pity. Not for himself, but for us. For what we've become—killing beings of intelligence and grace, just to extract machine oil. The kind the Russians used for lubricating ballistic missiles, weapons meant to exterminate life on land, too. In that moment, I realized—we are the insane ones."

It was there, in the shadow of that whale, that Paul vowed to dedicate his life to protecting marine life—not for people, but for the creatures themselves. That vow became Sea Shepherd's guiding principle: to defend life that cannot defend itself. They don't work for governments or corporations; they work for their clients, the billions of heartbeats in the sea.

All these years later, Paul and his team had succeeded in pushing whaling back to a handful of territorial waters—Norway, Japan, Iceland, and Denmark. The end was finally in sight. Because of their work, future generations might experience whales once again roaming the oceans of the world. And with their return, a new challenge was beginning to take shape: learning to live alongside these giants as they reclaimed the waters they once ruled. Paul leaned back in his chair, rocking gently, his gaze drifting beyond the Vermont hills, as if listening for something distant and ancient—the call of the sea.

I asked where Sea Shepherd needed the most help.

"Sea Shepherd France needs a ship for Operation Dolphin Bycatch, an upcoming mission off the coast of France," he said. "The fishing industry is destroying the coast, and thousands of dolphins are being killed in their nets with no consequences. We don't have a ship fast enough to reach them in time. We need speed. We need range."

That's when he brought up the M/Y *Sam Simon*—a docked ship that, with the right funding, could be the answer. For the next hour, we talked about France, about the battle unfolding offshore.

With Captain Paul Watson.
Credit: Dax Dasilva

Chapter 4 | **THE GHOST FLEET OF LA ROCHELLE**

"Let's get this ship back at sea," I said, shaking his hand, sealing my commitment to fund its operating costs for the next three years. Paul's face lit up. He pulled me in for another hug, and I left Vermont with a mission—to fund the *Sam Simon* and to travel to France to help however I could.

Before I left, he offered one last piece of advice, the kind that lands heavy but true.

"Dax, you'll need to grab the public's attention. There are two industries politicians fear: farming and fishing. There are laws, but no one enforces them. Politicians only move when the people force their hand."

He was right. The European fishing industry survives on massive subsidies. Without them, it would collapse under its own weight. But fish on the dinner plate keeps governments complicit.

I'd been moved by *Seaspiracy*, the documentary that lays bare the brutality of overfishing. Viewing it confirmed two things: the critical importance of Sea Shepherd's work and the power of film to stir the public. Watching Sea Shepherd intercept illegal trawlers off the African coast, protecting local communities, was a call to action.

Within six months, the paperwork was done. The ship was funded, refurbished, and ready. And I was headed to France, camera crew in tow, ready to tell the story of the devastation just beneath the waves.

Sea Shepherd M/Y Age of Union *in the Bay of Biscay.*
Credit: Age of Union

La Rochelle

It was a cold, overcast February morning on France's western coast when my film crew and I left the harbor in a Zodiac—a small, inflatable but dependable boat. Behind us stood the centuries-old stone watchtowers of the Vieux Port in La Rochelle, once sentinels against seafaring invaders. We motored into the Bay of Biscay toward the M/Y *Age of Union*—formerly the M/Y *Sam Simon*—one of Sea Shepherd's fourteen ships, collectively known as Neptune's Navy, that patrol and protect the world's oceans. Just months earlier, I had committed to fund this 184-foot vessel's operations for the next three years, supporting campaigns across the African and European coasts. With renovations complete and the crew preparing to set sail, I had come to see the ship in person.

The wind cut through me, cold and merciless, as we tore across the salt-whipped bay. Each spray of seawater stung my raw eyes, still burning from the red-eye out of Montréal. My body felt rattled and exhausted from the whirlwind of travel—Haiti just days ago, Congo before that, and

Historic towers of La Rochelle.
Credit: Dax Dasilva

Preparing for night patrols—zodiac boarding.
Credit: Dax Dasilva

the Amazon not long before. A blur of climate zones, time changes, and vaccinations had left me in a kind of physical limbo. I wasn't fully here, not yet. Just suspended—adrift between the places I'd come from and the one I was trying to reach.

Overhead, the herring gulls heckled us with loud, cackling cries, mistaking us for a fishing boat. They circled in hungry spirals, their white bellies and black-tipped wings gleaming as they danced on invisible air currents. Each bird adjusted mid-flight with sharp precision, never colliding, never breaking formation—chaos with choreography. They watched us, keen-eyed and expectant, not knowing we were here to protect the very waters they relied on.

As the Zodiac bounced over deepening water, the sea grew darker, silkier. Ahead, the ship rose on the horizon—steel-gray and resolute, like a warship. *M/Y Age of Union*. Seeing her name emblazoned on the hull, seeing our partnership forged into metal, brought a surge of emotion I hadn't expected. This moment, this vessel suggested by Captain Paul, was the culmination of decades of work. To stand alongside Sea Shepherd— to help defend the ocean with the most daring conservationists on the planet—filled me with awe and gratitude.

We pulled alongside the ship and climbed the rope ladder, one by one. On deck, Captain Alex Cornelissen welcomed us with a grin that could slice through fog. The tall Dutchman, CEO of Sea Shepherd Global, oversees the European fleet. His reputation is legendary, burnished by years of front-line work, including campaigns alongside Captain Paul Watson during the *Whale Wars* era. Both men had led daring protests against the slaughter of seal pups in northeastern Canada—actions that got them arrested under the Seal Protection Act and banned from entering the country, despite Paul being a Canadian citizen.

"Welcome aboard!" Alex boomed, his voice carrying easily over the surf.

"Great to finally be here," I replied, stepping onto the deck and shaking off the cold.

Alex clapped me on the shoulder. "Well, it better be, Dax. Let's get you dried off and show you around your ship."

My ship? I smirked. Not quite. But the words warmed me just the same.

He walked us through the updates with pride in every footstep. "We've overhauled the generators, added slip-resistant floors in the mess and scullery, upgraded the galley, and replaced every last door," he said. "We've also added a twenty-five-foot deployable boat on deck, fully equipped for inspections."

"You feel ready for the mission?" I asked, scanning the deck.

"Absolutely. She can hit eleven knots and reach zones we never could before. We're the only ones out here watching. And when the bad actors see us coming, they run. Every time. Most of them are fishing illegally: working in restricted zones, pulling in protected species, dumping the bycatch like it never happened. And out here, no one's watching. But we're going to change that."

The goal was simple: to haunt the waters like a ghost fleet, a constant threat to illegal fishing operations off Europe and Africa—a presence so feared that even in our absence, the thought of us would keep them in line.

The ship itself had its own story to tell. Originally built in 1993, it was a Japanese weather survey vessel named *Seifu Maru*—one of five oceanographic ships designed to monitor environmental pollutants like greenhouse gases, ozone-depleting substances, heavy metals, and oils. It worked Japan's waters and the North Pacific until 2010, when it was sold, renamed *Kaiko Maru No. 8,* and faded from record.

That's where the story gets juicy.

But by 2012, Sea Shepherd needed a long-range ship. Building one from scratch was too expensive and too slow. The *Kaiko Maru* was a rare find: sturdy, fast, ice-ready—and conveniently for sale. The problem? Captain Paul Watson was wanted by the Japanese government—zero chance they would sell him a ship. So, he got creative.

He formed a shell company in Delaware, which fronted another in Hong Kong. A Korean surveyor was hired to inspect the ship. Funds were secured through Sam Simon, *The Simpsons* co-creator and fierce animal rights activist. With fake paperwork, Bart Simpson royalties, and a bit of espionage, Sea Shepherd bought the vessel. It wasn't until after the handover that Japan realized it had sold a ship to its most persistent maritime adversary.

Renamed the *Sam Simon,* the vessel was immediately deployed to the Southern Ocean to confront Japan's whaling fleet. For years, Paul and his crew used it to block, track, and expose illegal whale hunts. But after Simon's death in 2015, funding dried up. By 2020, the ship was docked, idle and gathering rust.

That's when Paul brought it up during our recent visit. They needed $4.5 million to run it for three more years with a full crew. I didn't hesitate. Through Age of Union, we cut the check. The ship was reborn again, rebranded as the M/Y *Age of Union.*

Supporting Sea Shepherd was different from our work on land—securing forest concessions in the Amazon, mapping land titles in the Congo, and reforesting mountainsides in Haiti. This wasn't about planting trees or protecting terrestrial ecosystems. This was open water. Fast-moving, lawless, hard to police. But I knew it mattered. This ship would patrol against illegal, unreported, and unregulated (IUU) fishing; defend coastal fisheries from predatory supertrawlers; and expose the global corporations draining the oceans of life.

Its first mission: Operation Dolphin Killers.

In the Bay of Biscay, over ten thousand dolphins die each year as bycatch—casualties of industrial fishing. Massive trawl nets stretch miles, scooping up everything: dolphins, sharks, sea turtles, whales, seabirds. The dead are dumped back into the sea and dismissed with a word: "bycatch." A cold, bureaucratic term for carnage.

In 2018, researchers from the Pelagis Observatory in La Rochelle raised the alarm. Dolphins were washing up on shore at record rates. More than in the Taiji cove. More than in the Faroe Islands. France had the highest rate of dolphin deaths in the world.

The fishing industry denied everything. Claimed the dolphins were sick. That they'd died naturally. But autopsies said otherwise: The dolphins were healthy, their bodies shredded by nets. As air-breathing mammals, they can't stay submerged. They panic, fight, and suffocate. Their lungs burst.

Faced with this brutality, I partnered with Sea Shepherd France and brought in a film crew. We had to catch the perpetrators in the act. If we could show the public the truth, we could force the government to act. Fishing laws don't change quietly. You need outrage.

So, we made noise.

Night after night, we patrolled the bay in Zodiacs, shadowing trawlers and waiting for them to haul in their nets. We filmed everything. We knew many weren't reporting their bycatch—if they reported anything at all. The footage would tell the real story. And we had one hell of a story to tell.

Ocean Killers

Trouble had found its way to the French Atlantic. While we were still stationed along the coast, Sea Shepherd received intel that the FV *Margiris*—one of the largest supertrawlers in the world—was lurking in the Bay of Biscay.

To call it a fishing boat is a grotesque understatement. The Dutch-owned *Margiris* is the world's second-largest fishing vessel—a floating fortress weighing 9,500 tons and stretching 143 meters, roughly the height of a 47-story skyscraper. It hauls a net that is 600 meters long and 200 meters wide, dragging it through the ocean and annihilating everything in its path. Capable of catching and freezing 250 tons of fish per day, the *Margiris* is a commercial killing machine.

The bycatch is staggering. Everything caught in its wake—seabirds, dolphins, sharks, turtles—dies in the net and is dumped back into the sea. Globally, over 40 percent of the 160 billion pounds of fish caught each year is considered bycatch. That's hundreds of thousands of marine mammals dead because of the scale and indifference of industrial fishing.

The *Margiris* isn't a fishing vessel in any traditional sense. It doesn't fish—it harvests. It consumes the ocean in kilometer-wide swaths, swallowing entire ecosystems. Banned from Australia after public outrage. Banned from Chile, Ireland, and swaths of Africa. And yet, there it was—off the coast of France.

To call the *Margiris* a fishing boat is like calling a nuclear warhead a firecracker. It's the Death Star of the oceans—a floating factory of mass destruction. As I imagined its shadow stretching across the sea, headed into the Bay of Biscay, I thought of Oppenheimer's immortal words:

"Now I am become Death, the destroyer of worlds."

We dispatched the *Age of Union* to intercept. Once the *Margiris* was located, the crew launched rigid inflatable boats to get closer. What they found was horrifying: hundreds of thousands of dead blue whiting—small fish used in frozen food products—blanketing the water behind the ship. You couldn't even see the sea.

Normally, the *Margiris* would have gotten away with it. What happens at sea usually stays at sea. But not this time. We had a ship that could match its speed and range—and we caught everything on camera. Our team launched drones, capturing video and stills that went viral within hours.

Public outrage followed. France's maritime minister called the images "shocking" and launched an investigation. The *Margiris*'s representatives claimed the disaster was the result of a ruptured net—a "rare occurrence." But we knew better. EU law requires vessels to return to port and unload

A sea of death—Sea Shepherd photographs fish discarded by FV Margiris.
Credit: Sea Shepherd Global

unwanted catch—a costly and time-consuming process. Dumping the bodies at sea and carrying on is the easier option.

Overfishing is the single greatest threat to our oceans. Global fish consumption has doubled in the last fifty years. Today, we consume 22 to 24 kilograms per person annually. The ocean can sustainably support about 8 kilograms per person. We're fishing at nearly triple the planet's limit. The hard truth is: Eight billion people can't all eat fish.

Supertrawlers are the sea monsters behind this crisis—massive vessels dragging mile-long nets, hauling hundreds of tons of marine life every day. In 2019, Greenpeace found twenty-five supertrawlers, including the world's four largest, operating off the UK coast. Together, they spent over three thousand hours fishing in marine protected areas (MPAs). Protected in name only. As the deep sea is stripped bare, dolphins are forced toward shore in search of food—and into local fishing nets, where they die slowly, suffocating. It's a death spiral.

Most of this devastation happens far from land, beyond the reach of regulators or activists. Getting to these ships is nearly impossible without vessels like the *Age of Union*. Our presence acts as a deterrent. We can't be everywhere—but knowing we're out there changes the equation.

FV Margiris *dumps a haul of dead fish.*
Credit: Sea Shepherd Global

The company behind the *Margiris*, Parlevliet & Van der Plas, boasts an "excellent reputation for sustainable fishing." They claim their bycatch is "zero." Yet the *Margiris* has been photographed in Mauritania, docked at one of the world's largest fish-processing plants. From there, fishmeal is exported to feed aquaculture—shrimp farms in Asia and salmon pens in Scotland. Meanwhile, local African communities are outpriced, outcompeted, and left with empty nets.

The Mayor of La Rochelle

At a secret location along the west coast of France, the Sea Shepherd team brought me to their communal farmhouse—the quiet hub of their operations. The property hosted a mix of volunteers, crew members, and guests. Humble, lived-in, and unassuming, it was a sharp contrast to the scale of the global impact that radiated from this place. My crew and I had arrived to film several interviews for the documentary.

Waiting to greet us was Lamya Essemlali—Captain Paul's protégé, one of his closest confidants, and the face of Sea Shepherd France.

In 2006, Lamya co-founded Sea Shepherd France with Paul, and by 2008, she had become its president. A French environmentalist with a master's degree in marine biology, she'd spent time with WWF and Greenpeace before finding her true calling alongside Captain Watson. Moroccan by heritage and raised in the suburbs of Paris, she'd grown up far from the oceans she now risks her life to protect.

"How's Paul?" she asked, knowing I'd seen him recently.

"He's holding up," I replied. "He wished he could be here." We both understood why he couldn't—the risk of arrest remained too high.

Lamya nodded, her expression softening. "When I first met Paul, he said something I didn't know I needed to hear. He asked, 'Would you be willing to die for a whale?' I hadn't even seen a whale yet. But I knew my answer was yes."

We spent hours discussing the state of the seas. The challenges were immense, but with the *M/Y Age of Union* back on the water, there was a renewed sense of purpose—of momentum.

"With all the monitoring we do along the coast, not everyone's a fan," Lamya said. "This region has deep fishing roots. Some people think we're here to destroy their way of life."

"I can imagine," I said. "But this kind of devastation—it's recent, right? Industrial overfishing changed the game."

"You're right," she said. "It wasn't always like this. But when the supertrawlers came, the dolphins started washing up onshore—net injuries, one after another. We knew what was happening."

In 2016, when the Pelagis Observatory released their public report of spiked dolphin strandings, the message was clear: This was not a natural event. The dolphins were absolutely casualties of long drift nets dragging French waters.

"Ocean predators hunt selectively," Lamya said. "They take what they need. These nets? They take everything—fish, dolphins, sharks—whatever's there."

The mission of our film was simple but heavy: Hold the fishing industry accountable for its bycatch and show the real numbers to the public and policymakers. There was a dangerous "what happens at sea, stays at sea" mentality, and we were going to challenge it. Our hope was to push for commercial fishing regulations that required third-party inspectors and onboard video surveillance.

By the end of the week, we had most of what we needed. But we were still missing one critical piece: footage of dolphins caught in the nets. Without it, the story wouldn't be complete.

This was the hardest part—spending nights freezing on a small Zodiac, waiting for the devastating moment to unfold. But it was necessary. We needed proof. We needed to show the world what was happening when no one else was watching.

So, my film crew joined Sea Shepherd aboard the *Age of Union* for a week at sea. Every night, the Zodiacs launched, tailing fishing vessels for hours, watching as nets broke the surface. It was grueling work. The camera operators held their lenses steady in the cold, knowing that a few seconds of distraction could cost us everything.

That week, the Bay of Biscay came alive under a rare and surreal spectacle—a red tide of bioluminescent dinoflagellates. These microscopic plankton bloom in warm, nutrient-rich waters, and when agitated by waves or movement, they emit a soft, electric-blue glow as a natural defense. With every swell and ripple, the sea pulsed with light. Fish traced luminous paths beneath the surface, and the wake of our boat shimmered like liquid stardust.

I'd seen beauty in nature before—towering rainforests, volcanic ridgelines, reefs blooming with color—but nothing like this. The ocean felt alive in a way I hadn't experienced, like I was moving through something ancient and conscious. I sat on the edge of the Zodiac, mesmerized, the cold forgotten. It was as if we'd slipped into a dream. Van Gogh's *Starry Night* rendered in motion. Even he might have blamed the absinthe if he'd seen it firsthand.

And in the midst of our grim work—waiting for the nets to surface, bracing for the worst—it was a moment of quiet awe.

But beauty gave way to darkness. As nets broke the surface, the glowing water parted for the night's haul. Still—no dolphins. Each morning, the crew returned soaked and exhausted. Empty-handed.

Then, on the final night, everything changed.

"We got it!" Oliver's voice cracked through the radio as their Zodiac neared the ship. In the cabin of the *M/Y Age of Union*, we crowded around the monitor. The footage was crystal clear: a large fishing vessel pulling up dolphins in its nets—and then dumping the lifeless bodies back into the sea. It was sickening to watch, and even worse to celebrate. But this was the proof we needed. We had caught them in the act.

The story had its spine now. And the next step was to bring it into the light.

We scheduled an interview with Jean-François Fountaine, mayor of La Rochelle. For years, Sea Shepherd and the local fishing industry had been at odds. Five years ago, the mayor wouldn't have spoken to us. Nor would the fishermen. But as the ocean collapsed beneath them, their tone had started to shift. Perhaps they'd begun to realize their grandchildren might not inherit fish at all. That the oceanic way of life could end on their watch.

La Rochelle seemed more forward-thinking than most coastal towns when it came to conservation. Or so we believed.

During the interview, we showed Mayor Fountaine the footage. He watched in silence, then offered a restrained nod.

"La Rochelle was born from the sea—from fishing, from exploration," he said. "It's sad to see a dead dolphin. But fishing is hard work. We must be careful not to discredit the fishermen."

My heart sank. The evidence was right in front of him, and still, his sympathies leaned toward industry.

Documenting the mission—Sea Shepherd crew members share their front line experiences.
Credit: Dax Dasilva

"We can stop people from throwing plastic bags or cigarette butts into the sea," he continued. "That's local. But dolphin captures? That's not our jurisdiction. That's for the state to address."

As we interviewed more officials, a pattern emerged: No one wanted to take responsibility. The fishermen blamed the policymakers. The policymakers blamed the state. The state shrugged it off as incidental. It was a perfect loop of denial.

My crew left disheartened. But Lamya? She was furious.

Dead Dolphins in Paris

Frustrated by the French government's reluctance to change fishing regulations—even when confronted with undeniable proof—Lamya called Captain Paul for advice. Over the years, he had mastered the art of galvanizing public attention. According to his personal "laws of media," a story needs one of four ingredients to catch fire: sex, scandal, violence, or celebrity. Fortunately, we had two of them already. But Lamya was up against a formidable enemy—the commercial fishing lobby—and the broader public wasn't even aware dolphins lived along France's coast, let alone that they were dying in record numbers.

"You need to show the world what's happening," Paul said from his home in Vermont, his voice low and calm, as if plotting a storm. "Take some of the dead dolphins to the Eiffel Tower. Lay them out in the open. They won't be able to look away."

It was bold. But Lamya doesn't shy away from bold.

The Sea Shepherd France team retrieved several dolphin carcasses that had recently washed ashore and transported them to the Place du Trocadéro in Paris, directly across from the Eiffel Tower. There, with the

Iron Lady rising behind them, they arranged the bodies in full public view. Beside them, stark white signs read:

These are real dead dolphins.

Thousands die every year in France so that you can eat fish.

Crowds gathered quickly, confused at first, then stunned. Many had never seen a dolphin up close, let alone a dead one. Some didn't believe they were real. The idea that dolphins lived off the coast of France—let alone died by the thousands—was unthinkable to most. Lamya and her team stood with the display, calmly answering questions and explaining how these animals had died, what it meant, and why it mattered.

The public was disturbed. A few media outlets picked up the story. But it wasn't enough.

So, they doubled down.

Next, the team brought the dolphins to the steps of the National Assembly, where the Minister of the Sea and members of the press happened to be present. This time, the display landed like a grenade. Headlines erupted. The public demanded answers. But the Minister's reaction was not what anyone expected. She expressed shock—not at the dolphin deaths, but at Sea Shepherd's demonstration. She threatened legal

Dolphins killed in bycatch on display in Paris.
Credit: Sea Shepherd France

action against the organization for transporting and displaying the dead animals in a public space.

Police arrived shortly afterward and ordered the dolphins removed. Officers handed Lamya a document: a "law reminder," asking Sea Shepherd to sign.

She didn't flinch.

"We won't sign this," Lamya said, standing her ground. "We're not the ones breaking the law. Fishermen are required to declare their bycatch. They're not doing it. We're here enforcing the law that protects dolphins—not violating it."

She was right. Less than 5 percent of fishermen declared their bycatch. None had ever been penalized for failing to report it.

After the standoff, we returned to Sea Shepherd headquarters to continue filming. Along the shores of La Rochelle, where dolphins regularly wash up, we interviewed Lamya and Captain Alex Cornelissen.

"The bycatch numbers are far worse than anyone wants to admit," Alex said, his voice tight with frustration.

I nodded, still shaken. "It's illegal to target dolphins, but if you're pulling up nets full of them—nets set in areas where dolphins are known to hunt—how can they still call it an accident?"

"Exactly," Lamya said. "It's legal wordplay to protect the fishing industry. And even the language around seafood is designed to sever empathy. We say 'seafood,' not 'sealife.' You don't see restaurants advertising 'sealife specials,' do you?"

Her point landed hard. There was a profound disconnect between the fish displayed on ice in local markets and the suffering that came before it. If people truly understood what was happening beneath the surface, I wondered how many would eat fish at all.

With filming in France wrapped, we shifted our focus. We needed to show the other side of this story—what life looked like when dolphins were left in peace. Left to thrive. Our cinematographer, Will Allen—a seasoned underwater filmmaker—agreed the Red Sea would offer the perfect contrast. Clear waters. Protected habitats. A thriving dolphin colony.

Chapter 4 | **THE GHOST FLEET OF LA ROCHELLE**

The very next day, while the rest of the crew began their journey back to Canada via Paris, Will and I boarded a flight to Egypt. We were chasing something rare in the world of marine conservation: unspoiled beauty, and the chance to capture it before it disappears.

A Heist in Paris

Will and I chartered a boat from Egypt into the Red Sea, one of the most extraordinary places on Earth to film marine life. Known for its warmth and salinity—thanks to scorching temperatures, scarce rainfall, and the absence of rivers flowing into it—the Red Sea is home to some of the most vibrant and undisturbed coral reefs in the world.

We launched from Hurghada, a bustling port city at the mouth of the Gulf of Suez, and sailed deep into the open sea. Our destination: Sataya Reef, a remote marine sanctuary nearly a day's sail from shore. The reef is legendary, a place where wild dolphins surface around 10 a.m. each day, spend the morning waking, then spend the afternoon in a state of pure joy—playing, spinning, mating—until the sun disappears.

As we neared the reef, the sea came alive. Pods of spinner and bottlenose dolphins swarmed around the boat, sleek and agile, keeping pace with us like we were part of the pod. Their acrobatics felt like an invitation—a dare to match their grace. When we anchored and dove in, the water revealed a living kaleidoscope. Sunlight filtered down in gold shafts, illuminating clouds of jewel-toned fish weaving between vibrant coral formations. It felt like stepping into a secret cathedral of light and life.

Brilliant schools of angelfish, butterflyfish, unicornfish, and triggerfish spiraled around us. I hovered near a coral head and watched a pair of clownfish dance through the tentacles of a sea anemone. The symbiosis was mesmerizing—clownfish protecting the anemone from predators like butterflyfish, while the anemone sheltered them from harm.

Nearby, a parrotfish gnawed audibly on coral, the crunch of its beak echoing like a quiet metronome. Everywhere I looked, life thrived. It was like swimming through a dream.

We ventured beyond the reef into deeper water. A school of striped surgeonfish darted past—harmless grazers, but armed with a razor-sharp spine near the tail, capable of slicing like a scalpel. Even here, in paradise, nature kept its edge.

Soon, we found a pod of bottlenose dolphins just waking up. Dolphins sleep with half their brain alert, one eye open—a survival adaptation that's both fascinating and unsettling. They floated near the surface, still and calm, until, suddenly, they were awake—zipping through the water, spinning, playing, brushing against one another in fluid joy.

Will swam closer with his camera rig, years of experience making him part of the water. I watched as the dolphins twisted and chased, blowing bubbles and darting around us like children at recess. This went on for hours. I knew, even as it unfolded, that this was the kind of footage that could change minds—make people fall in love with the ocean again.

Back on the boat, I peeled off my gear and leaned against the railing, letting the wind dry the salt from my skin. There was a quiet contentment in the air—the stillness that comes when you know you've captured something rare.

Then the satellite phone rang.

I answered, and the voice on the other end shattered the calm. The team in Paris had ignored protocol. Instead of backing up footage and securing the gear, they'd gone straight into the city. They left the van—with over $200,000 worth of cameras and hard drives—unattended in a public car park. When they returned, the van had been broken into. Everything—interviews, ship footage, protest scenes, bycatch evidence—was gone.

I was furious. Sick to my stomach. All that work, all that risk—vanished because they couldn't wait to hit the nightclubs. I gripped the phone, trying to stay composed.

"You need to fix this," I said flatly. "Go find the equipment." I hung up and stared out across the sea, suddenly feeling very far from everything.

Will was still disassembling his gear, oblivious to the storm that had just rolled in.

"In all my years filming marine life, this is the best footage I've ever gotten of dolphins waking up and transitioning into play," he said, eyes still bright.

I tried to smile. "It was incredible," I agreed—and then I told him what had happened in Paris. His face dropped. We stood there in silence, two men on a boat in the middle of the Red Sea, after one of the best days ever—knowing we might not have a film at all.

Losing that footage felt like losing the mission. We brainstormed—maybe we could piece together something from the Red Sea alone, supplement it with outside clips—but the interviews, the protests, the incriminating footage... those moments were irreplaceable.

Still, we kept filming. Each morning, we set out at dawn, chasing pods, filming reefs, trying to capture as much as we could. Meanwhile, the situation in Paris got stranger by the hour.

The stolen gear had AirTags in two of the hard cases, and they were pinging. The signal led to a nondescript apartment building in a Parisian suburb. The team called the police, but without a specific unit number, the officers weren't interested.

So, the team took matters into their own hands.

They climbed to the roof and descended the fire escapes, phones in hand, watching the signal narrow to a single floor. That's when they stumbled into the building's maintenance room. Inside: tools, coveralls—everything they needed for a convincing disguise. Now dressed like janitors, they roamed the halls tracking the AirTags until they zeroed in on a door.

With that information, they called the police again. This time, the officers returned. They knocked, then kicked in the door.

Inside was a goldmine of stolen goods—cameras, laptops, jewelry, stereo equipment. And there, among it all, was our gear.

It turned out to be part of a small crime ring operating in coordination with parking lot security. When guests left their cars, the guards alerted the thieves, who struck within minutes. Our van had been the jackpot. But we got lucky—the goods hadn't been fenced yet.

Nearly everything was recovered: cameras, lenses, and—miraculously—all the hard drives.

When the call came in, I exhaled for the first time in days. I turned to Will.

"We're back in business," I said. "Everything's intact."

Those last two days in the Red Sea felt different—lighter. We kept filming, spirits lifted. We had our footage. We had our story.

By the time we wrapped, we had the film's title: *CAUGHT*.

It carried a double meaning—the fishermen caught in the act of killing dolphins, and the criminals caught with our stolen film. But deeper still, it was about what's at stake when we don't pay attention. What's lost when no one's watching. And what's still possible when we are.

Retiring a Legend

In October, I flew to Tel Aviv to join Captains Peter Hammarstedt and Alex Cornelissen for the final voyage of the M/Y *Bob Barker*. After thirteen years of service as one of Sea Shepherd's most iconic vessels, she was ready to be retired. The decision was bittersweet, but the sale of her steel would fund the very campaigns she had once sailed for—her legacy continuing through the lifeblood of new missions.

Built in 1951 as a whaling vessel, the *Bob Barker* had spent seventy-one years at sea. She'd served as a Norwegian Coast Guard vessel, an ecotourism ship, and a refueling barge before Sea Shepherd acquired her in 2009. Thanks to the generosity of *The Price Is Right* host Bob Barker, the former whaling ship was transformed into an anti-whaling weapon. For over a decade, she chased the Japanese whaling fleet across the Antarctic like a ghost from her own past.

Her campaigns were legendary. In one unforgettable year, her hull buckled and steel rails twisted as she wedged herself between an 8,000-ton floating whale slaughterhouse and a 5,000-ton refueling tanker—cutting off the lifeline and forcing the whalers to abandon their season.

And in 2015, she made maritime history. For 110 relentless days, the *Bob Barker* pursued the notorious poaching vessel *Thunder* across three oceans and more than 11,000 nautical miles. Cornered, outmaneuvered, and out of options, the *Thunder's* captain chose to scuttle his own ship—trying to erase the evidence before Sea Shepherd could seize it.

If the *Bob Barker* had ever carried karmic debt from her early days as a whaler, she had repaid it in full.

The **Bob Barker** *on mission, off the coast of Israel.*
Credit: Dax Dasilva

But time had taken its toll. Her hull was thinning, her systems aging. She had given everything, and now it was time to let her rest. Her final voyage would be a patrol in the Mediterranean—a swan song for the old warhorse.

Just outside Jerusalem, I met Captains Hammarstedt and Cornelissen at a kibbutz nestled along the central West Bank. The morning sun warmed the hillside, and all was quiet. A farm organizer handed us beers.

"Really?" I asked, surprised but not unwilling.

"Dax," said Captain Cornelissen with a grin, raising his glass, "this is one of those moments when it's perfectly acceptable to start the day with a beer."

From the kibbutz, it was an hour's drive to Ashkelon, a coastal city just ten miles from Gaza's northern border. The casual mood belied the tension. We had armed Israeli soldiers with us the entire time, both on land and at sea. No immediate danger, but no illusions either. We took precautions.

From the Ashkelon harbor, we boarded a Zodiac and motored out to the *Bob Barker*. Climbing the rope ladder, I stepped onto her deck for the first—and last—time. She looked worn. But to us, she was still magnificent.

"Wow, she's looking a bit rough," Alex said, running a hand along the railing. But there was a glint in his eye. Pride. Respect.

Onboard, the mood was reverent. This wasn't a mission—it was a farewell.

"It was the greatest honor of my life to be given command of this ship," Captain Peter said, standing on deck, eyes scanning the horizon. "I'd wanted to fight for whales since I was fourteen. This vessel gave me 500 tons of steel to negotiate on behalf of the hunted."

He paused, lost in memory. "I still remember the first time we ran her through the Antarctic. Wind howling. Deck iced over. Half the crew hadn't even seen a whale before. The other half were seasick the whole time."

"Sounds brutal," I said, laughing.

"Oh, it was," Alex added. "But when that first harpoon ship turned tail and ran, we knew—this ship had fight in her."

He grew quiet. "I spent four years of my life physically on this ship. Retiring her…it feels like losing a part of myself."

We stood there in silence, the weight of it all settling around us.

We toured the ship, reminiscing. The *Bob Barker* was a Frankenstein vessel built within a vessel. Her top decks had been welded over the original whaling platforms. Below deck, they showed me where the harpoon gun had once been mounted—a grim reminder of her past.

But now we were here to celebrate her legacy, not mourn it.

It also happened to be Age of Union's one-year anniversary. In just twelve months, we had supported ten conservation projects across the globe. The $40 million commitment was already making waves in the Amazon, the Congo Basin, Canada, and off the coast of France.

The Sea Shepherd chef baked a vegan birthday cake, and we stood around the galley, passing plates, smiling, and taking it all in. When I blew out the candles, I made a simple wish: that this moment—aboard the *Bob Barker*, with her heroic captains—would stay emblazoned in my heart. A reminder of why we fight to protect the wild.

The next day, the *Bob Barker* began her final voyage.

She was assigned to patrol the newly established MPA surrounding the Palmahim Slide—a critical reproductive zone for deep-water sharks

Aboard the Bob Barker *with Captains Peter Hammarstedt and Alex Cornelissen.*
Credit: Dax Dasilva

and a spawning ground for Atlantic bluefin tuna, one of the most sought-after and endangered species in the Mediterranean. These torpedo-shaped giants can reach thirteen feet in length and weigh 2,000 pounds. They live for decades, roam thousands of miles, and sit at the top of the food chain. But poor management and overfishing—especially in the Mediterranean—have pushed their numbers to the brink. Populations have collapsed by as much as 98 percent.

For the next several weeks, the *Bob Barker* would monitor the Palmahim Slide and other marine parks, detecting and deterring illegal fishing off the coast of Israel.

The day I left for Paris, a message came through on WhatsApp. It was from Captain Hammarstedt.

"We just busted three trawlers fishing in Greece's National Marine Park of Alonnisos."

The *Bob Barker* wasn't done just yet.

Première à Paris

Paris in the fall is as magical as it gets. The sun hangs low in the sky, casting a burnt-orange glow across the city, making even its most iconic landmarks appear cinematic. Golden leaves tumble through the streets, and everything looks as if it's been lit for a film. I arrived a week after the NKPR team—Natasha Koifman, Eric Hendrikx, and Victoria Baker—who had flown in early to finalize details for the Paris premiere. Eric, NKPR's Creative Director and brand storyteller, and Victoria, a senior director at the agency, had been instrumental in bringing this moment to life. It was through a decade of working with Natasha at NKPR—first on Lightspeed and then Age of Union—that I met Eric, and over time, our shared passion for storytelling and activism led us to co-create this book.

Chapter 4 | **THE GHOST FLEET OF LA ROCHELLE** 177

The premiere was held at Le Grand Rex—a dazzling Art Deco landmark modeled after New York's Radio City Music Hall and the largest movie theater in Europe. It was the perfect venue for *CAUGHT*. Thanks to NKPR's expert coordination and the support of Sea Shepherd France, tickets sold out overnight.

Lamya and her team had traveled to Paris for the event. After the screening, she and I would take the stage for a panel on ocean conservation. The film would speak for itself, but our goal was to make its message echo long after the credits rolled.

As the sun dipped beneath the Paris skyline, the crowd began to arrive. Lines snaked around the block. Inside, the theater filled quickly—journalists, environmentalists, business leaders, students, and citizens shoulder to shoulder in anticipation. Watching them stream in felt surreal, knowing that the story we had fought so hard to tell was about to play out on the biggest screen in Europe.

At the CAUGHT *premiere in Paris.*
Credit: Age of Union

The lights dimmed. The projector hummed. And then, in the final act of the film, Captain Paul Watson's voice rang out through the stillness:

"Don't worry about the future. Focus on the present. What you do now will define what the future will be. Your power is in the present."

The applause was immediate. Then came the standing ovation—*CAUGHT*'s second since its debut in Toronto. But this felt different. More than praise. There was a shift in the room. In their eyes, I saw it—urgency, reflection, a fire to act.

During the Q&A, Lamya took the microphone. Calm but unflinching.

"Today, we're fishing more and more, for smaller and smaller animals, with increasingly powerful technology," she said. "Billions in subsidies are keeping this destructive industry alive. It's unsustainable."

She paused. Let it settle.

"When we ask, 'What can we do for the ocean?' my answer is simple: If the fish on your plate isn't necessary for your survival, the best thing you can do for the ocean... is leave it in the ocean."

A hush followed her words. The kind that doesn't come from silence alone, but from truth landing hard.

This wasn't just a screening. It was a reckoning.

As we left the theater, still humming from the standing ovation, we climbed into a car and headed toward the Seine. The city blurred past in golden streaks, the buzz of the evening still thick in the air. When we stepped out near Pont Alexandre III, Eric nudged me.

"You killed it in there, Dax," Eric said, grinning. "Sold-out crowd, media everywhere—feels like something big is about to happen."

I exhaled, the night air cool against my skin. "Yeah. Feels like change is coming."

Natasha and Victoria walked just ahead of us, heels clicking softly against the stone as we followed them along the river. In the distance, the Eiffel Tower shimmered above the water and treetops. Victoria glanced at her phone. "If we hurry, we can catch the sparkle on the hour. Think we've got the legs for it?"

I laughed. "It's a haul from here, but let's move."

"Consider it post-premiere cardio," Eric said, already picking up the pace.

Chapter 4 | **THE GHOST FLEET OF LA ROCHELLE** 179

We crossed the bridge, the Seine glittering below like it was mirroring the sky. The city felt quiet now, emptied of applause but still holding its breath. We walked in rhythm, weaving between lampposts and the occasional passerby, until the Eiffel Tower rose into view, golden and poised.

Eric slowed slightly beside me. "You know," he said, his voice softer now, "I used to think saving the oceans was about… well, the oceans. But this journey with you—this film—it made me realize it's about something bigger."

I glanced over. "Bigger how?"

"Proving one person can do something. That this fight we're in—it's not naïve. It's necessary."

I nodded, letting that sit for a beat. "Guess we're both in that boat."

Eric smiled. "Yeah. But you didn't just make a film, Dax. You lit a fuse."

Just then, the clock struck one. And right on cue, the tower erupted—sparkling in a brilliant cascade that danced across the rooftops and shimmered on the river. We all stopped to take it in, standing shoulder to shoulder.

No one said a word. We didn't have to.

Sometimes, Paris speaks for itself.

The M/Y Age of Union *continues to protect the seas off the coasts of Africa and Europe.*
Credit: Age of Union

France Takes Action

I was back in Canada, not long after the Paris premiere, when Lamya called. Her voice was electric. "Dax, we did it," she said.

"What happened?"

"They had no choice but to act," she replied. "The government's putting a ban on fishing along parts of the Atlantic coast. We finally made them listen."

Lamya had recently filed a legal complaint against the government, citing the staggering number of dolphin and porpoise deaths. Combined with a damning report from Pelagis, a marine conservation observatory, it forced the French State Council to respond. In just one week, more than four hundred dead marine mammals had been found on beaches—bodies scarred by nets, boat engines, and fishing gear. The destruction was undeniable.

In response, the State Council ordered the government to establish no-fishing zones and implement stronger protections. It was a breakthrough. A real shift in the tide.

"I wasn't sure this day would ever come," Lamya admitted. "It's been years of fighting brick walls."

I stood at the window in Montréal, city lights blinking beneath the clouds. "Well," I said, "those walls just cracked."

"It's a short break," she said, "but it will save a lot of sea life, and it's a start."

And it was. Because the victory in France wasn't an isolated moment—it was part of a larger ripple effect sparked by *CAUGHT*, Sea Shepherd's relentless campaigns, and the ongoing mission of the M/Y *Age of Union*.

Since launching, the ship had become a force across European and West African waters. In just one year, it spent 138 days at sea, covering over 18,000 nautical miles. The crew, a mix of seasoned veterans and wide-eyed recruits, patrolled everywhere from the Bay of Biscay to the Gulf of Guinea.

Off the coast of West Africa, the ship worked alongside national authorities to combat IUU fishing. Eleven ships were boarded. Four arrests followed. In Liberia, the *Age of Union* helped detain the *Kanball III*, a supertrawler with serious safety violations. Its experimental fishing license was revoked—a decision that sent shock waves through the industry.

But perhaps the clearest sign of the ship's impact came during Operation Sierra Leone Coastal Defense. When the *Age of Union* appeared offshore, seventy trawlers fled back to port, afraid of being caught. For several days, the ocean was quiet. Tens of millions of sea creatures were spared—not because of enforcement, but because of presence. Sometimes, just showing up is enough to change everything.

"Every time one of these ships is docked, it's a win," Lamya told me.

I smiled. "The *Age of Union* is already proving to be a great investment."

"It's more than that," she said. "It's strength. It's presence. It's a voice."

After we hung up, I sat in silence for a while, letting it all settle in. The change we were making wasn't just measurable in miles patrolled or trawlers deterred. It was in the minds we were shifting. In the new urgency taking root.

And I thought of Captain Paul.

If he had only listened to statistics, he might never have taken up the fight to save the whales. But he didn't. He refused to accept a future written by others. He acted—in the present—and the world is different because he did.

There's a principle I've carried with me since the beginning of this journey. It's a simple idea from Jewish spirituality known as tikkun olam—the act of repairing the world. What resonates with me most is that it's rooted in now. Not in a fear of what's ahead, but in the belief that every small action, taken today, has the power to shape tomorrow.

That's what *Age of Union* is about. It's not about waiting for change. It's about choosing it. It's about showing up, in the fight, in the moment—knowing that every effort, every risk, and every act of care is part of something greater.

And it's only just begun.

"It seems to me that the natural world is the greatest source of excitement; the greatest source of visual beauty; the greatest source of intellectual interest. It is the greatest source of so much in life that makes life worth living."

—SIR DAVID ATTENBOROUGH

A leatherback turtle carves her place as day fades.
Credit: Brendan Delzin

Suzan Lakhan-Baptiste—guardian of leatherback turtles.
Credit: Brendan Delzin

Chapter 5

THE NIGHT WATCHERS OF MATURA

PROTECTING TRINIDAD'S LAST LEATHERBACK SEA TURTLES

There's a creature that haunts the forests of Trinidad, a being whispered about in folklore—half-human, half-goat—an enigmatic figure known as Papa Bois, the father of the forest, protector of its flora and fauna.

He is said to be a short, wiry old man of African descent, with cloven hooves and a beard of tangled vines. Don't let his appearance fool you. Despite his age, he's strong as an ox, faster than a deer, and covered in thick hair like that of a donkey. Small horns jut from his forehead. He carries a hollowed-out bull's horn, which he sounds to warn animals of approaching hunters. Papa Bois is also a shape-shifter. He takes the form of a deer and lures poachers deep into the jungle until they are hopelessly lost, swallowed by the very forest they sought to exploit.

Yet for all his wild mythos, Papa Bois is curiously merciful. He startles, but he spares. He clacks through the brush on hooves of warning, not vengeance. If I'd had a say in his story, I might have laced it with a bit more retribution. Maybe some Old Testament dread. Dismemberment. Castration. Entrails as a cautionary tale. Trial by fire.

But Papa Bois's story was never mine to write. The legend, like the land, belongs to Trinidad. Yet forest sentinels are still needed. Today, a determined and inspiring woman named Suzan Lakhan-Baptiste stands as one of nature's fiercest protectors. She doesn't chase men through trees—but she's spent decades chasing poachers off beaches. As the founder of Nature Seekers, she is the mother of turtles and the unyielding guardian of Matura Bay.

"You feel it, too, don't you?" Suzan asked, her voice steady, threaded with something heavier. We walked along Matura's strand, a long stretch of protected shore where the turtles came to nest. "The turtles…they make you think. About time. About survival. About what we're doing here."

I nodded as she told me more about the leatherbacks. Living relics—a species dating back over 110 million years—they had survived everything: tectonics, ice ages, even the asteroid that ended the dinosaurs. But now they were staring down humanity as the final threat. Their nesting beaches were vanishing, oceans warming, plastics choking their food chain, and lights along coastlines disorienting their hatchlings.

The history Suzan was handing me felt heavy in the air, as if it clung to the salt and wind. Her story was the reason we stood there, along this remote crescent of coast in Trinidad, one of the most critical nesting grounds on Earth for *Dermochelys coriacea*, the leatherback sea turtle. From March through August, the sands of Matura transform into a slow-

A tranquil stretch of Trinidad's coastline.
Credit: Brendan Delzin

motion epic—thousands of females, some as large as a compact car, hauling themselves from the sea in the dark to lay eggs in the dunes of their birth. Some nights, hundreds nest under the same moon, their deep, deliberate tracks scarring the sand like the grooves of time itself.

They are delicate giants. Leatherbacks are the largest of all sea turtles, reaching lengths over six feet and weighing up to 2,000 pounds. And yet, unlike their armored cousins, they lack a hard shell. Their backs are instead cloaked in a leathery, oil-slicked skin stretched over a mosaic of bony ridges—an evolutionary design honed over 100 million years. They have no claws on their fins, no crushing beak like the hawksbill or loggerhead. Their soft, scissor-like mouths are adapted for gelatinous prey. They feed almost exclusively on jellyfish, consuming them by the hundreds each day—making leatherbacks one of the ocean's most effective natural regulators of jellyfish swarms, especially in warming seas where these creatures bloom in disruptive abundance.

But it's their journey that borders on the impossible. Leatherbacks are the great marathoners of the marine world. After nesting, they vanish into the open ocean, traversing entire basins. Tagging studies have tracked females from Trinidad all the way to Newfoundland and Nova Scotia. They drift through the Sargasso Sea, ride currents along the eastern seaboard

Back to the sea—the leatherback turtle's journey.
Credit: Brendan Delzin

of North America, and often surface in Canadian waters, feasting in jellyfish-rich bays before the long swim south to nest again. These are not creatures of one nation or one sea; they belong to the Atlantic itself, touching shores across continents.

And still, somehow, they remember. Leatherbacks return to the same beach where they were born, sometimes decades after they first left as hatchlings. Scientists don't yet fully understand how they navigate such staggering distances across the featureless ocean, but the leading theory is that they imprint on Earth's geomagnetic field—a kind of natural GPS embedded in their DNA. Like salmon returning to natal streams or monarchs tracing invisible highways to Mexico, the leatherback's migration is a biological feat so elegant, so ancient, it borders on the mystical.

That miracle—that instinct to return, despite all odds—was what Suzan was helping to protect here. And standing beside her, as the breeze whispered through the coastal trees and the surf pulled steady at the edge of the sand, I felt the weight of it all. These creatures were not simply nesting. They were returning from a journey few on Earth could fathom—millions of years in the making, and hanging, now, by a thread.

We walked together along the rumpled strand of coastline on Trinidad's northeastern edge. It didn't look like the kind of place you'd find on a postcard—no manicured sand, no resort-ready gloss. It was raw. Seaweed clung to the shore in tangled heaps. The wind pressed in from the Atlantic, gusting through the almond and palm trees, whipping the fronds into a restless dance. The surf, though steady, rolled in softer here, buffered by the curve of the bay.

"Turtle police, crazy turtle woman—that's what they used to call me," Suzan said, her eyes scanning the horizon. She smiled at the memory, but her tone darkened. "People laughed. They didn't understand."

Matura had once been a slaughterhouse. Leatherbacks were butchered here by the dozens. Their meat was food. Their eggs, currency. Hatchlings were used as bait. Suzan lowered her voice as we reached a nest. "I still remember the smell of the carcasses," she said. "They were stacked. Rotted. No tourist would want to come here."

She had grown up in Matura. As a child, she mistook turtle tracks for tractor trails. Her mother laughed. That night, they walked to the beach and watched a mother leatherback dig into the sand and lay eggs beneath the stars. Something clicked.

"I always wanted to see them," Suzan said. "When I realized they were being killed, something in me snapped. I had to fight for them."

She did. Some nights, it came to fists. She walked the beach until dawn—warning, pushing back, protecting the turtles. That's how she earned the nicknames. There was no ecotourism then. No visitors. No outside support. "No one cared," she said. "No one imagined people would pay to see turtles. It wasn't even on the horizon."

But Suzan didn't stop. She got her family involved. Then neighbors. Then more supporters. They formed watch groups and patrolled the beach every nesting season. From there, Nature Seekers was born. What began as a handful of stubborn defenders turned into a movement. The killings slowed. The nesting returned.

Today, two to three thousand leatherback females return each year to lay their eggs at Matura, protected by law and by people. It took Suzan nearly fifteen years to have the beach legally designated as a critical nesting site. Visitors now require guides. But in the town, not everyone understood what she'd done.

That changed in 1993. Suzan traveled to Beijing to receive the United Nations' highest environmental award. When she came back, something shifted.

"They finally respected me," she said. "They respected what we were doing."

Former poachers became guides. Offenders became defenders. Nature Seekers became not only protectors of a species, but a pathway to livelihoods. Still, the threats evolved.

"Bycatch. Vessel strikes. Climate change. It never ends," she said.

We stood at the edge of the surf. Suzan pointed at the thick, rust-colored bands of sargassum that choked the beach. "It's killing the nests," she said. The floating seaweed had been washing ashore in ecological masses. Turtles couldn't dig through it. Hatchlings got trapped beneath it.

She explained the causes: pollution feeding algal blooms, sewage runoff, warming seas, and shifting currents. Thousands of truckloads of it had needed to be cleared in past seasons. But there weren't enough trucks. There wasn't enough anything.

Nature Seekers was severely underfunded. And the leatherbacks were running out of time.

"Dax, we've come so far," she said. "And done so much. With so little."

I could feel it—that quiet desperation that sits just behind triumph. Suzan had held the line for decades. But she couldn't hold it alone. Not anymore.

I knew why I was here. Not to observe, to act. The turtles needed more than admiration. They needed reinforcements.

Suzan's story was extraordinary, but it was never meant to be hers alone. She had bought the turtles time—an extra generation, maybe two. But if the trajectory didn't change, the ending was already written.

I thought of Paul Watson—of Sea Shepherd and the Neptune's Navy chasing whaling ships through the Southern Ocean. Paul rewrote the fate of whales. When the trajectory pointed straight to extinction, he veered it off course. Through sheer will, through confrontation, through years at sea, he gave us a future where whales might still exist.

Suzan was doing the same for leatherbacks. I saw it—the fights, the years spent walking the beach alone, the trade of a life for the survival of a species. She didn't have ships or a global fleet. She had Matura. A strip of sand and a small community willing to believe in something bigger than themselves. And she defended it with everything she had.

All she needed now was help—real help. More resources. More backing. She'd already moved the tide. But to hold the line, she couldn't do it alone.

This wasn't just about preserving a species. It was about helping a village protect what it had once exploited. It was about modeling what harmony with the natural world could look like.

As Carl Safina—MacArthur Fellow and one of the most vital ecological writers of our time—once said, "We are not protecting nature for nature's sake. We are nature protecting itself." From that perspective, Suzan wasn't just defending turtles—she was part of the living system fighting for its own survival. A force of nature answering its own call.

You plant trees for the next generation, knowing you'll never sit in their shade. That's what Suzan had done. That's what I hoped to do.

The tide was coming in now. The last rays of sun washed the Atlantic in gold.

Up ahead, a few leatherbacks began to emerge, their massive shells glistening in the sun's fading light. One by one, they hauled themselves out of the ocean. Ancient, slow, determined, as if the weight of millions of years rested on their flippers.

I watched as one turtle lumbered over a sandy dune, choosing a nesting spot. It was exciting to see, but Suzan assured me there was more ahead.

The night, she promised, would bring the real magic.

Bake and Shark

The day before I met Suzan in Matura, I had arrived in Trinidad with a few members of the Age of Union team—Mariette Raina, Chelsea Finnemore, and Adam Simms. It was Indian Arrival Day, a national holiday commemorating the landing of the first indentured laborers from India in 1845. The streets were alive with music and food stalls, a vivid celebration of heritage and endurance. Women in bright saris moved through the crowds, the scent of curry and roasting corn curling through the air. It was a reminder that this island is more than a place—it's a blend of histories. African, Indian, Indigenous, European, Chinese. A cultural convergence that didn't just define its festivals and food, but had bled into its identity as a nation of protectors—of nature, of community, of each other.

Brendan Delzin was waiting for us at the airport. A gifted wildlife and culture photographer, he knew this island better than most—its forests, its hidden beaches, its people, its stories. He had arranged a place for us to stay, but more than that, he opened doors we wouldn't have found on any map—calypso bars tucked into the backstreets of Port of Spain, elders drumming limbo rhythms in open yards, roadside stalls passed down through generations, and wild stretches of coastline where the past still whispered through the trees. He moved through Trinidad like someone tuned to its deeper frequencies.

Before we made our way to Matura to meet Suzan, Brendan showed us around two of the island's coastal gems: Maracas and Las Cuevas. These beaches were so pristine they felt cinematic—white sand edged by coconut palms and almond trees, steep jungle rising behind us in layered green. The waves came in soft, curling into north-facing bays, while the light played across the water in hues of jade and cobalt. The air was thick with salt and sun, with something timeless underneath it all.

We stopped for food—Trinidad's unofficial love language and the heartbeat of any proper lime. *Liming*, as it's called here, is the act of coming together—eating, laughing, hanging out. It's not just about passing time; it's how time becomes something richer.

I ordered a vegetarian version of the island's famed bake and shark. Traditionally, it's made with seasoned fried shark meat tucked into golden, pillowy bake, but mine came stacked with sweet plantains, cucumber chutney, shredded cabbage, and pepper sauce that demanded respect. Brendan handed me an aloo pie—spiced mashed potatoes wrapped in flaky pastry and fried until the edges blistered. Each bite carried the warmth of cumin and the fire of Scotch bonnet, a flavor map of the island's colonial spice routes.

A woman behind the stall fanned coals beneath a row of roasting corn, her bracelets jingling as she moved with effortless rhythm. Kids wove between vendors. A man played chutney soca from a Bluetooth speaker balanced on a milk crate. The air was thick with the smell of charred husks and fried batter, laced with sweet tamarind and something distinctly local—maybe anise, maybe nostalgia.

"This," Brendan said, gesturing around us, "this is Trinidad. You feel it before you understand it. People, food, rhythm, spirit—it's all the same thing here."

I wiped my hands with a napkin, still chewing. "There's this energy—it hits you the second you land."

Brendan leaned on the table, grinning as I folded up the empty grease-blotted paper.

"I could live on Trini street food," I said.

"Plenty of us do," he said. "And we live good."

Matura

That evening, our group returned to Matura Beach for a mandatory safety briefing. Before anyone was allowed near the turtles, all visitors gathered at Nature Seekers headquarters—a modest open-air building nestled just beyond the tree line. The orientation wasn't just protocol for tourists. It was protection—for the turtles. The rules were simple but nonnegotiable: no white lights, no flash photography, no noise, and no contact. Everything was designed to minimize stress on the turtles.

Each year, thousands of leatherbacks arrive on this stretch of northeastern Trinidad—on many nights, coming ashore in droves. To protect the site, visitor numbers are capped at one hundred per evening, all accompanied by certified guides.

Tonight, it was a smaller crowd—about thirty of us, including our group and several local volunteers: young Trinidadian women, sharp-eyed and engaged. Likely future recruits for Nature Seekers.

We gathered beneath a forest pagoda, our headlamps casting a dim red glow. The jungle pressed in around us, thick and breathing.

"White lights confuse the turtles," Suzan explained. "They follow it, thinking it's the moon, and lose their way. That's why we use the red lights."

Our lights flickered through the trees, soft and spectral, as we followed her down the forest path toward the sand.

What we saw as we stepped onto the beach belonged to another time. Dozens of glowing red beams scanned the surf line, and from the darkness, they began to appear—great shadowed forms crawling up from the sea. Leatherbacks. They looked unreal, like moving dunes rising from the tide, their slick carapaces glinting in the moonlight, pushing through the damp sand.

Along the shoreline, some turtles had already breached the dunes and begun their nesting ritual. Others were just beginning the laborious crawl from water to shore, propelled by instincts that predate written language and settled civilization.

We spread out along a 100-meter section, leaving the rest of the 8-kilometer beach undisturbed. This protection zone—guarded, managed, and fought for by Suzan—had become the last stand for the leatherbacks. A species that once shared the planet with *Tyrannosaurus rex* and had somehow, improbably, survived. Until we came along.

One turtle dragged herself toward us, slow but deliberate. I could hear her short, wheezing puffs of effort as she reached her nesting site and

The Nature Seekers team—guardians of Trinidad's leatherbacks and stewards of the coastline.
Credit: Brendan Delzin

began to dig. Her rear flippers moved like scoops, flicking away sand with a rhythm that felt both mechanical and sacred.

"Dax," Suzan called. "Come closer."

I stepped to the edge of the pit. The turtle had entered a trancelike state—her head lifted slightly, eyes glossy, movements automatic. Each egg slid out with a low sound, landing in the nest like a soft marble.

"She'll lay a clutch of close to a hundred eggs," Suzan whispered. "But with leatherbacks, only one in a thousand will survive to become mature."

The statistic hit like a stone. Leatherbacks face one of the highest mortality rates in the animal kingdom. Most hatchlings don't make it past the beach. Ghost crabs, birds, raccoons, stray dogs, and now, ever more frequently, human interference.

I was astonished to learn that a single female—reaching sexual maturity at thirty years—will lay four to seven nests per season, about ten days apart. Then she'll disappear into the ocean, not to return for another two or three years. And when she does return, she'll find this exact beach. Scientists believe they imprint on the beach's unique magnetic signature when they hatch—a kind of internal compass calibrated by geology. They carry that code inside them for decades, crossing oceans only to come back, often within meters of where they were born.

The moon cast a silver highway across the waves as more turtles emerged—each following that call home. A primordial ritual—millions of years old—unfolded before us with quiet gravity.

"This process," I said, barely audible, "it's...humbling."

Suzan nodded. "It's perfect, if we let it be."

We moved down the beach to another nest. A female dug with only one rear flipper. The other was gone—likely severed by fishing gear. Yet she kept working. A guide with a shovel stepped in beside her, gently mirroring the motion of her missing limb, helping finish the nest.

"She's done this before," Suzan said. "It doesn't stop her."

The turtle began to lay. Her body trembled with effort, her head rising with each breath. There was something elemental in her persistence. A will to continue, even maimed. Even alone.

I worried that we were intruding. Suzan saw my hesitation. "They've existed millions of years without us," she said. "But now, it's us tipping the scale. We owe them this. We owe them so much more."

Nearby, another guide crouched to tag a flipper. It was part of a long-term effort to track migration patterns. Roughly 70 percent of the leatherbacks spotted off Canada's Atlantic coast are believed to have nested here on this very beach, making them one of the longest-migrating reptiles in existence.

They are the widest-ranging sea turtles on Earth, crossing more territory than some whales. From the beaches of Trinidad to the jellyfish-rich waters off Nova Scotia, they migrate over 10,000 miles, linking nations, ecosystems, and cultures through a shared biological legacy.

It was staggering. Our countries shared custody of these giants. What happened here shaped the fate of those we claimed as ours.

The turtle lingered for a moment above the nest, then began to bury it with slow, deliberate sweeps of her flippers. We watched as she sealed the sand over her eggs—her work quiet, instinctive, ancient.

We call them mothers, but only by genetics. She will never meet her hatchlings, never witness the journey she has set in motion. After depositing her clutch beneath the surface, she turns back to the sea, her role complete. What comes next is survival at its most fragile.

Even the temperature of the sand carries consequence. Around a pivotal temperature of 29.5°C (85°F), hatchlings are born in roughly equal numbers of males and females. A few degrees warmer, and nearly all are female. A few degrees cooler, and most are male. But if the heat rises too far—as it's beginning to—it can end life before it begins. Climate doesn't just change the numbers; it shifts the future itself.

Those eggs will remain buried for roughly sixty days, incubating at a precise blend of depth, moisture, temperature, and pressure. If the conditions are right, the hatchlings will emerge under the cover of night. They'll dig their way upward in a synchronized effort, breaching the sand like a wave of tiny, determined miracles.

And then comes the sprint—across open beach, through driftwood and gull cries, dodging dogs and ghost crabs, toward the pull of the moonlit ocean. Everything larger is a threat. Even in the water, they must evade the jaws of fish, birds, and human consequence.

Only one in a thousand will survive. Maybe less. And that's before you factor in us—nets, lights, vessels, pollution, and climate.

Yet here she was, this battered survivor with only one fin, doing what her species has done since the age of dinosaurs. Not with hope. Just instinct. Just the memory of evolution embedded somewhere deep in her blood.

A few years from now, she'll return to this beach under a different moon to repeat what we saw that night. That's the hope. That's the gamble.

As the stars burned above and the Atlantic curled in rhythmic applause, I stood beside Suzan—no longer just a woman or a guide or a conservationist. She was part of this system, threaded into the island's DNA.

Leatherbacks are deep-sea voyagers. Scientists have tracked them plunging over 1,200 meters—nearly 4,000 feet—into ocean darkness, chasing jellyfish through pressure zones that would crush most life. They are built not just for endurance, but for mystery.

This wasn't tourism. This was a covenant. And we were all witnesses.

It was impossible not to feel awe.

The Hatchery

The next morning, Brendan and I visited the Nature Seekers hatchery—one of the group's newer interventions, designed to give at-risk hatchlings a better chance at life. Modest in size but meticulous in function, the hatcheries stood outdoors, just above the high tide line, protected by wooden framing. There were a dozen large plexiglass cubes filled with sand, each tagged with a matrix of dates and numbers. These were not display cases but surrogates—artificial nests housing egg clutches relocated from fragile sites where tides, encroaching sargassum, animals, or people threatened their survival.

Suzan called it the "maternity ward" of Matura. "It's still experimental," she said, lifting one of the large lids and exposing the pale crust of sand below. "They take about fifty days to hatch. We're learning what happens between the laying and the surfacing. What makes them strong. What doesn't."

The Age of Union team geared up for turtle nesting: volunteer, Mariette, me, Chelsea, Adam, volunteer, and Kevin. Credit: Brendan Delzin

Chapter 5 | **THE NIGHT WATCHERS OF MATURA** 199

"You're just in time," a technician said, pointing toward one of the boxes. "These little guys are just starting to hatch."

I stood beside the cube. A cluster of eggs was pressed against the clear barrier. At first, there was only stillness. Then a tremor. A shift. Eggs began to rupture—soft, leathery shells splitting open from within. Tiny beaks poked through, flippers twitching blindly. It looked chaotic, but beneath it was a choreography only evolution could script, unfolding like clockwork.

Each hatchling fought its way upward, instinct driving the effort. In the wild, this upward push through sand and shell debris is a trial by fire—what scientists call "predator swamping," a coordinated emergence that overwhelms predators by sheer numbers. Not all make it, but enough do. It's not mercy. It's math.

The technicians placed the turtles in shallow trays. But with the eggshells, half-buried beneath the shards of its kin, a lone hatchling struggled, clearly alive but failing. Trapped under the wreckage of its own beginning.

"This is what happens in nature," he explained with a resigned tone. "Sadly, not all hatchlings make it to the surface. It's just the way things are."

Using red light to observe nesting leatherback turtles naturally.
Credit: Brendan Delzin

My heart sank. I watched the little hatchling struggle, its tiny fins flapping feebly against the weight of the sand and broken shells. For a moment, I held my breath, willing it to push harder, to fight its way up. But its movements grew slower and more desperate, until finally they stopped.

I pointed. "He's still trying."

The technician studied it for a moment. Then he grinned. "That's the beauty of this place. We tip the odds. Want to give him a hand?"

Hell yes, I did.

I hadn't realized how tightly I was gripping the edge of the box until I let go. I climbed the stepladder and reached down, slowly clearing the sand from around the hatchling's head. Its eyes opened—wet, black, blinking against the light. It moved not with panic but resolve. I cleared a channel. It pulled itself free.

"You made it," I whispered, lifting it into my palm. Its flippers twitched against my skin—warm, soft, pulsing with new life.

"You saved him," the technician said. "Feels right that you release him, too."

We gathered the trays and headed to the beach. The tide was coming in. The surf pulled at the sand like a breath.

The technician dug a shallow trench—a symbolic channel. Crawling down the sand is part of the imprinting process. Scientists believe hatchlings memorize the unique magnetic fingerprint of the beach during this moment, creating a map in their nervous system. If they survive, they'll return decades later to this exact stretch of coastline—one of the longest navigational memories known in the animal kingdom.

We released them one by one. The hatchlings scrambled down the slope, flippers spinning like wind-up toys, drawn to the moonlit horizon. Some would swim for days without rest in a burst of instinct called a "swim frenzy," a survival strategy hardwired into their blood. If they made it past the shelf, they'd seek out floating mats of sargassum—mobile nursery grounds where they'd drift, feed, and hide.

I saved mine for last.

He was all beak and flippers and determination. He looked like Squirt from *Finding Nemo*. That's what I called him: Squirt.

I held him a moment longer. The wind off the water had cooled. I could feel his energy—a pulse of will wrapped in softness. He was so small but felt expansive, like a question thrown into the ocean.

He was a reminder: of the work Suzan had committed her life to, of the fragility of these ancient mariners, of how little control we actually have and how much responsibility we still carry.

I made a silent wish—that Squirt's journey would be long, wild, and unfinished—and set him into the trench.

He launched forward like he knew the way. As if the ocean had whispered his name. No hesitation. Just motion. A straight line into whatever came next, vanishing into the surf.

I stood still for a long time. Not just watching, but absorbing. I had spent years traveling to the front lines of environmental collapse—from jungles to coral reefs to cloud forests—but something about this moment lodged itself deeper. There was a spiritual geometry in it. A rhythm I hadn't heard until now.

"I've seen this before," I said quietly to Brendan, who had just lowered his camera. "You protect one species, and suddenly everything else starts to align."

Tiny flippers—rescued hatchlings returned to the sea under watchful eyes.
Credit: Brendan Delzin

He nodded. "It's fragile, isn't it? You pull the wrong thread, and the whole weave unravels."

I nodded back. "We can't let it fall apart."

"It'll be a decade before we see them again," Brendan said, eyes still fixed on the sea. "They vanish. No one knows exactly where they go. They just...disappear."

That mystery lingered in the salt air. A vanishing act written into their biology. Scientists call it the "lost years"—a decade of absence, when hatchlings drift in pelagic waters, rarely seen, rarely tracked. Not gone, just beyond reach.

There was something mythic in that. A creature born of sand and moonlight, vanishing into the blue with no promise of return. And yet some do. They find their way back across oceans, guided not by memory but by something older. Something elemental.

As I stood on that beach—bathed in salt, humbled by life—I realized Squirt was a metaphor for all of it. For the fragility, yes, but also for the wild, radiant defiance of life itself.

He was gone now, into the churn. Into the unknown—but not forgotten.

And for now, that was enough.

New life—a hatchling leatherback turtle.
Credit: Brendan Delzin

Matura Arts and Crafts

We left the hatchery and strolled the curve of Matura's beach, the surf hissing at our ankles. Suzan walked beside me, steady and sure. For over three decades, her presence had reshaped this shoreline—not just its ecology, but its spirit, too. Where poachers once prowled under cover of night, now there were guides, artisans, and students. Suzan had become more than a conservationist. She was Matura's trusted compass, sought for guidance on everything from turtle nesting cycles to mental health, from storm prep to school fees. An informal social worker. A spiritual matriarch.

She gestured toward a group of young women down by the dunes, laughing and sifting through baskets of washed-up debris. "See them?" she said. "Most started with beach cleanups. Now they're handling parts of the operation. Future guides, teachers, artisans. Some might run this place one day."

The pride in her voice wasn't performative. It was lived-in. Earned.

Protecting paradise—Matura Bay cleanup.
Credit: Brendan Delzin

In the shadow of Suzan's efforts, Matura had undergone a quiet, seismic shift. What was once a village known for turtle poaching had become a stronghold of stewardship. Leatherbacks were no longer hunted—they were celebrated. Local football teams took their name. School mascots bore their silhouette. And the crafts produced here—under the Turtle Warrior brand—were now a source of sustainable income. The turtles had become both totem and teacher.

"Suzan," I asked, "did you ever imagine this? That you'd save the turtles and somehow rebuild an entire community around them?"

She laughed, the sound rough-edged and honest. "No. I thought I'd get myself killed long before any of this caught on. You have to remember—this was their livelihood. And I was a woman telling them to stop. That didn't go down well. I was shouted off beaches. Threatened. There were fights. But I kept coming back."

We arrived at the workshop, a modest wooden structure set just behind the tree line. Inside, the air was rich with the scent of driftwood, scorched glass, and effort. Tools clinked. Hands moved with quiet choreography. This was where the transformation happened—where the cast-offs of the sea became something purposeful, even beautiful.

Art and conservation meet—glass beads made from discarded glass.
Credit: Brendan Delzin

Each season, before the turtles arrived, Nature Seekers organized community cleanups. Locals and volunteers from around the world combed the beach for plastic, glass, and marine debris. The collected refuse was sorted by type, washed, dried in the sun, and stored for artists to work with. What had once suffocated tide pools or strangled hatchlings now lined the shelves in jars—sorted by color, by grade, by future potential.

At a table, a woman bent over a flame, coaxing recycled glass into luminous beads. Her daughter sat beside her, threading colors onto string with a quiet diligence, while her son sorted fragments from a bin of beachcombed waste. Glassblowing had once been a family tradition, but now it was more than art—it was livelihood, inheritance, and resistance. These colorful new ornaments were protest songs forged in flame.

"These glass turtles," Suzan said, nodding toward the woman's work, "travel farther than our turtles. We sell them in the shop, in Port of Spain, online. Tourists buy them, sure—but more than that, people connect to the story behind them. They wear the tide on their wrist. They carry Matura with them. They tell people all over the world who we are."

I picked up a bracelet—translucent green beads with flecks of amber, like sea glass caught in sunlight. "It's beautiful," I said. "You'd never guess it came from a broken bottle tossed in the sand."

"Exactly," she replied. "And every sale supports the hatchery, the guides, the patrols. It helps us pay women like her," she said, pointing to the glassworker. "So she doesn't have to choose between feeding her family and protecting this beach."

The spirit of innovation here wasn't flashy. It wasn't branded or funded by a global NGO. It was born from necessity, stitched together with resourcefulness, stubborn hope, and the kind of entrepreneurial instinct that grows in places long overlooked. What struck me most was how much Nature Seekers had achieved with so little—how every bead, every hatchling, every community program was powered not by grants or glossy campaigns, but by an almost defiant sense of purpose.

It reminded me of something Paul Hawken once wrote: "The most radical thing you can do is introduce people to one another." Suzan had done just that—linking ideas, skills, and souls across generations. The cleanup crews became artisans. The artisans became advocates.

The community, once fractured by poaching and poverty, was now crosshatched by purpose.

They didn't wait for perfect conditions. They built with what washed in. Repurposed the wreckage. Turned obstacles into inventory. Glass shards into necklaces. Plastic trash into income. A nursery into a classroom. A single endangered species into a regional identity.

This was reinvention. The kind that rewires a community's sense of what's possible.

Suzan turned to me, her expression soft. "This place used to be a turtle graveyard. Now look at it. We're living proof that conservation isn't just about science—it's about community. About dignity. About not leaving anyone behind."

I nodded, still holding the bracelet in my hand. There was a lesson in it—not just about turtles or plastic or poverty. It was about transformation. The kind that starts small, almost imperceptibly, like a hatchling pushing toward the moon, or a bead pulled from the fire.

A kind that, over time, can change everything.

Kayaking the Salybia River

On my final day in Trinidad, Brendan and I set out on a kayak tour of the Salybia River, a snaking vein through one of the island's last untouched mangrove corridors. His camera, always nearby, hung loosely over his shoulder—an extension of his instinct to witness, to preserve.

We launched into the river under a soft morning haze, the hulls gliding quietly across the surface. The first few strokes were smooth, meditative. But as we ventured deeper, the current stiffened. The water tugged sideways at our kayaks, demanding precision. My shoulders began to ache, but I welcomed it. The resistance felt earned. Familiar.

Chapter 5 | **THE NIGHT WATCHERS OF MATURA** 207

The mangroves closed in around us, limbs interlocked overhead, blotting out the sky. The air was thick with the scent of damp soil and leaf rot. With every stroke forward, it felt as though we were slipping further into prehistory—a realm where time moved differently, more slowly, with more consequence.

"Feels like the Amazon, doesn't it?" Brendan said, his paddle slicing through the water with practiced ease.

"Yeah," I replied. "The kind of place that puts you back in your place."

I meant it. The smell of wet bark, the press of the canopy, the way the river seemed to think for itself—it all echoed my first journey into the Madre de Dios, where the jungle felt like a living, watching thing. Back then, every vine looked like it might strike, every splash made my chest tighten. The Amazon had made me feel like an intruder.

But here, drifting through Salybia's mangroves in a kayak—vest snug, friend close—it felt different. Not safe, exactly, but known. Things now felt more intuitive, like I'd come far enough to stop resisting the wild and start listening to it.

The river narrowed, forcing us to duck and weave beneath gnarled limbs. A pair of ibis streaked overhead—blurs of crimson against the

A river's journey over rocks and roots.
Credit: Brendan Delzin

green. A caiman surfaced beside us, barely more than a pair of unblinking eyes above the waterline.

We passed a tree boa coiled on a branch overhead, its camouflage nearly perfect. Herons stalked the shallows. Crabs scrambled over mangrove roots, vanishing into their burrows as we approached. The density of life was staggering—an orchestra of interdependence, each player vital.

Brendan lifted his camera toward a diving kingfisher. Snap. Perfect timing, I was sure. "This place," he said, "it's like our last secret. No roads. No resorts. Just nature."

I nodded, the burn in my arms grounding me. The river was beautiful, but it asked something of you in return—attention, humility, effort. Although the reward was something close to divine.

The cliffs flanking the river grew steeper, draped in vines and moss. A channel-billed toucan flitted between the branches, its oversized beak slicing through the canopy like a paintbrush. Brendan captured it mid-flight, laughing softly to himself. "I love places like this," he said. "The ones that don't owe us anything. Places that just are."

I understood. It mirrored my own reasons for being here. This wasn't just a diversion. It was communion. And I was different now—not just observing, but part of it.

The river carried us into a clearing where the water widened and light filtered through. We slipped into the cool shallows and let ourselves float. A few months earlier, this would've terrified me. But now, life vest wrapped snug around me and Brendan nearby, I felt safe. Not invincible, but steady. I closed my eyes and let the hush of the water rock me—the wind brushing the surface, the rustle of trees, birdsong drifting like smoke.

We climbed back into our kayaks and continued upriver. Soon, the sound of rushing water grew louder—steady and heavy, like a drumbeat behind the trees. We followed it until the river opened into a glade of rock walls and fern-covered cliffs. At its center, a waterfall spilled from above, cascading into a pool so clear it glowed aquamarine. Brendan pulled out his camera again, reverent as ever, framing the light, the texture, the stillness.

We didn't speak much. We didn't need to.

After a while, we turned back.

The mangrove roots reached down into the water like anchors, holding the land in place. Everything felt connected—the roots, the birds, the silence between us.

As the sun began its descent, the jungle shifted. The howlers fell quiet. And then it began—the return of the ibis. Thousands of them, rising and wheeling in the dusk, settling into their roosts like a rain of petals. The sky went crimson. The mangroves bloomed red.

Brendan exhaled. "We think we're just passing through," he said. "But places like this—they show us we're not separate. We're part of it. Same as the birds, the trees, the turtles. All part of one story."

We paddled the last stretch in near silence, the sky now inked in deep blues. The last of the birds disappeared into the trees. The monkeys stilled. The light softened. And the Salybia, patient and unhurried, carried us home.

The Promise

As the sun dipped beneath the horizon, casting a golden haze over Matura Bay, we gathered for a final dinner on the cliffs. The condo, perched above the endless Atlantic, hummed with warmth and salt air, the ocean breathing steadily below. Despite the heavy humidity, there was a lightness among us. Suzan, the Nature Seekers team, Brendan, and a few close friends sat together, sharing one last meal before our departure at dawn.

As night thickened and candles flickered in the breeze, Suzan began to speak.

"There were times," she said, her voice low, "when I almost walked away. It wasn't just the poachers. It was the loneliness. The ridicule. People laughed at me. Called me the 'crazy turtle woman.' Even friends drifted away. I was fighting a battle no one else believed in."

She paused, eyes fixed on the darkening sea. "One night, after a confrontation with poachers, I sat alone on the beach. I honestly thought about quitting. Then—almost like it was staged—a turtle emerged from the surf. She rose slowly from the black water, heaving her cumbersome body across the sand. It took her nearly an hour to cross just a few meters. She stopped often, resting between pushes, like the weight of the world was strapped to her shell. But she never turned back."

Suzan's voice softened. "And I thought, 'If she can keep going, so can I.'"

She turned toward me, her expression clear and composed. "That's when I stopped caring what people thought. I wasn't doing it for them anymore. I was doing it for her. For all of them."

The table fell silent. For the first time, I could feel the full gravity of what Suzan had carried—years of resistance, loss, persistence. Her cause had grown larger than turtles. It had become about endurance.

I stood. The room quieted.

"I just want to thank you all," I said. "For your work. For this community. For creating something that didn't exist before you dreamed it into being."

I paused, letting the weight settle.

"And because of that, I want to make a promise. I'm going to contribute $1.5 million to Nature Seekers over the next five years. This funding will support everything from nesting protection and climate research to community education and habitat restoration."

Suzan's eyes brimmed with emotion. The weight of that moment wasn't just financial—it meant the work would go on. The turtles would be watched over. The coastline protected.

"We're not just saving turtles," I said. "We're safeguarding the future—this ecosystem, this coastline, this community."

The clink of raised glasses followed. Suzan, usually calm and composed, let out a laugh—light and unguarded. It rose above the hush of the waves, the sound of someone who, for once, allowed herself to exhale.

Later, Suzan and I walked the beach one last time. The sand was cool, the moonlight stretched in silver ribbons across the surf.

"You've done something remarkable," I said. "This is your legacy."

She shook her head gently. "It never was just about the turtles," she said.

We walked in silence. And then I wanted to know. "What does success look like now?" I asked.

She looked out toward the horizon, thoughtful. "Success is when they don't need me anymore. When the community protects this place as their own. In ten years, I want the next generation to love these turtles like I do. In a hundred years…" She hesitated. "I hope they look back and say this was the moment it all turned. That the leatherbacks kept returning. That Matura thrived."

Her words hung in the air, as if caught among the stars.

We stood together, quiet, and I felt something ancient pass between us—the gravity of the Earth, the rhythm of time. I looked out across the water, beyond the surf's reach, into the dark, unknowable vastness. Somewhere beneath that ocean skin, Squirt was swimming—tiny, determined, disappearing into myth. Not lost. Not alone. Just claimed by the wild. Part of something that had always been there and would outlast us all.

Later that night, I sat alone on the cliffs, thinking about legacy, about Suzan's quiet war, about whether we as a species could truly change. Whether we could protect what cannot protect itself.

I thought of what Suzan had said: *"When you save one part, you end up saving it all."*

And beneath that moonlit sky, I believed her.

Hope isn't a wish—it's a decision.

And we had chosen it.

The Pitt River Watershed—one of British Columbia's last wild strongholds.
Credit: Alan Katowitz

Industrial footprint—log sorting on the Pitt River.
Credit: Dax Dasilva

Chapter 6

WHERE THE WOLF DRINKS FIRST

THE WILD RESTORED ALONG BRITISH COLUMBIA'S PITT RIVER

It was early fall, and the trees blazed with color—reds, yellows, and oranges too vivid to believe. It wasn't just the spectacle—it was the glow, as if the leaves had swallowed the autumn sunlight and were releasing it in a slow, smoldering burn. The air was crisp, biting at my ears and face, thick with the sweet scent of cedar and pine resin. I left behind the urban sprawl of Vancouver and drove out to Grant Narrows Provincial Park on Pitt Lake.

The drive through British Columbia felt like stepping into a living memory. This was the landscape that shaped me—the place where I first fell in love with nature and began to understand who I was. These peaks, rivers, and forests didn't just inspire awe; they rewired how I saw the world. Coming back, not as a visitor but with the intent to protect it, felt like returning to a sacred inheritance.

Danny Gerak met me at the docks. Built like a mountain man, he'd lived on the Pitt River for decades, stewarding the waterway with his wife, Lee. His father had taught him to fish here—his first steelhead, his first bear sighting, his first sense of wilderness. Danny had built their home here: the Pitt River Lodge.

"When we were kids, my dad took us camping here," Danny said as he started the boat. "He knew this was a place where you could realign your soul with the wilderness—and witness God's country as He intended."

We untethered and zipped across the mirrored surface of the lake, headed north toward the Upper Pitt River Valley.

"The ecosystems here are like nowhere else," Danny said, pointing ahead as the boat sliced through the water. The Pitt River is a wild and unpredictable channel that snakes through the valley before emptying into Pitt Lake—the largest tidal lake in the world, with a three-foot range. "Because of the geography, we get all five species of salmon, sea-run bull trout, cutthroat, and sturgeon. You're about to see something special."

Word got out. That's how it goes. Danny and Lee's lodge—tucked into the trees, warm coffee and waders at the ready—became a waypoint for those chasing wild fish in wild water.

I looked out across the lake—a vast body of water nestled in the shadow of the mountains. The cerulean blue of the lake reflected the deep emerald of the forest, all framed by snowcapped peaks. A flock of Canada geese crossed the sky. Mother Nature had painted a masterpiece here.

But at the north end of Pitt Lake, signs of industry appeared. The mouth of the Upper Pitt River serves as a sorting zone—timber stripped from the hillsides, floated into the lake, stored, and then shipped to sawmills. A stark contrast to the wilderness, and an early sign of what lay ahead.

"We're surrounded by protected lands," Danny said, gesturing to the mountain ranges encasing the valley. "National parks on all sides, but this valley is crown land—government-owned and leased to private logging operations. It's like having a fortress with a broken gate."

As we passed the log booms, frustration crept in—sharp, steady, familiar. Not just at the damage but at how routine it had become. Conservation reports and environmental assessments didn't touch this. They couldn't. The numbers never showed the rot beneath the bark, the silence where birdsong used to fill the air. The Pitt River Valley is bordered by parks—Pinecone Burke, Golden Ears, Garibaldi—names that sound like guardians. Danny and Lee had fought for those protections. But in the unguarded gaps, the machines kept moving. Government-sanctioned logging, clear cuts, no cleanup. The real offense wasn't the taking; it was the refusal to put anything back.

Inside the Upper Pitt River, the landscape turned enchanting. A wide valley rose steeply on both sides, its flanks cloaked in towering conifers that reached into a cloudless blue sky. I'd been in this region before, but it still surprised me. After traveling to the far corners of the world—the Amazon, Haiti, Democratic Republic of Congo, Trinidad—I'd somehow overlooked what was in my own backyard. British Columbia, I was reminded, is one of the wildest and biologically rich places on Earth.

The sounds of the river whispered old memories. Every ripple and every current stirred echoes of my teenage years—hiking, camping, finding peace in nature. I thought of Clayoquot Sound, where my brother and I linked arms with strangers to defend the old-growth forests. It left its mark on the land, and on me. But things were different now. Back then, I was just a kid with heart, standing for something I didn't yet fully understand. Now, those same trees felt less like giants and more like elders—steady, watchful, guiding me back in.

"It feels good to be back home, huh?" Danny said, glancing back at me as he eased off the throttle as the river narrowed.

"Home's the right word," I answered, nodding.

On the riverbank, a small herd of black-tailed deer gathered, drinking from the shallows and picking their way carefully through the reeds. A few paused, lifting their heads to watch us, ears twitching, and then returned to grazing along the edge of the water.

"Look at this," Danny said, a proud smirk curling on his face as Mother Nature put on a show. Across the river from the deer, a black bear ambled through the meadow, headed slowly toward the water.

"Will it go after the deer?" I asked, glancing back at the herd. There were a few young fawns among them—small, unsteady, easy targets.

"Doubtful," he said. "They don't usually bother with deer, not this time of year. She's here for the salmon—less effort to catch."

The bear seemed uninterested in us, crossing a bed of rocks toward the river's edge, her movements unhurried.

"How can you tell it's a *she*?" I asked, trying to see what he saw.

Danny pointed farther up the far side of the meadow, toward the tree line. "Over there," he said. "I saw them on my way to pick you up. I was hoping they'd still be around."

At the edge of the forest, two small cubs wrestled beneath a tree—grappling, tumbling, learning. One clambered up the trunk a few feet and then launched itself off like a stuntman. It might have been the cutest thing I'd ever seen. They spun and chased each other through the brush while their mother stood watch, eyes fixed on the river, scanning for dinner.

"We've seen grizzlies come back, too," he said. "Not many, but they're back. We get elk, cougars, even wolverines."

The river turned milky turquoise as we neared the lodge. "That's glacial silt," Danny said. Glacial silt is made up of tiny particles of rock, ground down by the movement of glaciers and carried downstream—so fine it stays suspended in the water, giving it that cloudy hue.

"The Chinook love it here," he said, pointing out fish I couldn't see, with a trained eye that could identify species and size at a glance.

"The river's chock-full of Chinook and sockeye right now," he said. "The bears and eagles love them, but we don't harass the salmon when they're spawning. We'll go for coho, which runs a bit later, and trout: bulls, rainbow, and cutthroat."

Danny knows the rhythms of Pitt River like the back of his hand. Once the snow melts in spring, visitors arrive for peak-season steelhead fishing, as the fish push upriver fresh from the saltwater—strong, silver, and full of fight. Summer brings the return of bull trout, drawn back by the snowmelt

Nature's grandeur along the Upper Pitt River.
Credit: Marietta Raina

Chapter 6 | **WHERE THE WOLF DRINKS FIRST**   219

runoff to their spawning grounds in the Upper Pitt. Later in the season, the river comes alive with all five species of salmon, funneling into the upper stretches and tributaries to prepare for the spawn. By fall, it's coho salmon, trout, and steelhead again.

"Catch and release only," Danny explained, steering us toward the lodge. I wasn't here to fish, but I was interested in the way they treated the river. "We use barbless hooks," he said, "and in this glacial-fed water, the cold helps the fish recover quickly. We even tag a few—some come back year after year, get caught again, released again."

We arrived at the dock and tied off. The lodge sat just beyond the trees—a sturdy log cabin facing the river, tucked into the valley like it had always belonged. A hand-carved sign swung above the front steps: *Pitt River Lodge.*

Inside, Danny's wife, Lee, welcomed us with the quiet confidence of someone who knew this place well. A bar of stone and timber anchored the main room. A wood-burning stove crackled in the corner, cutting the chill. There were a few guest rooms, a long dining table, and black-and-white photographs lining the walls—images of the valley before the logging roads came, before the trees fell.

Over dinner, we mapped out our plan for the next day. I told Danny I'd come to see a specific piece of land—one I'd heard about through conservation partners but hadn't seen with my own eyes. A place where the damage wasn't just visible; it was ongoing. Once alive with fish, birds, and thick vegetation, it was now—by all accounts—cut off. Failing. Dying.

"The Red Slough," Danny said, sipping his wine. "That's where you'll really see what's going on here. The land gets used, then left behind. No restoration. No repair. And it's tearing through the forest and the wildlife like rot."

I first learned about the Red Slough through the BC Parks Foundation. I'd been looking for meaningful conservation projects in Canada, and the Foundation stood out. Led by Andy Day, they'd accomplished a lot in a short time—scrappy and focused, like a startup with a mission.

Andy had shown me a list of high-priority sites—places in danger of vanishing beneath the pressure of BC's rapid development. At the top was the Pitt River Watershed: 733 acres of privately owned, ecologically critical land. Before it was privatized, it had been stewarded for generations by the Katzie First Nation.

This region is home to some of the largest salmon spawning events in the Pacific Northwest. But land development and climate change have taken a heavy toll. Each year, fewer salmon return. And when the salmon go, the whole system suffers. As a keystone species, they feed everything—bears, wolves, eagles, even the forest itself. Scientists have found traces of salmon DNA in the trees.

Now, with the runs in steep decline, the damage is undeniable. The animals feel it. The forest feels it. The Katzie feel it. Where they once fished year-round, they now cast their nets for just a few short weeks in August.

Danny leaned back in his chair, quiet for a moment, his gaze fixed somewhere beyond the fire. "You'll see it for yourself tomorrow," he said.

A bald eagle perched in the treetops.
Credit: Age of Union

The Pitt River Lodge.
Credit: Dax Dasilva

The Red Slough

As the pale light of dawn seeped into my room, I found myself wide awake, still on East Coast time. I slipped downstairs, craving a cup of coffee and the quiet of the morning. Danny was already in the kitchen, standing by the window, motioning me to join him.

"Gray wolf," he murmured, pointing out toward the mist-laden river.

I joined him at the window, squinting into the dim light. There, cutting through the gauzy haze, was the sleek silhouette of a wolf. Its coat, a rich gray against the morning fog, looked as if it had been lifted straight from a Jack London novel—a creature bound to the wilderness, wild and unapologetic. Clamped in its jaws was a massive fish, its first catch of the day.

Danny's voice was a low rumble. "They love salmon. That wolf's probably heading back to the den, maybe to feed its young."

I watched as the stealthy beast turned and melted into the forest with an easy grace, the salmon swinging from its mouth. It was like a scene from *The Call of the Wild*, a glimpse into a life where instinct was king, and survival depended on the land and the hunt. Here was a creature woven into the fabric of this valley, moving with a purpose as ancient as the trees surrounding us.

"Incredible," I breathed. "You weren't kidding when you said that everything feeds from the river."

I looked back out the window—gone. The wolf's silent departure was a reminder: Here, nature runs by its own ancient laws, and I was merely a visitor, sometimes lucky enough to witness its harmony for a brief, fleeting moment.

After breakfast, we set off on foot, through the dense undergrowth along a well-worn trail that followed the river's edge. The forest was alive, pulsing with energy. Every step felt like it was part of something larger—a connection to the ancient rhythms of nature. Towering cedar and fir trees stretched skyward, their canopies filtering the sunlight into a soft green

First light. Thick mist. The forest exhales.
Credit: Alan Katowitz

glow. Ferns carpeted the forest floor, and moss hung from the trees in thick curtains, creating an almost otherworldly feel.

As we walked, Danny pointed out various signs of wildlife—tracks and scat. "This valley is a highway for animals coming down from the mountains. Elk, wolves, bear—they all pass through here."

The dense forest crowded us on all sides, rich with earthy scents, the air vibrating with the quiet sounds of wildlife. Suddenly, a black bear appeared from the undergrowth. Danny held his hand up to signal silence, stillness, his eyes tracking the bear as it moved.

Closer than I was comfortable with, the bear's muscular body swayed slightly as it dug into the moist earth, likely in search of grubs or roots. The bear lifted its head, nostrils flaring as it caught our scent. For a tense moment, it looked straight at us, eyes glinting with a dark intelligence.

The bear turned its body toward us, raising its head and sniffing the air. My heart raced, but I took Danny's lead and didn't move an inch.

Danny leaned in close, his voice barely a murmur. "Stay still. He probably thinks we're just a couple of oversized snacks."

I shot him a look, but before I could reply, he continued with a grin. "Don't worry, our bears usually prefer a more local menu. But, hey, if he's into exotic cuisine today, I'll make sure he gets you first."

"Thanks for the vote of confidence, Danny," I whispered back, trying to sound braver than I felt. It *did* feel a little too close to be kidding around.

The bear moved a step closer, still sniffing. Danny glanced at me, raising an eyebrow. "Guess he's trying to decide if you're organic."

Before I could respond, the bear let out a low grunt, turned, and loped back into the forest. Danny let out a quiet chuckle. "See? He took one whiff and knew you weren't from around here. Probably thought, 'Nope, too fancy for my taste.'"

I exhaled, laughing softly despite myself. "I'll take it as a compliment. Maybe I smell like high-quality conservation."

Danny patted my shoulder. "Keep telling yourself that. Out here, it's survival of the wittiest. Just another day in the valley—and we only charge extra if the bear decides to join us for dinner," he quipped, beaming after the close encounter.

Chapter 6 | **WHERE THE WOLF DRINKS FIRST** 225

I nodded, the adrenaline still pulsing through me. It was no small thing, being reminded we're guests here.

We traced the riverbank, a mosaic of beauty where the clear, glacier-fed waters of the Pitt River flowed steadily toward the lake. It was here, standing by the river, that the real importance of the watershed began to sink in for me. The river was teeming with life. Its streams running from forests, shallow and cool, provided perfect spawning nests for the salmon. We watched as some fish moved slowly through the water, their bodies gleaming in the sunlight as they made their way upstream.

We stopped at a bend in the river, where the water slowed, creating a calm pool. Danny knelt, scooping up a handful of the cool water and taking a sip. I did the same, wondering if he was conscious of his part in the cycle of life on the river. I told him about what Paul Rosolie had shared with me on my first journey to the Amazon.

"You drink the water, and it flows through your body and hydrates you," Paul had said as we cupped water from the Las Piedras River and drank it down. "Then you sweat, and the water leaves your body, becoming vapor and returning to the sky. This is the moment you become part of the life

Along the Pitt River with Andy Day of BC Parks Foundation.
Credit: Alan Katowitz

cycle of the forest." I was excited to share this sentiment with Danny, as he hadn't heard it put that way before.

We hiked through the forest quietly, taking in the majesty of the place. All around were coniferous trees: moss-covered Sitka spruce, Douglas firs, yellow cedars. There was a familiarity to it all. I could almost smell the memories rushing back into my mind—these were the same species of old-growth forest that were defended in the Clayoquot Sound logging protests. But here, the trees were thriving and could be protected forever. In moments like these, it was easy to forget just how fragile it all was. But then we reached the Red Slough, and reality came crashing back.

We stepped onto the empty bank. The Red Slough was hushed and choked—once a living corridor, now barely holding on. Now, it was cut off by an abandoned logging road, isolated from the river's flow. The water was red and still, and the surrounding vegetation had withered. There were no signs of fish, few birds, little life.

"This is what happens when the water stops flowing," Danny said grimly. "This all used to be crystal-blue water filled with fish, and a peak area for wildlife to come for food and water. Some animals try to use it, but it's dying."

His words hit me like a punch to the gut. It was true. The pressure on the Pitt River Watershed had never been greater. Logging, development, climate change—all of these forces were converging, threatening to destroy what remained of this wild, untamed place.

I could feel Danny's frustration as we stared at the dead water. And to pour salt on the wound, so many groups had visited this area and spent a ton of money on conducting studies and assessment reports, but none of them had been able to fix the problem.

I remarked on this to Danny, who nodded. "That's the way it goes. They come in, collect data, write reports, and move on. But nothing changes. Each time, the cost of the reports probably could have repaired the river." He wasn't wrong; many environmental groups make a business out of reporting. They could spend hundreds of thousands of dollars to create paperwork and not move a single rock.

As we walked farther into the area, the landscape unfolded before us in a mixture of beauty and decay. On one side, the Pitt River, vibrant and alive, flowed steadily, providing sustenance to the wildlife that called this place home. On the other, the Red Slough, cut off from the main water source, lay in stagnation—a once-thriving artery now dried up and dying. The contrast was a reminder of how easily the balance of nature can be tipped and how critical it was to act before this ecosystem collapsed completely.

I turned to Danny as we stood by the bank of the slough. "So, what exactly needs to happen here to bring this back to life?"

"We need to restore the water," Danny said, "back to how it was before the loggers arrived. The Red Slough used to be a part of the Pitt River's natural flow, but roads cut it off. And after the loggers left this area, they neglected to put things back as they once were. If we can redirect the glacial water back into this slough, nature will do the rest—the salmon will return, the forest will grow," he continued. "And when the salmon come back, the bears will follow, the wolves, the birds."

The Red Slough, a vital wetland, cut off from fresh glacial waters.
Credit: Marietta Raina

I nodded. "We are going to fix this," I said, with a plan in mind to make that happen.

We left the Red Slough. Danny took us to a quieter part of the river, away from where the salmon congregated, to let me experience the water's force without disturbing the fish. After slipping on waders, we carefully waded in, feeling the chill of the glacier-fed water through the rubber. The river was deceptive—it looked serene from the banks, but beneath the surface, the current tugged with an energy that was hard to ignore.

I felt good, confident; although I couldn't swim, it didn't seem to be a factor. The river's beauty drew me in like a siren's call. I stepped deeper in, trying to keep my balance on the uneven riverbed. The rocks were slick, coated in algae, and as I shifted my weight, my foot slipped. In an instant, I was submerged, the icy water rushing over me, filling my waders

Prepared for the water, but the river had other plans.
Credit: Marietta Raina

as the current began to carry me downstream. My legs were swept out beneath me. Panic surged as I struggled, the force of the river making it impossible to find my footing.

Suddenly I felt a firm tug against the flow as Danny's grip locked onto the back of my jacket. With one powerful pull, he yanked me upright and out of the current's grasp, hauling me toward the bank. It was just a few feet, maybe more, and I marveled at how quickly one can be washed away. I stumbled to the shore, coughing up water, drenched, cold, and thoroughly disheveled. My pride took a hit, but I was relieved to be on solid ground.

Danny held onto my jacket until we stepped out of the river. He grinned and deadpanned, "Guess you didn't see the fish taking bets on you there."

"Don't worry," he said, patting me on the back. "That's happened to me plenty. You gotta respect it, or it'll remind you."

I managed a laugh, my hands still trembling from the adrenaline. "Lesson learned," I said, shaking off the chill. I was humbled. As the cold sunk deeper, the river's lesson left a mark that was likely to stay.

Danny nodded, his expression shifting to something more serious. "Out here, respect's the only thing that matters. It doesn't care where you come from or what you've done—just how you handle yourself in any given moment."

We hiked back to the Pitt Lodge. A change of clothes and a hot meal never sounded better.

Dinosaurs

That afternoon, Danny and I met up with Andy Day from BC Parks and took a helicopter to get a bird's-eye view of the Red Slough and the valley. From the sky, the landscape looked Jurassic. The damage was even more obvious. There were clear-cut patches of forest that looked like open wounds on the landscape, banks of gravel beds along the river that were once lush with trees. Old framed photographs inside the Pitt River Lodge revealed the truth—these rivers had been lined with trees offering shade, keeping the waters cool for the spawning salmon and other fish that once thrived in them. Remnant logging roads crisscrossed the valley like scars. Despite the damage, there was still so much beauty. The river wound its way through the valley like a blue serpent, and the surrounding forested mountains stood as silent sentinels watching over this place.

As we flew over the Red Slough, it was easy to see how the restoration could work. It was a matter of digging and pushing around some dirt—a lot of dirt.

Exploring far reaches of the river accessible only by helicopter.
Credit: Alan Katowitz

We put the helicopter down on a sandbank clearing along an upper stream. "You're about to see something wild," said Danny.

We walked a short distance to a wide, shallow stream that fed into the Pitt River. Hundreds, if not thousands, of coho salmon filled the river. Every ripple, every dimple in the rocky bottom was occupied by massive reddish-colored fish, holding their positions as the cool water ran past them.

It was like seeing dinosaurs.

The clear water made visible their yellow eyes, large teeth, and hooked mouths. Their bodies shimmered in the light as they wriggled in the water, the males distinct with red bellies and black heads and tails. Their bellies aren't always red; they transform during spawning season—potentially to attract a mate or to offer themselves as targets for predators in lieu of the silver females.

"They've just started spawning," said Danny. "The males are the first to show up in the streams. These guys spend a few years in the ocean, then they return here to spawn."

Andy explained how the salmon lay their roe. The females build spawning nests, called redds, in the gravel of a streambed. A salmon's redd may hold up to five thousand eggs. One or more males will fertilize

Surveying the valley from above with Andy.
Credit: Dax Dasilva

Chinook salmon spawning in shallow waters.
Credit: Dax Dasilva

the eggs, with the female moving on to create more redds. It's the dominant males that remain with the nests, defending them by chasing and attacking invaders.

Salmon are considered anadromous, which means that they live in both fresh water and salt water. They are born in fresh water, where they spend a few months to a few years (depending on the species) before moving out to the briny ocean. When it's time to spawn, they head back to fresh water. Very few species of fish have the incredible physiological and behavioral adaptations required to live in both fresh water and salt water—most fish would die quickly in these conditions.

Years after salmon are born in the streams and head out to sea, they return to the river in which they were born to spawn. There are theories about how they do this, but whether it's a powerful sense of scent, use of the Earth's magnetic field, or something else, we really don't know. What we do know is that salmon are a keystone species that have a disproportionately large impact on their ecosystem relative to how many of them there are. And when a keystone species disappears, there is a massive impact on everything else.

I felt a sense of connection to something ancient, something primal. These fish had been spawning here for millions of years, long before humans ever set foot in these forests. Seeing these creatures that survived epochs and were now diminished and displaced due to human intervention reminded me of the leatherback turtles that, for millions of years, traveled thousands of miles from Canada to nest on Matura Bay—and how humans had disrupted this natural process as well. I remembered Aldo Leopold's words: "To keep every cog and wheel is the first precaution of intelligent tinkering." Here, the salmon were the keystone cog—their bodies feeding the soil, their movements sculpting the rivers, their DNA flowing through every tree, every creature in the valley.

Danny looked over the stream he'd seen thousands of times with the same passion and awe as he must have felt the first time he visited. "It's like they're the blood running through the veins of this place. Without 'em, everything else just kind of...fades."

Seeing the coho stirred up similar feelings to watching the leatherback turtles nesting in Trinidad or seeing the lowland gorillas in the Congo.

These weren't just animals—they were ancient, powerful beings that had survived for millions of years, overcoming challenges that humans couldn't even fathom. And yet now, their survival was in our hands.

"Do they go back to the ocean after they spawn?" I asked.

"No, this is the end of their life cycle—after spawning, they die," Danny said, "leaving their future to the fry that can develop and survive predators. That's why it's so critical to protect the streams, so that the young survive and make it back into the ocean for the next generation cycle." I looked around at the thousands of fish that were concluding their life cycle, having fulfilled their purpose. It was heavy to consider.

Danny took us farther upstream, following a shallow creek off the river. It smelled horrid, like death—it *was* death. In just a few inches of water spread across the rocky creek, thousands of salmon lay dead in the sun. The carcass area was so thick that you couldn't see the ground beneath them.

"This is the result of clear-cutting and climate change," Danny explained in a somber voice. "The streams are warming up in shallow exposed areas, and they become parched and run dry in the hot summer months, leaving no way for some salmon to reach the spawning grounds."

It was a heartbreaking scene, shocking to see.

A bird's-eye view of the Pitt River Watershed.
Credit: Alan Katowitz

"All of those salmon that just kind of wasted away and didn't even have the opportunity to reproduce is just heartbreaking," said Danny, confirming that these coho had not yet spawned. "It's sad to watch the wild salmon deteriorate right in front of your eyes."

The surviving fry will hide in smaller, shallower creeks and pools, more vulnerable to otters and herons, some falling to the unseasonable heat.

"It's the worst we've seen in all my years in the Pitt River Valley," said Danny. The losses will cause lower rates of return in future spawns, affecting predators like bears, wolves, and eagles, and have an impact on the commercial and Indigenous fisheries that rely on the salmon that populate wild central British Columbian streams each fall.

The significance of the salmon's role in this ecosystem became more and more apparent to me. Everywhere we went—whether it was hiking through the forest, traveling upriver through the valley, or flying over the mountains—the thread that connected it all was the salmon. Their presence—or absence—had a ripple effect on every other living thing in the valley. I hadn't fully understood the scale of that relationship until I saw it with my own eyes.

We returned to the spawning area, the sun glinting off the surface of the river as salmon swam around, their bodies moving with the grace of a species that has navigated these waters for millennia. Danny, ever the expert, crouched down, pointing out a coho male already protecting its ground.

"Look at him," Danny said with admiration in his voice. "He's protecting the redd. She's likely just laid her eggs."

I watched as one large fish darted around, guarding the shallow nest that his mate had dug in the gravel. The female was nearby, her brownish body blending more easily into the riverbed as she rested after laying her eggs. The male, on the other hand, was on alert, chasing away any potential threat to the nest, his body already showing signs of wear. His life would end here, defending the next generation.

"But not before they turn into zombies," Danny said, waiting to catch my reaction.

"Zombies?" I asked, interested in hearing what came next.

As Danny explained it, salmon enter the rivers from the ocean in top shape—silver, sparkly, and healthy. But their physical condition deteriorates the longer they remain in fresh water. First, they turn dark as they prepare to spawn, and once they have spawned, most of them deteriorate rapidly and soon die. Some are still alive, but their bodies have already begun the process of rotting, and these deteriorating salmon are called zombie fish.

"Most zombie fish die within days of spawning," Danny said, "but some can last up to a few weeks, wandering the streams, gruesomely covered in fungus. They are the living dead of the fish world."

I shivered at the thought, but nature isn't always pretty. And once the salmon die, they are scavenged by other animals, or they decompose and release nutrients to algae, river insects, and the forests. And soon a new generation of salmon are born to begin the circle of life anew.

As we made our way back to the lodge, I felt a renewed sense of purpose. This wasn't just about buying land and restoring it. It was about helping to ensure that there would be more places for the salmon to spawn, and the valley they supported would continue to thrive for generations to come.

The Promise

The sun had long dipped behind the mountain peaks, leaving a soft twilight glow over the valley. The lodge was warm and inviting, a welcome reprieve from the brisk evening air outside. Inside, the woodstove emitted a fresh pine scent, casting flickering shadows on the wooden beams that stretched across the ceiling.

Andy, Danny, Lee, and I gathered around the harvest table with a few fishing guides, their faces illuminated by the dim candlelight and the flickering light of the fire. The conversation flowed easily at first; it was a moment of peace after the long day spent exploring the valley, the river, and the forest.

As we ate, I found myself reflecting on the day's events—the sight of the salmon fighting their way upstream, the silent majesty of the elk as they crossed the river, the way the forest seemed to breathe with life all around us. I brought up the Red Slough, its potential to be restored, and the work ahead.

Danny leaned back in his chair and rested his hands on his stomach, a satisfied grin on his face. "You know," he said, his voice thoughtful, "This place. It gets into your bones. The land, the river, the animals—they're all part of you, whether you realize it or not. Not unlike your story of the Amazon River, Dax."

"This land needs to be protected," I said. "And I've got good news. We're going to fund the purchase of the Pitt River Watershed for BC Parks and the Katzie First Nation to restore and look after—starting with rechanneling water into the Red Slough. Together, we're going to turn that water blue again and bring it back to life."

The room echoed with excitement, the gentle sounds of the crackling fire replaced by joyful voices. But the weight of the promise brought up some heavy emotions, too.

Danny leaned forward with a hand wrapped around his glass. "You know, Dax, I never imagined it'd be like this—someone like you coming in, seeing value beyond what you can fish or log," his voice thick with sentiment. "You have no idea what this means."

Lee smiled softly from across the table. "I think he does." Raising a toast, she said, "To the valley—may it stay wild and timeless, no matter who's watching." We clinked glasses, the room warm with a shared sense of purpose and hope.

"Thank you," Andy said, his voice barely above a whisper. "Thank you for believing in this place."

We sat at the table for hours sharing stories—about the bear encounter, the coho in the stream, and my "swimming" incident. There was laughter, along with a deep sense of friendship that only comes after a trip like this.

As the evening wandered and the bottles were emptied, I couldn't help but think about the future. About what this promise meant—not just for the next five years, but for the next fifty, the next hundred. The salmon, the eagles, the bears, the wolves—all of them depended on this land, on the health of the river. It would be impossible to measure the true success of protecting this land, but very easy to see its demise if we didn't.

Later that night, after everyone had gone to bed, I was pulled from sleep by the sound of wolves howling down by the river. Their voices drifted through the darkness, a low and haunting harmony that seemed to rise from the very bones of the valley. The mournful, echoing calls sent shivers through me, not of fear, but of reverence.

I opened the window to see if I could spot them. They were somewhere along the edge of the forest, hidden from sight, their howls rolling over the landscape and seeping into the quiet spaces between the trees.

I sat still, listening as their calls wove together, carrying an ancient language older than any human presence here. Perhaps they were calling to distant members of the pack, claiming their territory, or celebrating a kill. The sound was wild and unrestrained, a reminder of the life that moved, mostly unseen, through these dense forests and shadowed riverbanks. I thought back to London's portrayal of the wilderness as both a brutal and a beautiful force. In that moment, I understood what he meant by the wild's pull—an irresistible, untamed energy that called every living thing back to its origins.

In the stillness, I closed my eyes, letting the howls settle into my mind and heart. The wolves owned the night, and in that moment, it felt as if this land belonged to them, their voices the truest claim to its wild heart. *This is our home, too.*

In 2022, I partnered with the BC Parks Foundation, with Age of Union granting $6 million to protect those 733 acres in the Pitt River Watershed on Katzie territory and subsequently to support the Katzie First Nation Community in reconnecting the Pitt River mainstream with the Red Slough, revitalizing a key salmon habitat. Over the next two years, we oversaw the ecological restoration of 74 acres of slough and wetland. The establishment of the Katzie Guardians program would increase capacity within the Nation for stewardship of the land.

David Kenworthy, elected council member of the Katzie First Nation, attended the reintroduction of fresh water into the Red Slough. "Our ancestors must be proud of the work happening here to bring life back to the land and to the water," he said, the running water behind him an accompaniment to his prayer song. "It's been a very long time since a song and drum have been heard on this land." David sang a traditional song while beating a hand drum.

Mike Leon, a territorial guardian from the Katzie First Nation, stood on the riverbank and spoke with quiet authority. "We're returning the water from the Upper Pitt to the Red Slough," he said. "In our way, this isn't just restoration—it's a reunion. We're bringing the water back to where it belongs. Back to a sacred place."

Historically, the Red Slough held all five species of Pacific salmon. It was an incredibly biodiverse area that held major significance to the health of the ecosystem. When the forest service roads were built in the 1930s, they cut off access for the main stem of the Upper Pitt River to connect to the Red Slough, effectively cutting off the neck of the ecosystem. Life in the area diminished rapidly after that.

The restored habitat will pay dividends to the surrounding ecosystem, not only for aquatic species, but also for the terrestrial animals that rely on that ecosystem for their existence. Years of strategic planning, technical preparation, and serious moving of earth brought us to the moment of the initial water release.

"Our future generations will be using the water, which is our matriarch," Mike said, holding his hand over his heart. "This water is what has kept Katzie alive for thousands of years. It was stopped, and now we are giving it back."

Several young Katzie sang as the water began running into the Red Slough, their voices pouring out over the water and forest. "Our youth are here today, because someday, they will share this story," Mike said, "a day when the sockeye, Chinook, and coho are spawning here. And all the wildlife—all our relatives of nature are here using this special place."

It was a beautiful day for the Katzie. And a beautiful day for nature.

"In simple terms, the rainforests, which encircle the world, are our very life-support system—and we are on the verge of switching it off."

—PRINCE CHARLES

Above the forest floor, a gibbon pauses—mid-world, suspended in the green silence.
Credit: Mathias Kellermann

In Kalaweit—Age of Union Dulan Forest reserve.
Credit: Chanee

Chapter 7

THE SILENCE OF THE GIBBONS

FIGHTING FOR BORNEO'S VANISHING CANOPY

Chanee and I lay motionless in the mud, the relentless rain hammering down on us like a waterfall spilling over the dense canopy of the Dulan Forest. Above us, Maurice, a massive orangutan, was perched just thirty feet up, blending into the thick tangle of branches and leaves like a ghost. Our bodies were camouflaged in fatigues, barely distinguishable from the drenched forest floor. To me, it seemed as though Maurice hadn't noticed us, but Chanee knew better.

"He knows," Chanee whispered, his voice barely audible over the drumming rain. He had been tracking Maurice for two years, moving through the jungle with a gait and sound that were neither fully human nor fully animal. Maurice recognized him—not as a threat, but as something...familiar. As for me? I could only hope that Maurice saw me as an extension of that trust.

Suddenly, Maurice's long, powerful arm shot out, gripping a branch thicker than my wrist. With a swift, effortless motion, he snapped it from the tree and hurled it toward us. The branch crashed into the forest floor just a few feet away, spraying mud and leaves into the air. My instinct was to look up, but the rain streaming down my face blurred my vision. I could hear Maurice moving above us, his massive weight shifting the branches as if they were twigs.

I glanced over at Chanee, seeking some sign of whether we were in danger, but he just grinned. That wide, toothy smile only someone with a dark sense of humor would wear in the middle of a situation like this. "Don't worry," he whispered, "this is Maurice's way of saying hello."

The second branch, more like a log, hit even closer, inches from our heads, splattering mud all over us.

"Hell of a hello," I blurted into Chanee's ear, wiping the grime from my eyes.

Another crackling snap echoed through the canopy, and I flinched, waiting for the next projectile. But this time, there was no branch. Maurice wasn't trying to skewer us into the ground. I dared to look up again, and what I saw stopped me cold.

He was fashioning an umbrella.

Maurice clung to a thick branch with enormous leaves, holding it above his head to shield himself from the downpour. He leaned back almost casually, his intelligent eyes scanning the forest as if making sure we understood—this was his territory, his world. Like Bonne Année in the Congo, Maurice was the boss. The sight of him was mesmerizing.

A dominant male orangutan watches from above in the Dulan reserve.
Credit: Kalaweit

The sheer ingenuity of it was both awe-inspiring and humbling. I had read about animals using tools, seen films about their intelligence, but witnessing it firsthand like this—a creature with this kind of raw power, creating a solution to protect himself from the rain—was a revelation.

Chanee was laughing, the joy blaring through the mud and rain and leaves on his face. "Dax, you just witnessed something very special," he said, his blue eyes peering right into mine. "Are we humans as different from apes as we claim to be? And if we can admit the similarity, shouldn't we reconsider how we treat them?" It was one of humankind's earliest questions, one that, deep in the Dulan Forest, beneath the showering sky, a big red orangutan answered for us. Watching Maurice, I realized he wasn't just an ape surviving against all odds—he was the soul of this forest. And if he couldn't survive here, none of us stood a chance.

Three days earlier, I had touched down in Borneo, ready to visit Chanee and see the forest we were working together to protect. Now, I was lying in the middle of it, in the rain-soaked mud, watching as a wild ape not only recognized us but surely used a tool to solve a problem. If that's not a welcome to the jungle, I don't know what is.

Jasmine

The journey to Borneo was grueling: five days of travel for a few days on the ground. After a twelve-hour flight from Montréal to Doha, a lengthy layover, and another ten-hour flight to Jakarta, I found myself in the capital of Indonesia with time to spend. That unexpected pause came as a blessing—a moment to pay remembrance to someone who had profoundly shaped my early life: Jasmine, a wonderful Indonesian transgender woman whom I looked to as my godmother in my late teens.

Jasmine passed away in 2018, but she had often spoken of Jakarta, her stories woven with a longing for her homeland. In her honor I took a cab to Suropati Park, a quiet, serene place where I could picture her picking flowers and contemplating life. Jasmine was deeply spiritual, a devout Muslim, though you wouldn't have guessed it from her brash, larger-than-life persona.

You could make a movie about Jasmine—a non-demure and powerful person who took on a variety of roles in her life: dominatrix, protector, scandal-causer—but after much of that faded in her later years, she was, to me, simply family. She had become my guardian angel when I came out to my parents at age eighteen. My father had turned evangelical after divorcing my mother, and my mother—well, I thought she knew, but when I came out to her, she was shocked. In those lonely days, it was Jasmine who watched over me and my friends like a hawk in Vancouver's gay scene. Her razor-sharp wit, fierce loyalty, and fearsome persona made her incredibly fun to be around, and essential when times were tough.

As Jasmine got older, the years became less kind to her. Her income dwindled, and she developed brain cancer. With treatment, she overcame the cancer, but her body had weakened, and she developed diabetes. She didn't like asking for anything, but she didn't have to—she had looked after me all those years, and I gladly reciprocated. I paid her rent and expenses, but she would often spend the rent money on flights to Indonesia in search of alternative therapies for her diabetes. Then, after a few weeks, she would find herself stuck and call me, and I'd pay to bring her home. Evictions for not paying rent were common, leaving her homeless until I could help find her new digs. We argued about it, but there was always something mischievous about her, constantly testing boundaries. I always looked to Jasmine as a form of teacher in my life. And in a strange way, through those fights and her own struggles, she taught me resilience, empathy, and compassion.

I strolled through the park's flower gardens and sat near a fountain, remembering Jasmine during our early days together. She could make my heart ache—from laughter. After my parents came around, Jasmine became a fixture at our Christmas gatherings, turning them into the most joyfully chaotic events. She'd sweep in, dressed in full dominatrix gear, and when my dad would try to compliment her outfit, she'd smirk, "You really think I woke up looking fabulous like this?" If anything went wrong with her ensemble, she'd wave it off with, "Don't look at Mama Sutra, she's having a wardrobe malfunction!" Even as she fought brain cancer and later diabetes, she never lost her spirit—or her faith.

When Jasmine passed, with my parents at my side, I was the one who unplugged her from life support at St. Paul's Hospital in Vancouver. That moment still clings to me—this remarkable woman who had cared for me and my friends during our most impressionable years, who loved us in her wild, unapologetic way. Her body, worn by years of illness, lay frail and still. To my surprise, the imam granted her a proper Muslim burial—embalmed and shrouded according to her final wish. I hadn't expected such a gesture for a trans woman, but they honored it. It was a moment of unexpected grace.

Jasmine didn't fit neatly into any category, which is what made her so remarkable. She was my friend, my teacher, and my family. Even now, after she's gone, I'm still learning from her. One obvious lesson was to be unapologetically yourself and embrace it with everything you've got. But more to the moment at hand, Jasmine taught me that standing on the margins of society makes you resilient, that pushing against the forces that seek to control you is a necessity. Perhaps it was this same lesson that drove me to the front lines of conservation—to protect the Dulan Forest from an all-too-familiar fate.

As I walked along the rows of white flowers in the park, I plucked one for Jasmine and set it afloat in the fountain, watching as it spun slowly in the water. I whispered a prayer for her. Being back in Jakarta, not to bring her home but to honor her, carried a heaviness I hadn't anticipated—a quiet farewell to someone who had shaped my life in unforgettable ways.

Palangkaraya

From Jakarta, I flew to Palangkaraya to finally meet Chanee in person, after three years of working together virtually. Chanee, the mononymous founder and director of the Kalaweit Foundation, had spent decades rescuing and protecting gibbons in Indonesia. Until recently, his focus had been on building sanctuaries, but in 2022, with a million-dollar contribution from Age of Union, he was able to purchase the entire Dulan Forest—5,000 acres of dense, untouched rainforest, home to orangutans, sun bears, clouded leopards, and, of course, gibbons.

He greeted me with his signature energy the moment I stepped out of the gate. "You must be exhausted," he said with a grin, giving me the once-over.

"Nope. But I'm starving," I replied, brushing off the jet lag.

"Good!" He laughed. "Welcome to Borneo, Dax. Let's get you fed."

We grabbed my bag and headed to a Dayak restaurant along the Kahayan River. Chanee's wife, Prada, is Dayak, and he was already talking up the cuisine.

"You're going to love it. But just wait until we get home. My wife's cooking is the best." His excitement was infectious.

"We'll stay here in Palangkaraya tonight and leave early in the morning," Chanee explained, scanning the menu. "The drive will take six hours, but tonight—tonight we're having the best tempe mendoan in town."

He wasn't wrong. Thin slices of tempeh, battered and fried, came sizzling to the table with green onions, garlic, and hot chilies. It was exactly what I needed. Soon the table was filled—tamarind vegetable soup, spicy grated coconut salad, stir-fried water spinach, and steamed rice.

I hadn't thought much about how cuisine ties into conservation. But food brings people together. Around a table, with full bellies, conversations tend to flow in the right direction. I thought of Bourdain—his *Parts Unknown* episode in Borneo, where he celebrated Gawai, the annual Iban rice harvest festival. "Food is everything we are," he said. "It's an extension of nationalist feeling, ethnic feeling, your personal history, your province, your region, your tribe, your grandma."

I hadn't planned it this way, but I had arrived just in time for Gawai. We were in for a treat—holiday foods, traditional costumes, and the joy of a good harvest.

Our waiter approached with a smile and a well-used plastic jug, half-filled with a cloudy, brownish-yellow drink. "This is tuak," he said, overpouring two glasses.

"Are you sure about this?" I asked, eyeing the liquid.

Chanee chuckled. "Tuak is sacred to the Dayak. Two things you need to know: First, it should be made by the women of the Sea Dayak tribe—the original headhunters."

"Headhunters? You're joking."

"No joke," he said, deadpan. "Ngayau—the act of decapitation—was real. Some say it was practiced into the '90s."

I looked down at my glass, suddenly hesitant. "Comforting. And the second thing?"

Chanee raised his glass. "When someone offers you tuak, you drink it."

I smirked. "To the Dulan Forest," I said, lifting my glass, "a conservation project that wouldn't exist without your dedication."

Heading upriver with Chanee, founder of Kalaweit.
Credit: Dax Dasilva

"And to you, Dax," Chanee replied, clinking his glass against mine. "For believing in it."

I took a sip. The fermented juice hit like a punch. Not the best drink I'd ever had—but tradition matters. And it had a kick.

The rest of the evening flowed like the Kahayan River beside us. We ate, drank, and talked about the forest—the politics, the future, the work ahead. There was an ease between us, like old friends at a bar, far from the world. Bourdain would've approved.

We took modest rooms in a nearby village for the night. Mine smelled of damp earth and woodsmoke. Through the open window, I could see silhouettes of trees swaying in the dark. I could hear the river from my bed, its voice steady and alive, threading through the night like a lullaby.

Morning came too soon. Outside, roosters crowed, and villagers coughed and cleared their throats as they rose. I shook off the remnants of last night's tuak and packed my gear. Chanee's Toyota Hilux was waiting. We loaded up and hit the road. Kalaweit was calling.

Kalaweit

The journey was long, hot, and ugly—six hours through man-made scars cut into what had once been pristine forest, now stripped bare for a wide dirt road that facilitated mining and coal extraction. The landscape was littered with bulldozers, excavators, and dump trucks moving like some soulless swarm, removing every trace of the wild. As Paul Rosolie once told me while we were deep in the Amazon, this is how it always begins. Not with an explosion of industry, but with the slow, methodical carving of a single road. After that, the rest follows. The parasites—extracting palm oil, coal, and gold—come next, feeding off the bones of a dying forest, each taking their share until nothing remains but dust and stumps.

Chapter 7 | **THE SILENCE OF THE GIBBONS**

You could feel it—a sense of irreversible loss. Calling it a rapidly spreading cancer doesn't quite capture the incessant violence that we were witnessing. But make no mistake, this was a cancer.

Chanee caught my gaze, reading the weight of what I was seeing. This wasn't his first time driving through this desecration. He had been carrying this same burden for over two decades. Twenty-five years ago, he was just a passionate young Frenchman, barely out of his teens, arriving in Indonesia with a mission: to protect the gibbons. At the time, he didn't know that passion would tie him to this place forever. He married a local woman, started a family, and eventually became Indonesian himself. His citizenship allowed him to stay and continue the fight even after most foreign NGOs had been pushed out. Chanee didn't just work here; he belonged here.

We crossed the Barito River on a creaking ferry and then drove another hour before reaching a small village, where we boarded a speedboat that would take us the rest of the way to Chanee's home. The scene on the river was no better than on land. Barges towering with coal drifted past us in a steady procession, their destination clear—China and India, the world's hungry giants. Cranes dipped and rose in rhythm, feeding the endless appetite for resources, while tugboats darted about like insects, guiding the flow of their black treasure down the river.

Among the roots and shadows, Chanee moves through the forest he vowed to defend.
Credit: Kalaweit

Finally, after hours on planes, boats, and the battered roads of Borneo, we arrived at Kalaweit. I was wiped out, feeling every one of those hours deep in my bones. But the sight of the Age of Union seaplane jolted me awake. A sign hanging from the floating riverside hangar read "Borneo Flying Club." Inside, the bright orange ultralight craft, built in 2022 specifically for Chanee to pilot, awaited its next mission. He had spent a month in France learning to fly it before it arrived in Borneo to take on its role. It wasn't just a plane—it was a symbol of the work we were doing here, the commitment we had made. What an empowering moment—it reminded me of when I first saw the M/Y *Age of Union* anti-poaching vessel. Now we had a fleet.

Chanee's fourteen-year-old son, Enzo, was waiting for us at the dock. Enzo loved flying with his dad. You could already see that spark in him—he was following in his father's footsteps, dreaming of one day piloting the ultralight to patrol the skies above the forest.

We untethered the ultralight from its place inside the hangar and rolled it carefully into the water. Chanee knew the weather wasn't ideal for a flight—he even said so—but I could tell he was eager to show off the plane. In the afternoon light, it gleamed, its fiberglass body casting a shimmering reflection on the surface of the water. "Age of Union" was proudly emblazoned along the fuselage, with our names stenciled on the doors—his on the pilot's side, mine on the passenger's.

"Dax," Chanee said, his voice carrying a quiet excitement as we prepped the aircraft. "I've been waiting over a year to take you up in this. I can't wait to show you what we've accomplished, what you've helped us protect."

I smiled, settling into my seat. "So, you're comfortable flying this thing by now?"

He grinned. "Two hundred hours under my belt. I'd say that's enough to get us back in one piece."

It was a moment filled with pride, the culmination of so much hard work, but ultimately, we had to postpone. The weather wasn't on our side, and while the ultralight was nimble and agile, it was also vulnerable to the incoming front. Still, I could hear the seriousness in Chanee's voice—the significance of this moment wasn't lost on him, and neither was my being there.

Secured by Kalaweit and Age of Union, the Dulan Forest from above reveals what preservation looks like. **Credit: Dax Dasilva**

We climbed the hill to Chanee's house, nestled in the heart of the reserve. There was something surreal about it—a peaceful place of refuge in the forest, it felt very protected, and for good reason. Seventy-five people worked for Chanee, most from the Dayak tribe, indigenous to Borneo's interior. Yet just outside Kalaweit, there was tension. The Dayak and the Jakartan people didn't always see eye to eye, and those cultural conflicts bled into conservation efforts. Prada's being Dayak helped bridge the gap, but the history between these peoples ran deep, and history doesn't dissolve easily.

Before Kalaweit, Chanee's life had revolved around Palangkaraya, where he built his first gibbon rescue center on leased land. It was modest but effective—until the government changed. Then, as it so often does in places like this, the ground beneath him shifted. His media work, exposing the fires set by palm oil farmers to clear land for plantations, earned him dangerous enemies. You don't make friends with this kind of truth, especially when it hits the pockets of powerful corporations.

First came the threats. Then, one day, he came home to find his houseboat, the home where his family lived, destroyed by fire. Not long after that, a businessman bought the land where his sanctuary stood, dismantled it, and kicked Chanee off the property. It was a dark time for Chanee and the gibbons, but he refused to give up.

In places like Borneo—or the Amazon or the Congo—conservation isn't just about rescuing animals. It's about survival. Yours, mine, theirs. And here's the bitter reality: If you don't own the land, you can't protect it. That's the hard lesson Chanee learned, and it's the foundation of our partnership, the reason that we purchased the Dulan Forest. Chanee and I both knew that this was just the beginning.

Inside his current home, the air was filled with the comforting smell of home-cooked food. Prada was pleased that we'd enjoyed the local cuisine the night before, but she was confident that this meal would top it. And she was right. She had prepared a spread of rice, vegetables, and chicken, finishing with fresh dragon fruit. After hours of traveling through dusty and deforested land, Prada's offering tasted like more than just sustenance. It was a reminder of what we were fighting for—cultural traditions, local ingredients, and the deep connection between the land and its people.

Chapter 7 | **THE SILENCE OF THE GIBBONS** 255

Enzo came to the table with a model plane he'd just finished building, setting it down next to his lunch plate.

"I see you've got a thing for airplanes," I said, raising an eyebrow.

Enzo's chest puffed up with pride. He picked up the toy again, turning it in his hands. "Yeah, Dad says I'm going to fly with him in the plane soon."

Chanee nodded. "The more we grow, the more we need eyes in the sky. It's the best way to keep track of everything."

Enzo wasn't done. "I'll be a pilot," he declared confidently. "I go up all the time with Dad. I can start taking flying lessons soon."

"You better be careful, Enzo," said Chanee, grinning at his son. "One day you'll be flying this thing, and you'll look down to see me waving up at you, stuck down here with all the paperwork."

"I'll come pick you up so we can go flying," answered Enzo, solving simple problems with simple solutions—the apple doesn't fall far.

I laughed. "Sounds like you've got a busy future ahead, Enzo. Better start saving up for all those flying lessons."

Chanee chuckled, sipping his tea. "Or just stick to building a fleet of these models. A lot cheaper."

Kalaweit x Age of Union Reserve—rangers on the front lines of Indonesia's rainforest defense.
Credit: Dax Dasilva

Song of the Gibbon

From inside Chanee's home, we could hear the evocative, almost haunting song of the gibbons echoing through the forest. "They're singing together," he explained, a smile on his face. "It's usually in the morning when you hear this. When a male and female hold territory together, they'll sing a duet to the forest. It's a territorial call, but also a declaration of their bond. When all the gibbons join in, the whole forest becomes alive with sound."

He paused, letting me take in the idea of an entire jungle erupting into a symphony of gibbon song. "These songs are crucial for them—marking boundaries, broadcasting their relationship, and warning others where not to tread."

"It's amazing that you understand so much about their vocalizations," I said. "I guess that's why you call it *speaking gibbon*."

Chanee nodded. "Exactly. In the forest, the gibbons have a call that warns of predators. A quiet 'hoo hoo' can tell you if a leopard is nearby, and there's an even quieter call for an eagle. Knowing the difference can be life or death."

He took me to the care center where they kept rescued gibbons. The air was thick with humidity, the dense foliage surrounding us. The center is tucked neatly inside the forest, adjacent to a river, its towering enclosures blending into the landscape. Chanee's deep passion for these animals was unmistakable here. The gibbons weren't just creatures in cages to him—they were a reflection of his life's mission.

The enclosures, massive and well thought out, stand at around twenty-five feet high and just as wide, some even taller. They were constructed to allow the gibbons to swing, climb, and find privacy. Some cages have living trees growing inside, complete with pools for bathing and shelter from the elements. It isn't just about containment—it's about providing the closest approximation to a wild habitat while still protecting them. The open-air cages receive a careful balance of natural sunlight, forest views, and ample shade.

But no matter how thoughtfully designed they were, the enclosures are still cages, and these gibbons were never to be released. "Take these Bornean white-bearded gibbons as an example," Chanee began, stopping at their enclosure. "In the wild, they are very territorial and, with all the deforestation here, overcrowded in the remaining jungle. If we released them into the wild, the reigning gibbons of that forest would attack them right away. Plus, there is risk of these gibbons introducing disease to wild populations."

I peered inside the enclosure to see the gibbons, their black faces framed by white beards, their slender bodies, and their incredibly long arms. The way they moved—so effortless and fluid—hinted at their true nature. Gibbons bond for life, and they are bipedal on the ground, using their long arms for balance. But in the trees, they're extraordinary, swinging from limb to limb at speeds that would put any Olympic gymnast to shame.

Chanee's rescue center is not a small operation. Over a dozen employees were on-site during my visit, caring for more than four hundred rescued animals: gibbons, siamangs, sun bears, crocodiles, turtles, and even otters. All these creatures had been confiscated from the illegal wildlife trade, victims of human greed. The center includes medical facilities, with trained veterinarians ensuring the animals are well cared for, and a few small houses where the staff live on the property.

"These gibbons were stolen from the wild as babies," Chanee said, his voice lowering. "Sold as pets, toys, things to amuse people. Most don't survive. The stress kills them. If they make it to adulthood, they become unmanageable, and often their owners kill them."

He shook his head. "Only a small percentage ever make it here."

As we continued to tour the property, I could sense the weight these cages put on Chanee. It wasn't just the sadness of seeing wild animals trapped in captivity—it was the realization that despite all his work, he was still putting them in cages. And the pet trade was as prolific as ever, despite all his efforts to educate the public over the years. Chanee stopped, placing a hand on the cold steel mesh of one of the large enclosures.

Inside, a pair of gibbons sat nestled together, regarding us with curiosity, their soulful eyes reflecting a depth of emotion that only someone like Chanee could truly understand.

He didn't speak right away. Instead, his fingers lightly drummed against the enclosure, his gaze distant as he watched the gibbons' movements. It was as if they were communicating without words, something deep and unspoken passing between them.

"I've spent my whole life with them," Chanee finally said, his voice softer now, almost reverent. "These animals are my family. I know them better than I know most people. And it breaks my heart that this is the best I can give them."

His hand tightened on the cage, and for a moment, I saw the weight of decades pressing down on him. The pain of realizing that despite everything, the gibbons were still trapped, still cut off from the freedom of the forest where they truly belonged.

They swing in safety but not in freedom—gibbons rescued from the pet trade, now bound to sanctuary life. Credit: Mariette Raina

"They deserve better," he said, almost to himself. "We save them from the pet trade, from the fires, from deforestation, and yet...we cannot stop more from coming to us in the same manner." He stepped back from the cage, and there was a shadow of pain behind his eyes.

Chanee shook his head, a weary smile tugging at the corner of his mouth. "You know, when I was young, I thought saving them would be simpler. That we could just rescue them, release them back into the wild, and everything would be right again. But it's not like that. They've been damaged by people, and this"—he gestured toward the cage—"this is all we have left."

He sighed deeply and then added, "It's why the forest is everything now. It's not just about rescuing the gibbons. It's about making sure they never end up here in the first place. If we don't protect the land, there won't be anything left for them to go back to."

I felt the gravity of his words and the truth behind them. This wasn't just a rescue mission—it was a fight for survival. And Chanee, for all his passion and resilience, had been fighting this battle for far too long.

I placed a hand on his shoulder. "That's why the Dulan is so important. And it's just the beginning," I said.

Chanee's love for primates had started when he was just eleven. He was a naturalist in the making, years before most kids even think about the natural world. "The first primate I saw was a gibbon," he said quietly. "It was in a zoo in France. It looked sad—lonely. I felt that. I needed to help."

That experience set his life's path in motion. He spent years at the zoo, observing, learning, and speaking gibbon. "They're monogamous," he continued, "but the zoos didn't know how to pair them up. So, I made suggestions—move them between zoos, get them better social partners. It worked."

He smiled softly. "That was the moment I realized once you understand, you're responsible. Once you speak their language, you can't just walk away."

By sixteen, he'd published a book on gibbon behavior, and media attention followed. During one interview, he was asked about his ultimate goal. His answer was simple: "To see a real gibbon in the wild."

After reading the interview, French actress Muriel Robin called Chanee. "You want to see them in the wild?" she asked. "Then go. I'll help you." And with her support, Chanee made his first trip to Thailand to see gibbons in their natural habitat.

That trip changed him. The way the gibbons moved, their calls filling the jungle—it was like nothing he'd ever experienced. And it spurred him to action. When he returned to France, the headlines were filled with the news that two million hectares of forest had been lost to fires in Indonesia—the heartland of gibbons. It was clear where he needed to go.

Muriel didn't hesitate when he returned to her. "Go to Indonesia," she said. "I'll back you." And she did. To this day, she remains one of his closest supporters.

"I couldn't let her down," Chanee said. "When I was at my lowest, when everyone told me to come home, I remembered her faith in me. I had to keep going."

For over twenty years, Chanee built sanctuaries for gibbons, raising funds and awareness. Kalaweit became home to three rescue centers: Borneo, Sumatra, and the Mentawai Islands. Each one was packed, a clear result of the unchecked pet trade. As the forests disappeared, the gibbon trade flourished. There was a direct link between the two.

He constructed enclosures that mimicked the wild and educated the public on one fundamental truth: Gibbons belong in forests, not homes. But the pet trade didn't stop. More gibbons kept coming, and Chanee began to feel that his sanctuaries were more like "gibbon trade-in centers" than actual solutions.

It gnawed at him. "We've saved their bodies," he said, "but we've failed their spirits."

That's when Chanee's mission changed: Save the land, and you save the gibbons. The Dulan Forest Project was born out of the simple realization that if the forests could be secured, gibbons wouldn't need rescuing. It was a preventive approach, not a reactive one. The only way to truly protect them was to protect their homes. To buy all the land—that's where our paths crossed.

But Chanee had hit a wall, proposing a simple, pragmatic concept to European investors that they declined to support. "If people can buy land to mine coal and gold, why can't we buy land to protect it?" It was a concept that didn't take root. Until we met.

I first heard about Chanee in 2021. It was the early days of Age of Union, and his work stood out to me immediately. He and I shared a common vision: pragmatic, results-driven, adaptable conservation. We weren't interested in throwing money at a problem. We were interested in securing land and saving animals. I pledged to support Chanee in the purchase of the Dulan Forest.

Sending a million dollars via wire transfer to someone I hadn't met in person took a leap of faith. But I believed in Chanee and what he was doing, and I was confident that he would use the funds as he promised. And standing here now at the rescue center with the gibbons and seeing

A gibbon near the Kalaweit sanctuary.
Credit: Kalaweit

the Dulan Forest firsthand confirmed that what we were doing was critical.

At the far end of the center, Chanee stopped, staring into a cage at the gibbons inside. He was quiet for a long moment, and when he finally spoke, his voice was low and strained.

"We've saved their bodies," he repeated, "but we've failed their spirits."

Maurice

The next morning, Chanee and I were up before dawn, the forest still draped in a thin veil of mist. The gibbons' songs echoed through the trees, a chorus of hoots and howls that seemed to call and answer from the far reaches of the jungle. It was a sound like no other, a living symphony that made the forest feel alive.

Andrew Kalaweit, Chanee's eldest son, had arrived the night before and would be joining us. He was already a conservation YouTube sensation with more than two million subscribers, just home from his film studies in Paris.

Chanee handed me a set of camouflage fatigues to match theirs. I laughed to myself, wondering who we were hiding from—poachers, miners?

"No, it's not for people," he said, grinning. "It's for the animals. The less they see of us, the better."

We ate a quick breakfast and set off by speedboat, heading north along the Barito River toward the Kalaweit ranger station. The river was calm, and the towering trees that rose from its banks looked like ancient guardians, their roots twisting into the mud. As we weaved through small inlets, the forest closed in around us. The air was thick with humidity, the heat already oppressive even in the early morning.

Chapter 7 | **THE SILENCE OF THE GIBBONS** 263

When we arrived at the guard post, we transferred to a smaller boat for the next leg of the journey. I was given a larger seat—no complaints, as I am bulkier than the average Indonesian. The swampy forest soon gave way to the dense, towering trees of the Dulan, and we arrived at Butong Lake, a stunning stretch of water framed by massive trees reaching for the sky.

The trek through the Dulan was nothing short of grueling. Brutal heat pressed in on us as we set off on foot, our camo-clad figures blending into the forest. Every move felt like a test—the thick, damp air clung to my

Boating through the mangroves.
Credit: Chanee

skin, each step through the mud like pulling against the earth itself. The smell of wet leaves and rich soil filled my lungs as I fought off swarms of mosquitoes.

I slipped at one point, landing hard against a tree trunk, grunting in frustration.

"Softly," Chanee reminded me, glancing up at the canopy. "Orangutans are shy." He hoped to show me an orangutan in the wild, but chances were slim—shy was an understatement. Orangutans are ghosts in the forest, able to hold still for long periods without making a sound.

The hike stretched on for hours. The terrain was relentless, and I found myself wondering if we'd even see any wildlife. Just as I started to question the journey, Chanee stopped at a camera trap he had set up to monitor the area. We huddled around his iPad as he pulled up the footage.

What we saw left me speechless.

Clouded leopards, pigtailed macaques playing and tumbling like children, a sun bear sniffing the camera before wandering off, and even a Sumatran tiger padding confidently through the jungle, its powerful jaws open in a yawn. The sheer biodiversity of the Dulan Forest was astounding, and knowing that these animals roamed nearby sent a thrill through me—though the presence of a tiger was sobering.

Then Chanee pulled up a video clip that made my heart skip. Maurice.

"There he is," Chanee said, pointing at the screen. The massive orangutan moved slowly through the forest, his flanged face marking him as the dominant male. His reddish hair glowed in the sunlight filtering through the trees, his every move deliberate and calm.

"I've been following him for nearly two years," Chanee added. "I don't usually see him with guests, though. It's more common when I'm alone."

According to Chanee, Maurice was far more curious than most orangutans, often taking time to watch Chanee in return. Chanee decided to habituate Maurice not to humans in general but specifically to him by behaving in ways atypical of human patterns. "Every animal has its own definition of what a human is and how they act. If I behave outside of those expectations, the orangutan might spend more time trying to figure me out," he explained.

For example, when a gibbon sees a human approaching on the ground, it instinctively leaves. But if a gibbon encounters a human in the trees, it spends much longer observing, trying to understand what's happening. With Maurice, Chanee avoided making recognizable human noises—talking, walking, or using a machete. These sounds signal danger. Instead, Chanee blended into the forest, moving in ways that didn't fit Maurice's perception of human behavior.

Chanee had spent countless nights sleeping on the forest floor, becoming part of the landscape as he observed Maurice. "With some luck, we might see him today," he said.

Hope flickered in my chest. But I was also satisfied with the camera trap footage showing me that there were so many wonderful animals in the forest.

We continued our hike, the forest closing in around us with its ancient energy. Chanee pointed out an orangutan nest high up in the trees, but it seemed empty. Still, just knowing that Maurice was out there was enough to keep me going. Surveying his world, I felt small—humbled not by the forest's size but by its quiet strength. This forest, like Maurice, was ancient, wise. We weren't saving it; it was offering us a chance to protect something much larger than ourselves.

After another hour of trekking, we stopped for lunch beneath a towering kapok tree, its massive trunk providing shade. Prada had packed pasta in a creamy potato sauce, a simple yet satisfying meal after hours of exertion. As we ate, the sounds of the forest grew louder—gibbons calling, birds chattering, the forest announcing itself in full force.

"Is that because we've been still for a while?" I asked.

"No," Chanee replied, pulling his hood over his head. "They're warning us about the rain."

And sure enough, the sky opened up. The rain came down in sheets, turning the already treacherous terrain into a nightmare. The mud became even more unforgiving, and visibility dropped to almost nothing. I slipped and stumbled more than once, but Chanee and Andrew moved through the forest like they were born to it.

By the time we reached the boats, I was exhausted, drenched to the bone. For Chanee and Andrew, this was just another day in the Dulan.

We finally arrived at the ranger station. The rangers, all members of the local Dayak community, welcomed us warmly. Many of them had once worked as loggers or palm oil farmers, but now they were the forest's protectors, patrolling the area on horseback to guard against illegal activities.

The station itself was simple—two main structures, one communal with a kitchen and gear storage, the other a sleeping area with bunks. I was exhausted and glad for the chance to relax until dinner. I dropped my gear, washed up, and climbed into one of the bunks. Although the mattress was hard, the air was thick with humidity, and the jungle sounds filled my ears, I dozed off.

That night, Chanee rejoined us at dinner after six hours in the jungle on his own. It was well after dark, his face caked in mud, his clothes damp and stained, but the look on his face described his determination to find Maurice. "He made a nest for the night," he said, almost whispering as if afraid the forest might overhear. "We'll check it first thing in the morning."

At first light, we were back in our camouflage gear, moving through the jungle like shadows, slogging through the mud. After an hour of trekking, we approached Maurice's nest. We stopped, barely breathing, and waited.

The rustling came first. A stirring in the trees. Then, there he was. Maurice descended from his nest with the ease of a creature completely at home in his world. He stretched, his long arms reaching for the sky, one arm lingering as if holding on to the last remnants of sleep before he dropped it and began to amble on all fours across the forest floor.

Every move was deliberate, graceful despite his size. He moved like a king surveying his kingdom. Maurice climbed up into a tree, tore a strip of bark from the trunk, and began to munch on it, the crunching sound filling the stillness of the morning.

I could hardly breathe. Maurice was a symbol of everything we were fighting to protect—the soul of the Dulan Forest itself.

Chanee nudged me as Maurice moved higher into the tree, effortlessly snapping branches as thick as my wrist to reach a bunch of rambutan, plucking the spiny red fruits one by one, savoring his breakfast. He perched there, ten meters above us, effortlessly balancing on a branch, holding another in his free hand while he ate. His face, framed by his massive cheek pads, softened. His eyes were gentle, thoughtful even, as they scanned the forest. His gaze was always moving, always watching.

Chanee couldn't resist. He made a series of soft kissing and snorting sounds, a familiar call to Maurice. The orangutan paused, looked in our direction, and then continued his climb. For a moment, he descended toward us, then changed his mind and swung back up into the branches, as if to remind us that he was still in charge. It was clear that there was a kind of respect there—Maurice trusted Chanee enough not to bolt at the sound of his voice.

Then it started to rain. At first, just a few drops on Maurice's long, sparse hair. But soon the downpour began in earnest. We remained still on the forest floor to watch Maurice's reaction. That's when he formed the umbrella from a branch.

We watched Maurice until the forest visibility all but vanished, then made our way back to the ranger station. Nothing could wipe the smile from my face.

Borneo Flight Club

From the ranger station, we began our journey back downriver, our mud-streaked camos clinging to us like a second skin. Our next destination was Buntan Baru, a serene village nestled deep in the heart of Borneo. This place held a special significance for Chanee—it was here that he discovered a pristine 1,500-acre haven, untouched by the relentless creep of the palm oil industry and accessible only by seaplane.

Too often, villages like Buntan Baru fall victim to the systemic scourge of palm oil plantations. The forests are razed, replaced by endless rows of monoculture to feed the demand for palm oil found in nearly half of packaged products at the supermarket, despite the existence of viable alternatives. The fallout is devastating. Animals that wander into the plantations are shot, while villagers who sold their ancestral land find themselves consigned to grueling labor for the very plantations that displaced them. It's a lose-lose situation from the start, and Chanee knew this all too well.

"When I get depressed," Chanee said, solemnly steering his attention and pointing north, "I fly that way, into the northern Kalimantan region. It's massive and pristine, millions of hectares of untouched forests and no roads to reach it from here. But in the seaplane, I can land there." The northern region is yet untouched by commercialism and heavy human intervention. Those forests are ruled by the clouded leopard and orangutan. It's places like this that we still have time to protect on a large scale.

Recognizing the ecological value of Buntan Baru, Chanee moved swiftly, buying the land from the villagers at the same price the palm oil companies would have offered. But instead of taking it, he deeded the land back to the villagers with one condition: It would remain protected, never sold, and preserved for future generations.

This innovative approach safeguarded the land from future corporate takeovers. By putting ownership in the hands of the villagers, Chanee made them the protectors of their own future, while Kalaweit stayed one step removed from the line of fire.

As we made our way into the village, I noticed several tall, peculiar towers that seemed out of place. "Chanee, what are those?" I asked.

He chuckled, running a hand over his face. "Those are bird towers—for bird nest soup. The villagers took the money we gave them for the land and invested in these. They play artificial bird sounds to attract swiftlets, and once the nests are made from their saliva, they're harvested and sold to China for soup. It's a delicacy."

The constant drone of artificial bird calls filled the air, competing with the natural sounds of the jungle. The towers were impressive, but they felt like a metaphor for the forest itself—exploited, turned into something that serves a distant economy, disconnected from the land they were built upon.

Chapter 7 | **THE SILENCE OF THE GIBBONS** 269

As we walked through the village, sweat dripping down my face, I couldn't help but marvel at how our conservation efforts and the village's modern pursuits coexisted. Chanee reassured me about meeting the mayor while we were still caked in mud and grime from the forest.

"Dax," he said with a grin, "showing up like this, looking like we've been in the jungle, gives us credibility. They know we're in this fight, not just showing up in suits."

Inside the mayor's office, we were greeted warmly despite our appearance. The staff, dressed in their finest, didn't bat an eye at our muddy boots. Over tea and cookies, we discussed the future of the village and the critical importance of conserving the land. I spoke of my admiration for their commitment to preserving their home, emphasizing how their decision would impact not just the present, but generations to come.

Later that day, the weather cleared, offering us the perfect window to fly. From the sky, the contrast between the lush Dulan Forest and the surrounding devastation hit me harder than anything else. The coal mines, palm oil plantations, and gold mines were relentless, gnawing away at Borneo's forests. As Chanee and I climbed into the seaplane, I felt a sense of calm, knowing that we were fighting back in our own way.

The Borneo Flying Club.
Credit: Kalaweit

"The ultralight is perfect for this work," he said as we took off. "It's low-cost and easy to maneuver." He smiled, clearly at home in the cockpit. "But it's vulnerable. Bad weather could bring us down fast."

From the air, we could see the stark line where the forest ended and industry began. The fight to protect this land felt more urgent to me than ever. If we hadn't acted when we did, the Dulan would already be gone. Flying over the forest we were working to save gave me a new perspective—not just on the land, but on the importance of aerial patrol. This was the front line, and every inch of land protected was a victory.

Just beyond the Dulan reserve, coal mining pushes closer—one road at a time.
Credit: Dax Dasilva

Chapter 7 | **THE SILENCE OF THE GIBBONS**   271

Looking down at the endless miles of deforestation, I felt the weight of it all. If we didn't secure more land, everything Maurice represented—everything Chanee and I were fighting for—would vanish, like so many other species before him.

Chanee pointed to a national park below us, where palm oil plantations crept up to the borders. "That's the future we're fighting against," he said. "If we don't keep expanding, the forest will disappear." As we soared over the confused land, I realized that this wasn't the end of the mission; it was the beginning. Protecting the Dulan wasn't a victory we could rest on; it was a promise we had to keep, over and over, for every forest, every species, and every person willing to stand up and fight.

That evening, over dinner, I had news to share. "You've done something special here," I said, garnering Chanee's attention. "This place...the Dulan...it's more than just a sanctuary. It's hope."

Chanee smiled the kind of tired smile that comes after years of hard work and countless obstacles. "It's an excellent start," he said. "But there's so much more to do."

In town for a strategy meeting—discussing next steps in defending the Dulan Forest.
Credit: Dax Dasilva

I nodded, feeling the weight of his words. The challenges ahead were immense—the palm oil plantations, the mining, the relentless march of industry—but after spending time here and seeing Chanee's success with the forest, I knew we were on the right path. We had made a difference, even if it was a small one. And that difference was growing.

"I'm not done yet," I said, the decision forming in my mind as the words left my mouth. "I'm going to pledge the funds to secure more land—700 hectares. We need to protect every inch of this forest before it's too late."

Chanee's eyes widened, but then a look of calm resolve settled in. He extended his hand, and we shook, sealing the promise between us.

"We'll make it happen," he said with gratitude. "One step at a time." The moment felt significant—not just for me, but for Chanee, for the gibbons, and for the future of the entire forest.

The purchase of the final 700 hectares in southern Borneo was a monumental win for Kalaweit and for the future of the region's biodiversity. With that acquisition, we secured 3,000 hectares of protected land—vital habitat for tigers, sun bears, orangutans, and countless other species. It was the last available wilderness in the region, but it was enough to make a difference.

This expansion offset the carbon footprint of Age of Union's Black Hole Experience, a mobile immersive experience we launched in North America, inspired by the physics and spiritual properties of black holes. Working with artist Kelly Nunes, we created a one-of-a-kind mobile exhibition with a commitment to remain carbon neutral. The Dulan Forest became a key piece in that pledge.

I'm profoundly grateful for the journey that led me to Chanee and Kalaweit. To be part of his mission is to witness real change in action. Chanee is a visionary, constantly evolving and adapting to the challenges of conservation. His family, with their social media platforms and YouTube channels, reaches millions, spreading the message of rainforest preservation.

Chanee has taught me something invaluable: You can't solve these problems from a distance. You have to be on the ground, working side by side with local communities, creating tangible, lasting change.

The next morning brought a torrential downpour. Rain pounded the roof of Chanee's home as we packed up in silence, the jungle outside lost in a mist of falling water. I was zipped into my rain gear when Enzo burst into the room, eyes bright.

"Enzo wants to know if you'll come back when he gets his pilot's license," Chanee said, smiling. "He wants to take you flying over the forest."

I turned to Enzo. "Absolutely. I promise. And by then, let's make sure we've protected even more land—for the gibbons, and everyone who calls this place home."

I hugged Chanee and said goodbye to his family. As the rain softened, my thoughts drifted back to Maurice—the way he moved through the canopy with quiet command, as if he were the spirit of the forest itself. He reminded me that every inch of forest we save matters. That these victories, though hard-won and often small, carry weight.

Maurice was still out there. Watching. Surviving. And as long as he did, maybe we had a chance too.

Spelunking through limestone caves, searching for traces of extinct giants beneath the surface.
Credit: Will Allen

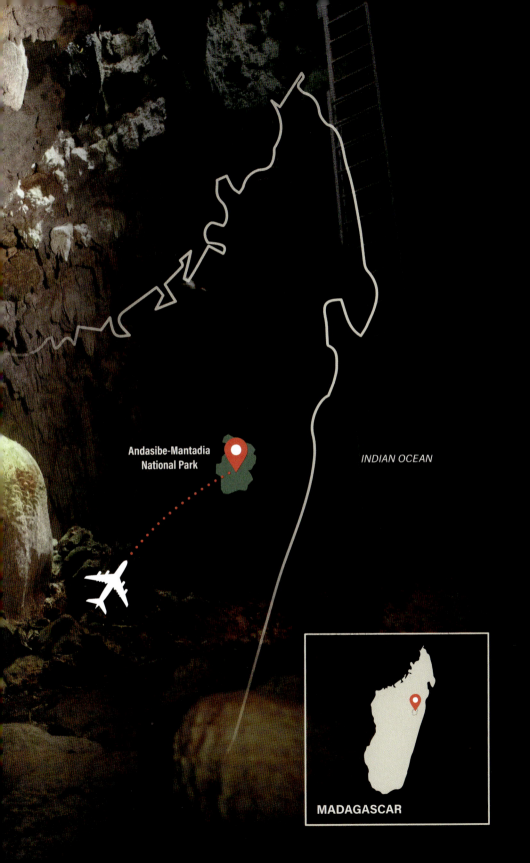

Across Madagascar's red dust, a chameleon drifts like a living brushstroke.
Credit: Will Allen

Chapter 8

WHISPERS OF THE INDRI

A JOURNEY THROUGH MADAGASCAR TO THE EDGE OF EXTINCTION

If I ever found myself stranded in the wild—lost in a dense jungle or a spiny desert, unsure whether the surrounding flora and fauna would save me or seal my doom—there's no question who I'd want by my side: Dr. Russell Mittermeier.

I'd heard the stories—legends, really—of Russ's encounters with danger. Tales of navigating Indigenous turf wars in Papua New Guinea, of surviving—after being trapped in the remote wilderness—for weeks with his son Michael ("Mick"), living off the land until their eventual rescue. With his encyclopedic knowledge of the natural world, Russ could find food, build shelter, and read the landscape like a map. After spending a week traversing Madagascar with both of them, I can say with certainty that none of those stories were exaggerated.

Dr. Russell Mittermeier is one of the most accomplished conservationists of our time. A Harvard-trained primatologist, herpetologist, and global biodiversity strategist, he has discovered more than two dozen species, authored hundreds of scientific papers, and helped establish more protected areas than nearly anyone alive. The former president of Conservation International and now Chief Conservation Officer at Re:wild—a global conservation organization founded by scientists and actor Leonardo

DiCaprio to protect and restore the wild—Russ has spent over fifty years on the front lines of the world's most endangered ecosystems. His fieldwork spans more than sixty countries, but Madagascar is the epicenter of his life's work.

Russ invited me to visit the island he now calls home. He's dedicated his life to preserving Madagascar's extraordinary biodiversity—most urgently, its lemurs. Madagascar is widely regarded as one of the world's most critical biodiversity hot spots, but it's also suffering one of the fastest and most extreme rates of ecological collapse. With over 90 percent of its original forest already lost, the country is in free fall—ravaged by deforestation, illegal mining, and unsustainable agriculture. What's left of the forest is disappearing fast, and with it, the lemurs.

"You need to come," Russ told me. "Madagascar is at its tipping point—one of the only places on Earth where we could lose entire evolutionary lineages in the space of a decade."

That's not theoretical. That's reality.

I took his recommendation and flew to Antananarivo with photographer Justin Kingsley and filmmaker Will Allen. Russ and Mick met us at the airport with smiles as bright as the Madagascar sun.

"Welcome to the land of lemurs, chameleons, and baobabs!" Russ grinned, his enthusiasm infectious. Dressed in his iconic Nat Geo-style vest with a lightweight backpack slung over his shoulder, he looked every bit the seasoned adventurer I'd imagined.

Mick—an expert botanist who'd spent years exploring Madagascar's ecosystems—was just as prepared, eager to guide us through the island's dense flora and surreal biodiversity. The adventure had officially begun.

Russ isn't one to waste time. "I had the palace and museum tour planned for tomorrow," he said, "but since you're here now and the day's still young, let's get started!" He gave us little chance to catch our breath. That's Russ's pace—go, go, go.

After a quick bag drop at the Carlton Hotel, we were off. First stop: the Queen's Palace and its museum. The original palace was destroyed in a fire in 1995. Now, its artifacts and relics—alongside skeletons of extinct species—are displayed in what feels like a shrine to what's been lost.

The extinct flightless elephant bird that once inhabited Madagascar.
Credit: Dax Dasilva

Inside, we stood beneath the skeletal remains of the elephant bird, a ten-foot-tall flightless giant that once thundered across the island. Nearby, the fossil of a giant lemur, a gentle creature that once roamed Madagascar's forests.

"These lemurs were the size of a male gorilla," Russ said. "Madagascar was home to a whole host of giants. But as humans spread across the island, the larger animals were the first to disappear—just like we're seeing today with rhinos, tigers, elephants." His voice trailed off. "But tomorrow, we'll go see some living animals. You're in for a real treat, Dax."

I couldn't wait.

Back at the hotel, the sun was beginning its slow descent over Lake Anosy, casting the water in molten gold hues. A soft breeze carried across the surface, breaking it into shimmering ripples. Justin, Will, and I sat out on the terrace outside my room. A Madagascar wagtail perched on the railing, its white and black feathers luminous against the pastel sky.

No fear, just respect. Russ holds a native snake, calm and curious in the wild.
Credit: Will Allen

Bougainvillea flowers spilled down the walls in vibrant pink and violet. It was a moment of calm in a place where the wild still whispered.

The next morning, we rose early and headed for Andasibe-Mantadia National Park, deep in the Eastern Rain Forest. We had planned to take a helicopter, but it was New Year's Eve, and with a shortage of aircraft on the island, ours had been claimed—requisitioned by the president. So, we drove.

It was during that four-hour drive through the highlands that the scale of Madagascar's deforestation hit me. Hills that should have been thick with forest were stripped bare. No canopy. No shade. No sign of the dense, living world that once thrived here.

"This used to be rainforest," Russ said, gesturing toward a landscape of exposed clay and sparse scrub.

For centuries, swidden agriculture—slash-and-burn farming—has stripped Madagascar of its native forests. First introduced by Indonesian

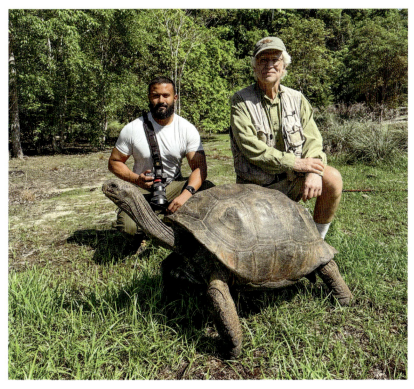

In the company of wisdom—Russ kneels before a creature that remembers more than we ever will.
Credit: Dax Dasilva

settlers around the year 600, the practice clears land for crops like upland rice. But the soil here is shallow, the nutrients quickly depleted. Within a few years, the land is exhausted, and the cycle begins again: more burning, more clearing, more loss.

Later, in the 1950s, the World Bank introduced eucalyptus as a fast-growing replacement for native trees, aiming to fuel railways and commerce. But eucalyptus proved a poor substitute—an invasive, water-hungry species that offered little to wildlife and choked the soil of its last reserves. The ecological cost was staggering.

"I've seen environmental disasters before," I said, watching the landscape blur by. "But this feels like the worst-case scenario. It's like looking at Haiti's future if they don't turn things around soon."

Russ nodded. "It's a warning. We already know what's going to happen in other regions if we don't act. Madagascar is a textbook case. Ninety percent deforestation. Second only to Haiti. If you want to see the consequences of ecological mismanagement—this is it."

I turned to him. "Why here, Russ? Why not the Amazon, or somewhere with more forest left to study all the biodiversity?"

"It's a naturalist's dream here," he said. "A wildlife experience you won't find anywhere else. And there's not a poisonous snake in sight—well, not one that'll kill you quickly, anyway," he added with a grin.

Then his tone shifted. "But more importantly, I don't believe in giving up on any species. These animals evolved here after Madagascar split from Africa 180 million years ago. Now, after centuries of exploitation, it's our responsibility to put things right."

As we continued east, the roadside attractions became part of the education. A crocodile farm. A reptile park. We saw ploughshare tortoises—some of the most endangered reptiles on the planet. On the black market, Russ said, one could fetch up to $100,000. It was hard to reconcile the gentle creatures before us with their obscene valuation in the illegal wildlife trade.

But what made this road trip extraordinary wasn't just the landscape or the wildlife; it was the Mittermeiers.

Russ—methodical, generous, impossibly well-read—could identify any species on sight. Mick, with his deep botanical knowledge, layered in details about everything we passed—plants, fungi, soil chemistry, native uses. Their rhythm was fast. Their banter, nonstop.

Between the two, their grasp of the island's vast microclimates and ecosystems was staggering. No insect buzzed by without someone calling out its Latin name. No plant was too small or insignificant to escape their notice. And when it came to the animals, they knew them all.

"What's this species—in Latin, please?" Russ would ask, pointing to a bright caterpillar with pink tubercles.

"Too easy—*Antherina suraka*," Mick responded.

"Okay, hotshot, but what butterfly does it become?" Russ asked.

"Nice try, Dad. It's a silk moth, not a butterfly," said Mick. "That's the Madagascar bullseye moth."

Russ grinned. "Thought I had you that time."

Between their playful competition, there wasn't a moment on that journey when I wasn't learning something new.

I asked Mick how he'd ended up choosing plants.

"I realized early I couldn't beat him at his own game," he said, nodding toward his father. "So I chose botany. Dad's a primatologist and herpetologist. My brother's an ornithologist. We divided up the kingdom."

I laughed. "The Mittermeiers cover it all."

Lemurs

We finally arrived in Andasibe—a lush green pocket of primary forest and a rare refuge for Madagascar's largest lemur, the indri. The contrast was staggering. We had crossed miles of dry, deforested terrain where nothing remained but stripped hillsides and skeletal earth. Now, it felt like we had stumbled into another world. The air was thick, alive, buzzing with energy. Above us, the indri's barking calls echoed through the canopy. It was a welcome that needed no translation.

Russ, suddenly energized by the forest's hum, grinned as we stepped into the shade of the towering trees. "Ah, the indri," he said, with a tone that held a mix of reverence and excitement. "It's a hard choice, but probably my favorite genus of primate. It's a privilege to be this close to them in the wild."

The indri, famous for their haunting calls that echo through the treetops.
Credit: Will Allen

A curious diademed sifaka—one of Madagascar's most striking and endangered lemurs.
Credit: Will Allen

Not high in the trees, several of them watched us. Their black-and-white fur reminded me of a panda's, and they didn't seem alerted or in any need to flee as we approached. Then the soundscape shifted. The high-pitched barks gave way to softer, almost intimate kissing sounds—it was a ghostly yet human sound.

"What's happening?" I whispered, not wanting to disturb the moment.

Russ leaned in, smiling. "The songs of the indri are among the most sophisticated vocalizations in the primate world," he said. "But this particular tune? That's their way of showing affection. What you're hearing is the gentle side of their social world."

I stood in awe, watching as the indri launched themselves effortlessly between trees, each leap spanning up to thirty feet. They moved like poetry.

"I've never seen anything like this," I admitted, unable to take my eyes off them. "I see why you love them so much."

Limbs like levers, eyes like moons—a Verreaux's sifaka grips the bark with quiet elegance.
Credit: Will Allen

"I'll share three reasons," he said. "What fascinates me most about the indri is their vocalizations—unlike any other mammal besides humans. They can use rhythm in their calls, and those barks you heard earlier? They can last for minutes, sometimes coordinated between individuals. It's hauntingly beautiful."

I listened carefully to the forest. "That's incredible," I murmured. "It sounds like they're singing a duet."

"Exactly," Russ said, nodding. "And there's more. The indri are monogamous for life. If they lose a mate, they'll seek out another, but only after a long period of mourning. It's a bond we rarely see in the animal kingdom."

The weight of that statement hung in the air. It seemed humans could learn a lot more than we think from lemurs.

"And the third?" I asked.

A collared brown lemur peers from the foliage.
Credit: Will Allen

Russ's expression softened. "Every morning, after sunrise, the indri will face the sun, legs crossed, backs straight, their hands resting low with palms outward, almost like they're meditating. It's a moment of stillness that looks uncannily like sun worship. Some scientists hesitate to call it that, worried about being too anthropomorphic, but the Malagasy believe that's exactly what it is—the indri honoring the sun."

I watched intently at an indri on a tree branch just a few feet from me. It studied me with its yellow eyes. I loved the idea of these creatures, so deeply attuned to their world, facing the rising sun as though in quiet prayer.

"It's almost as if they understand something deeper, something beyond our grasp," I said.

Russ's eyes flickered with a knowing look, and I continued, thinking aloud: "If we accuse ourselves of being too anthropomorphic—assigning spiritual behavior to animals—isn't that just the same as denying the

The smallest primate—the gray mouse lemur.
Credit: Will Allen

possibility? Who are we to say that there aren't animals capable of some form of spirituality?"

Mick stepped up to take a closer look at the indri. "You're starting to see it, Dax," he said. "There may be more to all this than science can explain."

As the indri continued their soft calls, I felt a strange compulsion to mimic them. After the next indri call, I called back. To my surprise, they responded. I repeated my call, and again, the indri answered, as if we were in conversation.

Russ noticed. "You're talking to them," he said. "It's not by chance; the indri are incredibly intelligent."

But as we continued our walk through the forest, the beauty of the moment gave way to a heavier reality. Russ's voice grew somber.

"As remarkable as they are, the indri are critically endangered. And most scientists believe it's already too late to save them."

I stopped, my heart heavy. "But we aren't going to give up on them."

Russ exhaled. "That's why we're here."

The challenges are immense. The indri reproduce slowly. Females only give birth every three years. And while there were once cultural taboos against hunting them, those traditions are eroding. Extreme poverty, the collapse of cultural norms, and immigration have all contributed to their hunting. In some places, indri meat is considered a delicacy.

"Their fate is tied to human efforts," he said. "And we've pushed them past their limits. Without serious intervention, they don't stand a chance."

We spent the rest of the day exploring the forest, with Russ and Mick sharing details about what we saw.

We encountered diademed sifakas, or "crowned lemurs." Russ called them the most colorful and attractive of all the lemurs, with their silky silver bodies and fox-red legs.

Farther in, we spotted a group of black-and-white ruffed lemurs snacking on fruits and flowers. These lemurs, critically endangered, have seen their population decline by 80 percent in the past thirty years. But what amazed me most was that they are the largest pollinators on Earth, vital to the survival of Madagascar's traveler's tree. They drink nectar, and as they move from tree to tree, they spread pollen. The survival of these trees—and many other species—depends on the lemurs.

As we walked through Andasibe, Russ shared stories of local efforts to protect the lemurs and their habitats. "Ecotourism is the key," he explained. It's likely the only sustainable way forward for Madagascar. If they can create programs that protect these animals and bring revenue to the local people, they can preserve what's left. But it's a tough battle. Madagascar is a poor country with a weak infrastructure, and the government struggles to enforce protections.

It became clear that the future of these lemurs—and this entire ecosystem—rested in the hands of the local communities. The guides who worked in the forest were part of that effort, forming associations that managed community reserves. They were scrappy. With very little funding, they were preserving vast stretches of forest.

That night, after hours on our feet, Russ turned to me at dinner with a grin. "Grab your headlamp. We're going for a night walk."

We strapped on lights and stepped into the dark.

Madagascar changed at night. Chameleons turned white and curled into sleeping spirals, tails looped tight. They glowed in our headlamps.

Celebrating New Year's with our Madagascar crew: Justin, Will, Russ, Mick, and me.
Credit: Dax Dasilva / Age of Union

Then we found her—Madame Berthe's mouse lemur. The smallest primate in the world. No bigger than a thumb. She sat frozen on a twig, eyes wide like planets.

"She only lives here," Russ whispered. "Nowhere else."

Then he explained: In this forest, and only here, grows a specific liana vine. On it, a single species of white flower bug feeds on sap. That bug produces a sugary "honeydew." And that honeydew is critical to the Madame Berthe's diet.

A vine. A bug. A sugar drop. A lemur. This is how the world works.

Madame Berthe's mouse lemur was discovered in 1992. She's already critically endangered. If deforestation continues, she'll be extinct within ten years. There are no captive populations. No backups.

Every animal we saw—lemur, chameleon, bird, insect—lives on the edge of disappearance. The beauty of that forest walk was shadowed by its fragility.

Back at the Mantadia Lodge, we made it to midnight—barely. A champagne toast. A few tired smiles. And sleep.

The new year had arrived. But for Madagascar's wildlife, it felt less like a celebration and more like a prayer.

Berenty

The next day, we boarded a pair of small aircraft headed for the Berenty Reserve—a private enclave inside a vast sisal plantation in Madagascar's arid south. From the air, the landscape below shifted dramatically. Closed-canopy tamarind forest gave way to open scrub. Then the spiny forest appeared—strange, towering, otherworldly. It felt like descending onto another planet. Of all the landscapes I encountered in Madagascar, this one was the most surreal—and it quickly became my favorite.

Sisal fields stretched endlessly across the earth, regimented rows of sword-shaped plants. Hardy, efficient, and almost militaristic, they grew like bayonets in formation. These fibers were used to make rope, paper, and textiles and supported many local communities. And while much of this land had been cleared long ago, the plantation had done something rare: Between blocks of sisal, wide buffers of native spiny forest had been left intact. Not by accident. By design.

Baobabs too big to fell stood as ancient monuments, rising above the green blades like mythic watchtowers. And in the preserved forest corridors, biodiversity still thrived. It created an odd rhythm—rows of cultivation followed by wild pulses of endemic life. In a country where deforestation has wiped out nearly everything, it felt like a blueprint for coexistence. Not perfect, but promising. I couldn't help but wonder if Borneo might benefit from this kind of compromise—agriculture that breathes.

As we entered the reserve, I lit up. Ring-tailed lemurs were everywhere—on the trails, in the trees, walking with tails held high like flags.

"These are some of the most terrestrial lemurs," Russ said. "Unlike the

"Dancing" sifaka lemurs move across the ground with an elegant, bipedal sideways leap—a unique adaptation to life in Madagascar's trees. Credit: Andrey Gudkov

indri, they spend nearly half their time on the ground. Their tails act like visual signals to keep the troop together."

A mother with two babies clinging to her back moved past us, her amber eyes watching intently. She trotted across the trail with an unbothered confidence. There was something magnetic about them—their charisma, their awareness, their swagger.

"Like the indri, they're also highly vocal," Russ added. "Different calls for different functions—cohesion, alarm, territory."

As if on cue, a loud chattering erupted overhead.

"That's a repulsive call," Russ said. "Something's made them uneasy. Probably Mick."

Mick shot him a look. "Careful, old man. I'll remember that."

Then Russ, grinning, launched into an explanation of one of their stranger behaviors.

"Stink fights," he said. "Mating season. Males have scent glands on their wrists and shoulders. They rub their tails through the glands and waft the stink at one another until one backs down."

Children of Berenty—keepers of culture, seeds of change.
Credit: Will Allen

Mick didn't miss a beat. "Dad used to do that to get his spot on the couch."

We burst out laughing.

Soon after, we saw two male lemurs mid-duel, tails raised, circling each other like fencers in a standoff. The smell, Russ assured us, was "indescribable."

"They'll keep going for an hour sometimes," he said. "The scent gets stronger with every pass."

"Sounds exhausting," I said. "And stinky."

"Both," Russ confirmed.

Deeper into the reserve, we encountered Verreaux's sifakas—the dancing lemurs. Specialized for arboreal life, they can't walk like other lemurs. So, when forced to cross the ground, they perform a side-stepping ballet—arms raised, feet kicking out, like dancers floating sideways.

They moved like ballerinas—graceful and controlled. Nearby, a juvenile sifaka swung from branch to branch, clumsily testing its skills under its mother's watch. At one point, it grabbed her tail, mistaking it for another vine. She scooped it back with maternal reflexes.

The landscape was just as surreal. Alluaudia plants surrounded us—candelabra-like spines reaching toward the sky. What looked dangerous and inhospitable to us was effortless for the sifakas. They leapt thirty feet through the thorny maze like it was nothing.

As much as I was falling for Madagascar's lemurs, Russ and Mick made sure the rest of the island's biodiversity didn't go unnoticed. They pointed out birds, insects, fungi, and reptiles at every turn, deepening my appreciation for the island's complexity.

Later, as we passed through the gallery forest, Mick pulled a long, slender leaf-nosed snake from a tree branch.

"Here, Dax!" he said, smiling wickedly.

I backed up. "Nope. Give it to Will."

Will didn't flinch. He took the snake in one hand. It coiled casually around his wrist. A moment later, Russ walked up with a boa constrictor and handed it to Will's other hand.

Now holding two snakes, Will looked at us. "At least they're not venomous."

Russ tilted his head. "Actually, that one is. But it has rear fangs, so... probably fine."

Will laughed nervously and gently set the snakes back in the brush.

Later that afternoon, we met the Tandroy, the "people of the thorns," a nomadic group indigenous to Madagascar's south. On Berenty, they've long worked alongside Benedicte, the reserve's French landowner. She provides jobs, education, and healthcare for many, including the Tandroy. Conservation here wasn't abstract—it was tangible. The Tandroy were the forest's guardians.

One of the Tandroy men offered us a swig of local moonshine. It smelled like diesel. Will took a cautious sip. His face turned inside out. "Like swallowing a live match," he coughed.

We all howled with laughter.

"This," Russ said, gesturing around at the smiling kids, the lemurs dozing on tree limbs, the careful balance of community and ecology, "this is what conservation looks like when it works. It's not just about saving animals. It's about giving people a reason to protect them."

At Benedicte's home, we met her tortoises—dozens of radiated tortoises that had been rescued from poachers. Over twenty-three thousand had been confiscated in recent years. Many of them were sleeping in her house.

Before we left, I hugged her. "I don't know who's going to carry this on when you're gone," I said. "But it's extraordinary."

She smiled. "We'll find a way."

Just before departure, our Tandroy friend returned with hand-forged spears and axes. They were beautifully made, traditional tools passed down through generations. Without thinking too far ahead, I bought three—one for each of us.

"You're going to have fun getting those through customs," Russ said. Then, smiling, "Don't worry. I've done it a few times."

He told us about his collection of more than 150 tribal blowguns, each one smuggled home piece by piece.

That night, Russ wrapped the spears and axes in towels and duct tape until they looked far less suspicious. To determine who'd carry them through customs, we did the only sensible thing: rock, paper, scissors.

Of course, I lost.

A Spelunking Adventure

We flew from Berenty to Morondava on the western coast of Madagascar, where we drove the famed Highway of the Baobabs—sentinel trees rising from the ground like living monoliths.

Baobabs are unlike anything else on Earth. These ancient giants have adapted to the island's extremes by becoming natural reservoirs, storing thousands of liters of water in their swollen trunks to withstand the long dry seasons. When the land around them withers, the baobabs endure—producing nutrient-rich fruit that feeds both wildlife and humans. If there's any tree that resembles a dinosaur, it's this one—the tree of life, as the locals call it. Their girth alone often spares them from chainsaws during mass deforestation.

"Baobabs predate the splitting of the continents," Russ said, gazing up at one of the towering elders.

Kirindy Forest—12,500 hectares of dry forest and one of Madagascar's most important ecological reserves—was next on our list of stops. But even here, in this rare stronghold of biodiversity, the threat was ever-present. Locals, desperate for farmland, had turned to fire. And the flames were creeping closer.

"The loss of dry forest here," Russ said, "is one of the most tragic things happening in the world right now. If we don't act, this entire ecosystem could vanish in five to ten years."

Thanks to support from Re:wild, the reserve had boots on the ground—twenty-five local rangers and four armed guards patrolling for land clearers and poachers. It wasn't enough, but it was something.

"If we lose Kirindy," Russ said, "we lose everything that depends on it."

From there, we flew to Anjajavy in the northwest. The landscape changed again: white sand beaches, pristine forest, and bungalows perched above the surf. It felt like a break.

Will and I were sick—most likely from a sketchy roadside meal en route to Kirindy. We needed rest. But Russ had other plans.

"We're going spelunking," he said.

There was a cave nearby—deep, wild, and full of surprises. Geological formations. Fossils. Maybe even a few ghosts.

The trail to the cave led us through a swampy forest that felt more alien than terrestrial. Mud sucked at our boots. Dozens of crab holes pocked the path, and land crabs the size of grapefruits peered up at us, claws raised.

"This feels like a sci-fi set," I said.

"They're harmless," Russ replied, grinning. "Just sifting the soil."

At the cave mouth, we geared up in harnesses, helmets, and headlamps and descended into the dark. The ladders were steep. The air cooled fast. Wingbeats brushed my face. Bats, everywhere.

In Peru, I'd once balked at sleeping beneath a bat-covered roof. But I'd changed. The journey had recalibrated my sense of fear and awe.

Madagascar's iconic baobabs—sentinels of time rising from red earth.
Credit: Will Allen

At the bottom of the cave, scattered in the dust, were the bones of giants—skulls of extinct sloth lemurs, long vanished but still looming in Malagasy legend.

"Humans arrived here around two thousand years ago," Russ said, crouching by a skull. "And that's when these guys began disappearing. They were part of the forest's engine. Their loss changed everything."

Giant lemurs once moved through the canopy like gorillas—big, strong, graceful. Now, they're ghosts. Looking at their remains in the quiet of that cave, I felt it: the full weight of extinction. These weren't just animals. They were evolutionary epics, each one ending mid-sentence.

Madagascar's biodiversity is still unlike anything else on Earth. But it's on the brink. The work that Russ and Re:wild are doing—alongside the local communities fighting to preserve what's left—isn't just noble. It's necessary. Urgent. It's a defense against silence.

The next morning, we took a boat into Narinda Bay, where the "mushroom islands" rise like floating mesas—massive rock plateaus balanced on thin stalks, carved by erosion, time, and rain.

These formations were home to lemurs, native baobabs, and one of the rarest birds on the planet: the Madagascar fish eagle. Fewer than three hundred remain.

"I'm not much of a birder," I said, "but this feels like a bucket list sighting."

Russ nodded. "You're lucky. Not many people get to see one."

That evening, we gathered on the beach for dinner. The sky was ablaze with color—lavender, flame, gold. Spiny lizards darted between the boardwalk planks. A Madagascar day gecko clung to a tree trunk, so vivid it looked painted on.

It felt like this world was showing off—one last burst of beauty before the final leg of our adventure.

Chapter 8 | **WHISPERS OF THE INDRI** 299

Lazarus Species

The Anjajavy International Airport is a casual affair—a red dirt landing strip and an open-air thatched-roof bar, with go-carts ready to take you from the bar to the aircraft. Planes take off over the clear waters of the Mozambique Channel with views of mainland Africa on the horizon.

We arrived on time for our chartered flight inland to Antsohihy, but departure time here refers to when the pilot has finished his aircraft preparations—and his lunch. This was regular scheduling, according to Russ, so we sat at the bar and ordered a baobab juice, a drink made from baobab fruit that had quickly become my favorite.

As we waited for the pilot, I asked Russ what we were doing next. We had been constantly on the move, and I couldn't keep track of his itinerary.

Russ leaned in. "Dax, have you ever heard of a Lazarus species?"

"I know the Bible story," I said. "Jesus raised Lazarus from the dead, right?"

A pair of Madagascar pochards in the dormant volcano lake—once thought extinct, now symbols of hope restored. Credit: Will Allen

He nodded, a smile tugging at his lips. "Exactly. In conservation, we use the term for organisms we thought were long gone—extinct—but are rediscovered. Seeing one is like glimpsing a ghost."

Mick chimed in, his tone factual. "Although technically, they weren't dead. They just managed to avoid human detection."

I thought back to something I'd read. "Like the coelacanth, right? That ancient fish they found after sixty million years?"

"Precisely," Russ said. "We're going to see one—a duck, no less."

Russ was referring to the Madagascar pochard—considered to be extinct in recent times. But during scientific explorations twenty years ago, a Malagasy biologist named Lily-Arison Rene de Roland rediscovered the pochard. There were fewer than one hundred pochards in the world, and they lived on a lake inside the crater of a dormant volcano. We were headed to see this rare bird, and Rene was coming with us.

We flew to Antsohihy, unpacked most of our gear at the lodge, and prepped for a helicopter trip to Bemanevika, a shanty conservation camp at the base of the volcano. There, we would begin our hike up, over, and into the dormant crater. This area was so remote and accessing it was so challenging that the lake was visited by fewer than thirty people per year.

I took the minimum—a water bottle and camera. Will, on the other hand, is a bit of a doomsday prepper, always ready for every possibility. He had a fully loaded survival backpack—satellite phone, water filtration kit, fire starters, nutrition packs, first-aid supplies, and more. But when we got to the helicopter, the pilot gave the backpack one look and said, "Nope—too heavy. Just the essentials. It's only a few hours."

Looking glum, Will reluctantly left his gear behind. With a camera over his shoulder and water bottle in hand, he now looked as unprepared as the rest of us.

The chopper couldn't take all of us in one trip, so Russ, Mick, and I flew first while Rene, Justin, and Will waited for the pilot to return and make a second run.

Pochard ducklings. Credit: Will Allen

As we hovered over the mountains, I looked down at the lush green valleys. Everywhere we had been, Madagascar felt like another world altogether, a relatively small island containing so many different microclimates—especially here, in an area too remote for industries to extract from.

Reunited with our team at the Bemanevika base camp, where conservationist guides were stationed to protect the wildlife, we started our ascent up the volcano.

The forecast was grim. Our bush pilot gave us a stern warning: "If the weather turns bad, you need to come back. I cannot fly in bad conditions, and we will have to stay here."

I nodded quickly. The last thing I wanted was to get stranded on a volcano in the middle of nowhere—not exactly on my bucket list.

We hiked about five miles, circling the volcano until we reached the ridge. From there, the view was breathtaking. Down inside the dormant mountain was a massive pristine lake surrounded by thick rainforest.

We descended into the forest, passing ancient palms and vines that tangled their way up into the canopy, the air damp and cool after a recent rain. The silence began to break as birds announced our arrival. We were walking through a land that time had forgotten.

Russ and Mick were still in competition as we made our way down to the lake.

"This gray emutail?" Russ challenged, pointing out a small long-tailed warbler. "*Bradypterus seebohmi*," answered Mick without looking.

A spectacular blue-and-white bird danced and sang nearby. "*Cyanolanius madagascarinus*," Mick said, this time without being quizzed by his father.

Satisfied for the moment, Russ continued hiking toward the shore and then spotted something in the reeds. "And this little fella?" he asked.

"That's a common snipe," Mick said, feeling unchallenged—the stocky brown bird's long, slender beak was a dead giveaway.

"Incorrect!" exclaimed Russ, startling me with the newfound pep in his step. "This guy is a juvenile Madagascan snipe—still showing fringing along his upper-wing coverts."

It had finally happened. I had no idea what fringing coverts were, but Russ had stumped Mick at name-that-bird and was basking in the glory.

Along the marshy shoreline of the lake there was a dock—odd branches tied together with old twine, reaching through the reeds to form a canoe launch. Through the reeds, we could see a few birds on the water, and the Mittermeiers were back at it—naming Madagascar grebes, Meller's ducks, a Madagascar rail. I took out my camera and started snapping pictures.

The real prize revealed itself near the center of the lake—a small group of mahogany-colored ducks with striking white eyes. The Lazarus species: Madagascar pochards—few, but alive and well on the water.

And there were babies—ducklings. Several juveniles trailed their mother. My heart melted as I watched them scoot around and practice with their wings, chasing each other, feeding. Ducks once thought to be extinct, now present and beautiful before us on this remote, nearly inaccessible lake.

Then it started to rain. The pochards loved it, flapping their wings so that we could see their hidden white interiors as the droplets hit the surface of the water. Rene, Justin, and I returned to the shore, while Will and the Mittermeiers continued filming.

With the rain still only a drizzle, I wanted to see if we could find a rare owl that Rene had told us about. Rene led Justin and me through the thick, wet forest. He quickly spotted and pointed out the camouflaged bird roosted low and conspicuous.

"This is another bird once thought to be extinct," Rene explained, pointing out the Madagascar red owl, rediscovered in this region about thirty years ago. "They are only found in this region of Madagascar." The owl's heart-shaped white face twitched, and it briefly opened its big black eyes, then drifted back to sleep, nuzzling into a puff of gray feathers. It was beautiful to see, and a bonus—another rediscovered species.

The drizzle turned into a full-blown downpour, and the sky darkened ominously. I could hear the pilot's warning echoing in my mind: *If the weather turns bad, you need to come back.* Anxiety crept up my spine as I looked around. The pilot had already glanced at the sky several times, frowning deeply.

"We have to go," I said to Justin, urgency in my voice.

Without hesitation, Justin agreed. "Yeah, let's move."

We went back to the lake, but Will and the Mittermeiers didn't seem fazed, photographing and observing in the torrent.

I wasn't comfortable with waiting. Neither was Justin. The pilot seemed serious. He would need to make two trips, and I wanted to be on the first.

The trek back was brutal. Mud clung to our boots, and the path—barely visible—slipped beneath us. I could feel my heart pounding as we descended through the dense forest, the mist thickening around us. My mind kept returning to the others on the lake. Would they make it back in time?

We reached the helicopter, soaked to the bone. The pilot shook his head. "The mist is getting worse. We have a very narrow window. We fly now, or we stay here."

I glanced back, wishing I could somehow signal to the others. Several calls to Russ's phone went unanswered.

"Let's go," I said, climbing into the chopper with Justin.

The pilot took off and we flew low, navigating between mountains and through the thick fog. As we passed over the volcano ridge, we saw Will, Mick, and Russell just starting back down the trail. Will waved at us as we circled the volcano and headed into the mist. I imagined them stopping to inspect every lizard, frog, and bird without paying heed to the one instruction we'd received from the pilot. My mind wandered until the pounding rain brought me right back into the moment.

The rain hit the helicopter windows like a barrage of pebbles, the wipers futile against the onslaught. Our pilot's knuckles tightened on the controls, eyes scanning for a break in the fog. My heart pounded louder than the rotors, waiting for either disaster or a sliver of clear sky. I could feel the chopper being pushed around by the strength of the tempest.

"I don't think we can make it," said the pilot. "But we also cannot go back. I'm going to try to fly low."

He seemed relatively cool, but everything happening felt very dangerous. Our chopper blowing around in the wind. No visibility. Then a mountain would appear. I wished I had stayed on the lake.

Through the storm, the pilot masterfully navigated through tiny clearances and eventually down to a river, flying very close to the ground, just above the water. Somehow, he followed the river and made it back to Antsohihy.

After we landed, the pilot broke the news.

"I can't go back," he said. "The weather's too dangerous. I'll try in the morning—it might not even be possible then."

Russ, Mick, and Will were stranded on the volcano. There was nothing we could do. I tried Russ's satellite phone again.

No signal. No word. Just rain.

Boarding a helicopter in Antsohihy, Madagascar.
Credit: Will Allen

Stranded

Back on the volcano, Will, Russ, and Mick descended the ridge, spotting the helicopter above them on its way out. They paused to admire a salamander, then a chameleon, and then a snake. Eventually, they made it back to camp. Russell's satellite phone rang.

"What do you mean, he's not coming back for us?" Russ barked into the phone. He was disgruntled, but this wasn't his first rodeo. He knew what it meant.

They would stay the night at the shanty camp and, with luck, be picked up in the morning. Will was displeased about being without his survival pack—but he did have Russ and Mick.

Using ropes, they crossed a river into the camp. The guides offered them an extra tent and pads to sleep on. One guide began hulling rice and prepared some food.

According to Will, Russ wasn't fazed in the slightest; he had been stranded in far worse conditions. Five minutes later, he was showing off a chameleon endemic to that valley, and then a rare caterpillar. Next came a visit from a troop of common brown lemurs. They were less habituated to humans but comfortable enough to approach and snatch a few cashews from Russ's hand.

That evening, they shared rice and stew around a fire on the dirt floor. It wasn't much, but it was enough to keep them dry and off the muddy ground.

Back at the lodge, I couldn't sleep. The rain had caused a power outage. I was concerned about our friends. I knew they'd be fine with Russ, but being separated didn't feel great. When the lights flickered on occasionally, I discovered a colony of giant cockroaches all over the floor of my room. I decided the lodge probably wasn't in much better condition than the shanty camp where the others were.

In the morning, the pilot found clear skies and picked up the guys. None of them had slept, either. They were fine—just exhausted from a rough night in the mountains. And Will was still a bit peeved about having to leave his backpack behind.

The rain had stopped, and the landscape around us slowly emerged from the mist, but the tension lingered—an unspoken reminder of just how close we had come to disaster. Relief washed over me, but it wasn't the kind that brings peace. It was the kind that forces you to reflect on the precariousness of it all—our lives, the mission, the creatures we'd come here to protect.

Our survival in that moment felt like an echo of the fragile survival of the species we'd seen over the past few weeks. The Lazarus species—the Madagascar pochard, the red owl—those once thought lost to time but somehow holding on. Their existence was a defiance of the odds, a quiet rebellion against the tide of extinction that threatens so much of the planet's biodiversity.

I thought about the wildlife we'd encountered: the lemurs with their playful energy and bright eyes; the tortoises, a testament to resilience. In so many ways, their survival mirrored our own—fragile and uncertain, but possible.

This journey reminded me that conservation isn't just about protecting animals or land. It's a fight against time, against unpredictability, against all the forces that conspire to wear down life's persistence. And it's a fight that never truly ends. Each victory, each rediscovered species, each protected habitat is a moment of relief—but also a reminder that the work is far from done.

We had made it out of a dangerous situation. We were lucky. But for the species we are fighting to protect, luck isn't enough. Conservation is about more than just survival—it's about creating the conditions that allow life to thrive in spite of everything.

And so, as we prepared to leave Madagascar, my mission felt clearer than ever.

That night, after the others had gone up to their rooms to pack, I met with Russ on the hotel's patio, the hum of conversation from the other guests fading into the background.

"Russ, I've made a decision," I said, looking at him across the table. "I'm going to donate a million dollars to Re:wild's projects here."

Russ raised an eyebrow, a smile playing on his lips. "That's incredible, Dax. Thank you. You'll be making a real difference here. We can do a lot with that."

I nodded, feeling the gravity of my choice. "Everything we've seen—it's all connected. The people, the wildlife, the land. It needs protecting. I want to be a part of that, and a part of what you guys are doing."

And then I said, "I'd love to get some perspective from you—a view of how you might see my future in conservation." It was a big question, but the most important one for me to ask. I had built up a huge admiration for Russ over the past few years—especially on this journey together.

Russ looked at me with the kind of respect that only comes from shared experience. "You know, Dax, you thrive out here in the field. If you partnered with us at Re:wild, you'd be bringing something that only comes from having stood where we stand. You've actually seen these conservation sites firsthand. You've felt it—the land, the species, the urgency. We could use your help selecting new projects, guiding strategies."

I nodded, grateful for the moment. We discussed a potential partnership between Age of Union and Re:wild—a way to be part of something much bigger, with more capability to protect more biodiversity.

"I'd like that," I said. "Let me get back home and see what that could look like."

I raised my whiskey for one last toast with Russ. What an honor to be here and see all the work he was doing. I realized this was the beginning of something much bigger. The projects we'd visited over the past few weeks, along with the momentum of the projects I had invested in over the past few years, were just a glimpse of the impact we could have together. It wasn't just about what we'd seen or where we'd been—it was about where we were going.

I knew then that the adventure had only just begun.

Drifting beneath the canopy on the Xingu River—lifeblood of Amazonia and guardian of Indigenous land. Credit: Edson Grandisoli

Jane Goodall after receiving a blessing from Chief Juma Xipaia in the Xipaya village, Amazonia.
Credit: Richard Ladkani

Chapter 9

BLESSINGS IN AMAZONIA

A NATURE WALK WITH JANE GOODALL AND CHIEF JUMA XIPAIA

My first journey to the Amazon was life-altering—spiritually awakening, and a clear affirmation of my life's mission to fight for a healthier planet. But if you had told me then that I'd one day return to the rainforest alongside my hero—Dr. Jane Goodall, the world's most iconic defender of the natural world—I would've laughed it off as fantasy.

The Amazon, though, has a strange way of bending time and fate. And somehow, two years after my first trip with Junglekeepers in Peru, I found myself boarding a plane to Brazil beside the most revered environmentalist of our time.

Jane needs little introduction. Her groundbreaking research with chimpanzees in Gombe redefined not only how we understand primates, but how we understand ourselves. She turned quiet observation into global movement, science into empathy, and a chimpanzee's twig into a mirror reflecting our shared origins. At ninety, she still travels the majority of the year, imparting her message of hope into microphones across the planet. To conservationists—and to many others—Jane is royalty.

Her reach extends far beyond the halls of science. She's woven into the cultural fabric—a figure as present in academic journals as she is in classrooms, coffee table books, and global summits. Her approach to conservation is both fierce and tender, grounded in a profound respect for the emotional and social intelligence of animals. She challenges us to reconsider our relationships with the living world. Jane hasn't simply spotlighted the secret lives of primates—she's issued a rallying cry to protect biodiversity before it's too late.

Here's a quirky detail not everyone knows: Jane travels with a small entourage of plush toys, including a monkey named Mr. H. Tucked under her arm through airports and across borders, this fuzzy globetrotter has visited more than sixty countries. Over the years, thousands have squeezed Mr. H for luck and inspiration. He was a gift from Gary Haun, a blind magician who defied the odds and mastered his craft without sight—living proof of the indomitable human spirit Jane so often champions. She keeps Mr. H close as a symbol of Gary's credo: that perseverance can pave the way for possibilities unseen.

What I love most about this story is Jane's belief in magic—not the pull-a-coin-from-your-ear kind, but the kind that winks at you from the cosmos. Jane has the universe on speed dial, aligning stars and stitching fate with a wink and a nod. Those close to her call it "Jane magic"—a kind of cosmic mojo that seems to conspire in her favor, rolling out the red carpet for life, chance, and the most serendipitous crossroads.

Which is why I believe we were meant to meet.

Jane's power lies not just in her intellect—it's in her presence. The meeting was supposed to be brief. Just a handshake and a thank-you, orchestrated by our mutual friend, marine wildlife photographer Hussain Aga Khan. But from the moment we met backstage at the David Suzuki Foundation Gala in Montréal, it felt like picking up a conversation we were always meant to have. She already seemed to know everything—my work, my beliefs, even my spiritual path. There was mischief in her curiosity and kindness in her cadence.

The room around us blurred. We talked about faith, about stories, about purpose. I shared the details of the film I was co-producing with Leonardo DiCaprio's production company, Appian Way. The director was Richard Ladkani, whose documentaries *Sea of Shadows* and *The Ivory Game* had left an indelible mark—especially the latter, which may well be the reason African elephants still walk this Earth. Jane and Richard are longtime friends, and she already knew he'd be filming in the Amazon.

"Oh, I just love Richie," she said, her eyes warm. "You know, we've traveled all over the world together." Then she leaned in, her voice a whisper: "Perhaps *we* should go together."

A few days later, her trusted colleague Susana Name emailed me: **Jane wants you to travel with her.**

Jane magic.

The Red Roller

I took a flight from Montréal to Ronald Reagan Washington National Airport to meet with Jane and Susana. Amid the formalities at the check-in counter, I found myself in a squabble with the customer service agent over printing out my boarding pass. Just then, an unmistakable voice reached my ears from behind—it was Jane's.

"Oh, don't check this man in," she said, with a mischievous smirk. "He's just trouble." She patted my shoulder. Jane was being silly, but it probably wasn't helping my position with the desk agent.

"Hi, Jane," I said, turning around to give her and Susana hugs.

"What is this monstrosity?" Jane asked, throwing a perplexed glance at my bag—a 100-liter Patagonia duffel with no wheels that I had purchased just for this trip. "Oh dear, is there a body in that? You could possibly fit two in there," she giggled. I looked down and saw Jane's small red carry-on suitcase with wheels. My face turned flush like the case.

"Mine is easy to spot, it's light, and it's *fast*," she said, showing off her prized bag with a smooth push and pull of the handle. The red roller seemed to be taunting me as well, as it rolled to and away from my feet.

Susana had one, too. I didn't get the memo.

"Richard said there are no smooth walkways where we are going," I said. "He told me to get the biggest bag I could carry." The two women snickered, rolling their luggage, both bags now jeering at me.

"Did Richie say anything about the airports?" Jane asked, her smile deepening in amusement. I could tell that she was enjoying herself. And to her point, I had already lugged the damn thing through two airports, and we hadn't even left North America yet. It *did* feel like I was hauling two bodies around. "Dax, I guess that's how you got those big muscles," she said. I laughed and turned back to finish with the check-in desk.

Jane's appearance seemed to make a difference for the desk agent. I could tell she recognized Jane, and she immediately changed her tune, graciously completing my check-in and accepted my behemoth bag. With my boarding pass in hand, I turned and offered to help Jane and Susana with their suitcases.

"No, I'm a big girl," Jane said, still grinning. "I've traveled all over the world—and this bag has wheels." She really didn't want my help, or anyone's, for that matter. Throughout the trip, Jane would always refuse physical assistance from others, insisting on doing things for herself—the Jane way.

Then, in a blurry-red flash, she sped off with her red roller toward the gate. Susana and I chased after her.

The Miracle Couple

In Santarém, in the western part of the state of Pará, the air was thick and nuclear hot—like a punch in the face. It tasted of soil.

Our hotel sat at the confluence of the Tapajós and Amazon rivers, a popular tourist destination. Thanks to the crystalline waters of the Tapajós, Santarém has more than sixty miles of pristine beaches, including the village of Alter do Chão, often called one of the most beautiful in Brazil. As brutal as the heat was, our riverfront setting offered a lifesaving breeze. I took a few minutes to myself and stared out at the milky-blue Amazon, colored by the sediment the river carries from the Andes in the east.

That night, Jane invited a small group of us—Richard, Anita, Susana, me, and our translators and fixers—for a kickoff toast to send us into the forest with good energy.

"Let's toast to this journey into the forest," Jane said, raising her glass, "with the miracle couple and our newest friend—Dax."

She calls Richard and Anita the miracle couple—for good reason.

On December 26, 2004, the Austrian couple were vacationing on Ko Phi Phi in Thailand when a deadly tsunami hit, dragging them into the sea along with thousands of unsuspecting locals and tourists. The waves destroyed 70 percent of the island's buildings. As they surged and receded, cars, boats, and buildings were reduced to wreckage—and thousands of lives were lost to the chaos and flooding.

Richard's account is harrowing. He recalls a moment in the madness when he and Anita locked eyes, realizing they might not survive. Then the wave hit. They were stripped apart in an instant. He was pulled underwater, tumbled and slammed into debris, unable to tell which way was up. A faint patch of light became his guide—he swam toward it, surfaced just long enough to gasp for air, then was pulled under again. This happened again and again, each breath barely enough to keep him alive.

Eventually, he was hurled into a smashed building, where he managed to surface. But the nightmare continued. Anita was nowhere to be found, and he was surrounded by bodies and wreckage. For a long time, he saw no other survivors. He crawled from the ruins, tended his wounds, helped others, and held on until rescue teams arrived. Among the few who lived, some tried to assist—others turned to violence, looting, even murder.

Richard endured twenty-seven hours in this landscape of death before military helicopters arrived. He was rescued quickly—there were few left to save. Only about 2 percent of those on the beaches survived. For hours, he feared Anita was gone. He searched relentlessly—until, at a rescue station, they were reunited. Anita had suffered serious injuries, but she was alive.

Back in Austria, they vowed never to be separated again unless by choice. Richard would continue making films in the field; Anita would manage their projects. Then came a film that would change the course of their lives again.

Richard was hired as a cinematographer on *Jane's Journey*, a documentary about the world-renowned primatologist and UN Messenger of Peace. He traveled with Jane across the globe—Tanzania, France, the UK, the US, Greenland. The film was shortlisted for an Academy Award and won the Cinema for Peace Award. During filming, Jane challenged Richard to take a deeper consideration of the impact of his work.

"Richard, you survived that tsunami for a reason—for a higher purpose. You have a message to share, to help save the future of our planet," she told him.

Inspired, Richard and Anita launched Malaika Pictures to spotlight the world's most urgent environmental crises—starting with elephants. A *New York Times* article titled "Ten Years to the Extinction of the African Elephant" drove Richard to direct *The Ivory Game*, a high-stakes investigative documentary about the illegal ivory trade and the looming extinction of African elephants. With Leonardo DiCaprio as executive producer, the film was shortlisted for an Academy Award and won multiple awards. Most importantly, it played a key role in ending China's legal ivory trade.

His next film, *Sea of Shadows*, documented the fight to save the vaquita—the world's smallest whale—from extinction, while exposing an international crime syndicate. Now, in the Amazon, Richard was directing *Yanuni*—the extraordinary story of Juma Xipaia, an Indigenous chief from the Brazilian Amazon, who rises from a remote village in Xipaya territory to the political front lines of climate justice. The film is produced by the Ladkanis and DiCaprio, with me serving as executive producer.

That night, we had dinner on the hotel terrace just steps from the river, surrounded by lush greenery and bright flowers. Brilliant birds soared across the water, riding the wind above the current. We feasted on local-caught fish, fresh vegetables, and juices. Jane, who doesn't eat meat, was content with rice, beans, and juice—the same meal we'd grow used to for the rest of the trip.

As the sun dipped behind the tree line, the sky lit up in amber and red, the river shimmering with reflected light. Nightfall brought a shift—an orchestra of unseen creatures rising from the jungle in song, as the rainforest took over again.

The Xipaya

In the sky, just outside of Santarém, our pilot—a reformed gold miner turned environmentalist—pointed out a somber view below: stretches of barren land and poisoned waters along the Tapajós River, where mining operations had devastated the river and its surroundings. The illegal airstrips that served these camps were prevalent. Lead-colored rivers were lined by greed-driven camps, treeless and dead, where pristine forests and vibrant rivers once thrived. We soared over hundreds of small islands that peppered the river. "Those are not typically visible," he explained. "The water level is extremely low right now because of extreme dry seasons and climate change. But soon the rains will come, and the river will flood and reclaim the islands."

Flying over a mining barge—extractive industry carving through the lungs of the Amazon.
Credit: Dax Dasilva

"This will stay with me forever," Jane's voice trembled, shocked to see the polluted lands and poisoned waterways.

"We are now above Indigenous protected territories," the pilot said. My heart began to replenish with hope. As far as I could see, it was green, green, and greener—lush forests divided only by bountiful, undisturbed rivers.

Our wobbly little plane juddered up and down as we sped toward a narrow dirt landing strip surrounded by forest. We flew in fast, hitting the runway with a few bounces. The pilot popped open the door, and the aroma of the jungle rushed inside. It was wet and rich, the scent of billions of trees rooted in some of the most fertile soil on the planet. I stepped out of the plane and looked outward at a lost world of untouched jungle, a place that hosted all secrets of life if we could protect it long enough to understand.

Jane and I took in the energy of the landscape as we neared the Xipaya village, the shared excitement of our visit to the Amazon readily apparent. We took a moment to celebrate a milestone. I realized it was Age of Union's second anniversary. To commemorate the occasion, Jane and I filmed a short video that we shared on social media.

"Conservation isn't just about climate change," she reflected, "it's also about the symphony of life we call biodiversity. These two are inseparable—if we lose one, the other will surely follow." I nodded, adding, "Conservation is our first line of defense in the climate battle."

Jane's gaze met mine, earnest and intense. "Only through collaborations like ours can we hope to turn the tide. I've often said that humans aren't exempt from extinction," she said. "And I'm grateful our paths have converged. Congratulations on your anniversary, Dax, and let's not forget Mr. H's three decades of advocacy."

Jane's witticisms weren't lost on me. I acknowledged Mr. H's silent but significant presence. "He's been quite the companion. There's much to admire in such dedicated service."

With Jane in Amazonia.
Credit: Richard Ladkani

… Chapter 9 | **BLESSINGS IN AMAZONIA**

Juma

The journey to Kaarimã was a passage through time. We traveled by river in a traditional longboat, the tranquility of the waterways a stark contrast to the usual bustle of boats near commercial ports. Here in Indigenous territory, strict regulations keep outside traffic at bay. Visits like ours happen only with special permission.

As we settled into the rhythm of the river, Jane's eyes scanned the forest for signs of life—and the jungle obliged. Brilliant blue and yellow macaws streaked across the sky, turtles stretched their necks on sun-warmed logs, and butterflies hovered like confetti in the humid air. A troop of spider monkeys chased one another through the canopy. Bird calls echoed across the river's glassy surface.

"Just look at the diversity here," Jane said, her eyes wide with wonder. "Ecosystems like this are the lifeblood of our planet."

I nodded, following her gaze. "You can feel the heartbeat of the untouched world here. This is what we're fighting to protect."

"Yes," she replied. "And the resilience of nature gives me hope. But it's fragile, and we must continue to be its voice."

It was the dry season, and the river was dangerously low—sixty feet lower than Richard had seen it just six months earlier. Our boat bumped across shallow rock beds, and islands that once peeked above the water now rose like small mountains of sand.

We arrived at Kaarimã, unpacked the boat, and hauled our gear onto the sandy shore. The village sat nestled just beyond, a circle of thatched homes surrounding a central community hall. Open-air structures, built with traditional methods but upgraded with solar panels and Starlink internet, stood as symbols of resilience and adaptation—Indigenous wisdom powered by modern tools.

A small group of Xipaya came to greet us. And then, the moment I had been awaiting since we left Washington, D.C.—Jane and Juma, meeting at last.

Juma stood at the center, cradling her infant daughter, Yanuni—her name meaning "Victory." Beside her stood her mother, Dona Lucia, dressed in brilliant yellow with birds and florals stitched across the fabric. Juma was regal, rooted. A chief of her people, a medical student, and a rising force in the Indigenous movement. In 2018, she became the first member of the Xipaya to speak at the United Nations, bringing human rights violations in the Amazon to the global stage. She's battled corruption, defended her lands against industrial encroachment, and carried the voice of her community with unwavering resolve.

And yet here she was—barefoot in the sand, smiling in the comfort of her village.

As Juma stepped toward Jane, the air seemed to shift. They faced one another—still, silent, fully present. You could feel it in your chest. This wasn't just a meeting. It was recognition. Two women, separated by continents and generations, joined in a moment that felt almost ceremonial. The air vibrated with the weight of it.

Juma broke the silence. "I cannot believe your energy," she said.

The two embraced, smiling.

Then came Hugo, Juma's husband. Once a soldier, now a forest guardian with IBAMA, Brazil's environmental enforcement agency. His work confronting illegal loggers, miners, and poachers is dangerous, relentless, and often underpaid. He doesn't speak much English, but when he looked into Jane's eyes, time paused.

"I don't believe you are here," he said, awed.

"I'm very glad to be here," Jane replied softly. "Nice to meet you."

"Nice to meet you," Hugo said, finally breaking the moment.

What passed between them needed no translation—two warriors of the wild, meeting across language, bonded by purpose.

To put it bluntly, Juma and Hugo are badasses. They lead with strategy and strength, fighting for their homeland while navigating the complex corridors of government and international activism. They use every platform, every tool—from village councils to COP summits—to protect their people and forest. They are not just defenders of a place, but messengers for all of us, reminding the world what's truly at stake.

The Kaarimã welcome was warm and generous. We shared a communal meal of fruits and vegetables, exchanged stories, and laughed freely. The Xipaya had prepared a new lodge for our stay, complete with bedrooms for Jane, Susana, and me, two washrooms, and a central open area with hammocks for the rest of the team. Just outside, a wide patio became our favorite spot for afternoon reflections over a wee dram.

That night, a villager warned us of recent jaguar sightings. Both Juma and her sister-in-law had recently given birth, and it was believed that the cries of their infants had drawn in the apex predator. The signs were clear—fresh paw prints in the sand, low growls at night, fleeting glimpses at the forest's edge. To deter the jaguar, red lights were installed along the perimeter. In the animal world, red signals danger.

Jane was fascinated. "I've always half-joked," she said, curving her fingers into claws, "that if I die in the wild, it'll be all claws and teeth."

I shivered at the thought. Jane, of course, had requested the red lights be turned off—just in case she might catch a glimpse.

The Xipaya village.
Credit: Dax Dasilva

Juma has a jaguar tattooed on her body. In her native language, her own name means "Jaguar."

"Why not turn the jaguar from a threat into a protector?" she asked, her voice calm but purposeful. "I want the jaguar to be a guardian of our people and this forest."

Later, on the lodge porch, stories continued into the night. Jane, ever the storyteller, recounted a visit to a remote tribe in Taiwan where she dressed in ceremonial canary yellow—a far cry from her usual greens and khakis. We laughed and imagined the jaguar watching from the shadows—not as predator, but as witness, protector, and perhaps even ally in the great balance of the Amazon.

The first meeting between Dr. Jane Goodall and Chief Juma Xipaia—guardians united by the forest.
Credit: Richard Ladkani

Three generations of Xipaia strength—Juma's mother, Juma, and her son carry the past, present, and future of the forest. Credit: Richard Ladkani

Blessings

At sunrise, Juma and her family brought baby Yanuni to the Iriri River. It was time for her baptism—a ceremonial welcome into the forest. We stood on the bank as Juma stepped into the water, holding her daughter close. Yanuni's tiny feet touched the warm current for the first time, and Juma whispered blessings over her child. This moment—a Xipaya mother offering her child to the spirit of the river—was one of the most sacred and hopeful things I've ever witnessed. It felt like a promise, a prayer for the future of the forest and the generations who will protect it.

Later that morning, Jane expressed a desire to take a solitary walk through the Amazon. It's a ritual of hers—no matter where she is in the world, she finds time to be alone with nature. This would be her first solo walk in the Amazon, and she was visibly excited. But as she prepared, the film crew instinctively grabbed their gear and followed. And so did we. Jane's quiet retreat quickly turned into a procession.

And then Juma arrived.

Carrying Yanuni at her chest, Juma joined the group, her face adorned in ceremonial paint. Two black lines stretched from the corners of her mouth toward her ears, turning her smile into something mythic. Ocher streaks ran from her eyes to her temples. Her braids were draped in feathers—yellow and red macaw plumes that framed a single large hawk feather. She looked radiant. Powerful. A bridge between worlds.

As we walked deeper into the jungle, two macaws burst from the canopy, squawking overhead until their vibrant wings disappeared into green. A feather fluttered down and landed at my feet. Red, yellow, and blue—like a message from the forest itself. It stirred something in me. I remembered a moment in Madre de Dios, when a flight of macaws passed overhead and I felt my life's path affirmed. Now, walking alongside Jane Goodall, through the Amazon once again, that feeling returned.

Juma led us deeper into the forest, her steps sure and quiet. "This is where I come when I need strength," she said. "The forest heals. It teaches. It guides."

Chapter 9 | **BLESSINGS IN AMAZONIA** 327

We followed in silence.

At thirteen, Juma had declared her life a battleground. "My entire life will be a fight," she once said during a filmed protest against the Belo Monte Dam. That dam diverted 85 percent of the Xingu River, devastating Indigenous communities and ecosystems. It was approved without consultation and built without the participation of the very people it would displace. Homes were demolished, traditional diets were upended by processed food, and villages were left with chronic health problems and no infrastructure to manage the resulting waste.

Juma fought it all—and paid the price. Threats on her life forced her into exile in Switzerland for a year. Even now, in Brasília, she travels with security. She's fluent in multiple languages, educated in medicine, and

Juma baptizes baby Yanuni in the Xingu River—a sacred act of continuity, belonging, and ancestral blessing. Credit: Richard Ladkani

capable of articulating the complexity of Indigenous struggle with precision and power. But it's more than that—when Juma speaks, she carries the weight of the forest in her voice. She sees straight into your soul. Being with her is like standing in the presence of something elemental.

Yet despite her strength, she's vulnerable, too. When the fight ends, she cries. She needs the forest. It's where her spirit is replenished.

Juma dipped her fingers into her face paint and marked each of us—first Jane, then me. A blessing of the wild. She welcomed us into the forest as kin.

Then, in a voice both soft and commanding, she told us to lie down among the trees, to listen.

"Feel the forest," she said. "Listen to its heartbeat. Accept nature into your heart—the trees, the animals, Mother Earth. Let this place fill your soul."

Bird calls rang through the canopy. Leaves rustled in the wind. The river murmured in the distance. I leaned back against a tree, closed my eyes, and let the forest take over. I drifted into sleep.

When I woke, I felt empowered. Somehow, more connected to the forest. And filled with gratitude.

A blessing from Juma.
Credit: Richard Ladkani

Forest blessing.
Credit: Richard Ladkani

That afternoon, we took a small boat to get a closer look at the sandy islands where scarlet macaws gather in abundance, using their curved beaks to nibble at the clay along the water's edge. Jane finally found the solitude she'd been seeking. She stood still, binoculars in hand, tracking the vibrant birds as they dipped and soared across the river. A few of us wandered the shoreline, feeling safe and calm—until we came across a yellow-spotted river turtle, torn apart. A brutal reminder that the jaguar is always near.

Over dinner, jaguar stories flowed. One of our team had seen one at the edge of the forest that morning. Two villagers believed one had shadowed them silently on a walk to the river. Suddenly, a deep roar echoed from behind the lodge. We jumped. Hearts raced.

Then came laughter.

It was Juma's young son, Tuppak, grinning with a toy voice box in his hands—perfectly timing a prank that left us laughing with relief and a little awe. Even here, even among warriors and spirits, mischief still had its place.

The Cloud Contingent

A night's sleep revealed that no matter the shelter, mosquito nets, full-coverage clothing—the jungle's fervor finds a way. The blistering heat was a persistent companion, and creeping, crawling bugs were undeterred adventurers; my body was a smorgasbord for the multi-legged nibblers. I was riddled with bites, a constellation of tiny red dots that burned fiercely. Dona Lucia offered a traditional tincture that soothed the incessant itching. There was no relief from the relentless heat.

Jane, on the contrary, had made peace with the bugs, waking up unscathed. After a good night's sleep, she repeated her longing for solitude in the wilderness—this time, no cameras. She wanted to go camping, a small expedition.

Just a few of us, Richard explained.

"We'll keep it intimate," he said to me. "Jane wants time to reflect. I think an overnight on the sandy islands will do the trick. There will be just five of us, if you'd like to join us."

My first reaction was to stay behind in the village. I had seen what the jaguar did to that turtle on the island shore, and I wasn't interested in being untethered by claws and fangs in the night. I also wanted to respect Jane's wish for privacy. But Jane nudged me to join, and the chance to share a special wilderness experience with her pushed my hesitations aside. It would become my favorite memory of the trip.

In a tin boat, Juma's father, Chico, threaded us through sandy keys in the river. The sky was screaming blue, and the breeze provided a welcome respite from the scalding heat. Chico pointed out an osprey, a large raptor they call a river hawk. The grassy shallows along the banks provided good hunting for the predating bird, as well as a large heron standing in the weeds, patiently watching the water beneath its stilt legs.

A moment with Jane on an Amazonian river island.
Credit: Richard Ladkani

We found an island with a long sandy beach—perfect for camping. Chico would return the next day to pick us up, leaving us with a GPS satellite phone in the event that we needed help. Jane and I had tents, while the others brought hammocks. I had never slept in a hammock, and Jane, after many years of using them, no longer found them comfortable. We set up camp higher up in the sand, near a barrier of tall grass. Richard strung his hammock between two small trees.

Jane grabbed her binoculars and headed to a cove on the beach, perfect for observing the river's feathered community. She sat peacefully at the shoreline, a glassy river in front of her reflecting the fiery orange sun that seemed just inches from dropping below the jungle canopy across the Iriri River. The water carried the songs of thousands of birds as they soared and fluttered, taking their places as the sky closed its curtains for the night. The sky went from blue to pink to violet to purple in a matter of minutes, and all became silent for a few moments. Then a new orchestra took over, a symphony of frogs, cicadas, howler monkeys, and other nocturnal critters staking claim to the night.

At night, our campfire created an enclave of flickering firelight and shadows. We passed around warm plates filled with rice, beans, and veggies, taking our places around the fire. I relished seeing Jane's and Richard's joyful faces glowing radiantly beneath the early night sky. We chatted and laughed, feeling like we were the only people on the planet. Then Jane proposed a special toast.

"The cloud contingent," she began, her voice rising above the crackle of the fire, "is where I imagine all our loved ones gather, watching over us, once they have passed on." Her eyes met each of ours in turn. "Every day at seven, I toast to them—mother, family, friends—all those who've journeyed on."

Jane came up with the concept of the cloud contingent as a way to help her reconcile the passing of her mother. Over time, she has shared this tradition with others who feel the sting of loss, creating a space of remembrance and connection. "It's a time we can be together each day and think of them," she said, her eyes soft with remembrance.

We raised our cups in salute to the celestial gathering of souls departed. I thought of my friend Jasmine, who had been on my mind since Jakarta.

"Here's to those who remain with us in spirit," I said, the firelight dancing in the amber of my glass.

A mouse scurried through our camp, nearing the fire and sprinting over the blanket I was seated on. I jumped up, and so did Richard. Jane didn't flinch. "Oh, that little mouse is looking to join us for dinner," she said calmly, tossing a few grains from her plate in its direction.

"Smart mouse," I said, as I shook out my blanket.

"They certainly are," Jane said. "Have I ever told you about the Hero Rats of Tanzania?"

"No, but I can't wait to hear this," I said, settling back down.

"I once met a man in Belgium working on his PhD on the landmine situation left behind by the African civil wars. He was working on strategies for the extraction of active landmines, a major problem in some areas. He recalled having two pet rats when he was a little boy and how they would always find food that he hid around his bedroom. For his research, he decided to see if the rats could detect TNT—and it worked. The only issue was that it takes nine months to train the rats, and their lifespans are only two to three years."

Jane took a sip of whiskey and continued. "That's when he learned of the Gambian giant pouched rat that lives eight to nine years," she said. "They're much larger, like this." Jane stretched her hands a lot further apart than I had expected. "Dax, they can be three feet long with their tails. And they are so delightful. Because of the work they are trained for, they call them Hero Rats."

Jane told us about one of the Hero Rats named Magawa, who ultimately received a People's Dispensary for Sick Animals Gold Medal, which is the animal equivalent of the George Cross, becoming the first rat to receive the award. Before retiring, Magawa had detected seventy-one mines and thirty-eight explosives, clearing over two million square feet of land in Cambodia and preventing many injuries and deaths.

"These types of rats live in solitary, not in groups," Jane continued, "and when they pick up the scent of explosives, they scratch the ground and receive a reward. But they won't eat their treats on the spot; they hide them away in their cheek pouches for later. The very clever ones go back into their little homes with their cheeks completely stuffed." She puffed up her cheeks and clapped them with her hands.

Leaning in closer to the fire, with a mischievous smirk, she said, "And the males are quite funny because they have the biggest balls—absolutely humongous for their size." She held out both hands as if she were holding a plum in each.

"They *must* have huge balls to be searching for landmines," Richard said, with perfect timing. Everyone burst into laughter.

As the night deepened, so did our stories. I shared my own call to the wild—the first time I saw macaws in flight, and the spiritual message I received in Peru, telling me I was on the right path and to keep going. I spoke of my evenings at Junglekeepers, sleeping beneath colonies of bats, and how I overcame my fear of snakes by riding in a van with a massive boa constrictor in a sack at my feet. Somewhere along the way, I had become more connected to the natural world—closer to it than ever before.

Jane chuckled softly, "Indeed, sometimes our legacy includes sharing space with less welcome company."

Jane sits in quiet reflection as the Amazon sky dissolves into dusk.
Credit: Richard Ladkani

"Well, it's not anything to be worried about tonight," I said, pointing out the unlikeliness of bats in my tent. I hadn't seen a single snake on this trip, unlike in Peru, where they seemed to be everywhere.

"Don't be so certain, Dax," she advised, a gentle jest. I thought of the dead turtle on the shore. Richard reminded me that we were well within snake, caiman, and jaguar territory.

Jane was right. But the beast that attacked me that night wasn't an animal—it was my tent.

Jane's setup was a dream: a breathable mesh shelter that let the breeze in and kept the bugs out. Mine was the opposite: a sealed oven with no mesh, no airflow, just heat. A sweltering, suffocating sauna. Within minutes, I was drenched in sweat and growing irrationally angry. I ripped off my shirt and pants, stripping down to my skivvies like a madman. Groaning, grunting, throwing things—I was an ogre in a nylon cave.

And then I saw them: two enormous cockroaches skittering along the edge of the tent.

That was it. I snapped.

I burst out of the tent, screaming. In my underwear.

Much, much later, I'd come to appreciate the humor in it all—a growling, half-naked man leaping from his tent in the middle of the night like a lunatic. I'd understand why everyone around the bonfire erupted when they saw my acrobatic exit from that sweltering nylon sweat lodge. But in the moment, I was rattled—bug-shocked, overheated, and totally over it.

Defeated, I asked the crew to rig me a hammock on the beach.

Sleeping in a hammock seemed like a terrible idea—a guaranteed recipe for a twisted spine and a sleepless night. I couldn't have been more wrong. Richard showed me the trick: Sit in the middle, swing your legs up at a diagonal, and lie flat. The pièce de résistance? A rolled blanket under the knees.

I was floored. A piece of cloth and two trees had outperformed every tent I'd ever known. Suspended in air, I stretched out and let go of all residual rage toward the tent—and the two cockroach squatters who now called it home.

Chapter 9 | **BLESSINGS IN AMAZONIA**

Above me, a yellow half-moon hung in the sky, casting silver across the river and painting a second universe in the Iriri's glossy surface. At the heart of it all, the bonfire crackled, breaking the ambient rhythm of fish splashes, night bird calls, and the chorus of cicadas. A warm breeze rocked the hammock gently. I let it carry me into sleep.

By morning, the fire was revived and fresh coffee brewed. My retelling of the previous night's meltdown earned a round of giggles—and when I got to the part about the cockroaches, we all lost it. It was hard to leave that little island. I wanted to stay in the glow of that fire and laughter a little longer. But our ride back to Kaarimã was waiting.

We doused the flames, packed our things, and climbed into the boat, the river pulling us back toward the forest.

Hugo

In Kaarimã, while Jane and Richard ventured into the forest to film, I sat down to lunch with Hugo Loss. Richard had already spoken of his brave missions with IBAMA, but hearing Hugo tell the stories himself, by way of a translator, brought a new weight to them.

"We are nature's bodyguards," Hugo said. "The last line of defense against those who seek to harm it."

As an IBAMA agent, Hugo leads paramilitary-style operations against illegal gold mining in the Amazon. He spoke of midnight raids—stealth teams navigating rivers under cover of darkness, ducking gunfire to storm mining barges that poison waterways with mercury and cyanide. Once the miners are removed, the team piles mattresses and oxygen tanks in the barge's center, ignites the heap, and flees as flames consume it. The barge sinks in a final act of reckoning.

Hugo's incredible stories of fighting illegal mining were inspiring.
Credit: Richard Ladkani

"This isn't a job," Hugo said. "It's a calling. With a job, you give your time. For this, you give your life."

He pulled back his collar, revealing a tattoo of a burning excavator. "When I fight, the spirits of the forest fight with me. I destroy the mining platforms, and the river swallows them. We fight together."

The scale of the damage is staggering. During the Bolsonaro presidency, illegal mining exploded. Privately funded barges gouged the riverbeds, dumping mercury and cyanide into the ecosystem—poisoning fish, wildlife, and people. Entire communities that depend on the river now bathe and drink in toxic waters. Children lose teeth and hair. Neurological, immune, and organ damage is widespread.

And the destruction doesn't stop at the waterline.

When mining barges cloud the river, sunlight can't reach aquatic plants. Plants die, fish suffocate, and starvation sets in. With their traditional food sources gone, Indigenous families are forced to seek work in the very mining and shrimping camps that displaced them—resorting to buying overpriced processed foods shipped in from cities, which introduces a cascade of health and social issues.

And then come the villages. Around each illegal mining operation, small towns sprout. Women, often local, take jobs as cooks or cleaners, but the pay is meager. Many turn to sex work at night to support their families. These boomtowns bring deforestation, roads, imported goods, and violence. And when the mining dries up, what's left is worse than nothing: poisoned water, wrecked forests, and broken communities.

"This is a cancer," Hugo said. "You must kill the tumor before it spreads."

His team's raids are strategic strikes meant to hit the financiers where it hurts. "Millions are invested in these barges," he said. "We destroy them so thoroughly, the loss outweighs the profit. That's our only leverage."

From the air, we saw the destruction. Flying in the Greenpeace plane, our pilot pointed out rivers turned lead-gray by mercury and sludge—lifeless scars on the land. Hugo looked down and said quietly, "The river's song is being silenced."

IBAMA agents infiltrate these camps disguised as miners, drinking in taverns and gathering intel. With approval, Richard joined Hugo's team to document one such raid. But Hugo gave him a warning first:

"Your chances of returning alive are 50 percent. You're not a soldier. You carry a camera, not a gun."

Richard called Anita to explain the risk. Then he went.

During the night raid, the team stormed a mining barge by boat, captured the miners, and stacked furniture and fuel in the center. After dousing it in fuel, they lit it up. As they tried to retreat, their escape boat got snagged on a chain tethered to the burning barge. Trapped. Richard filmed as agents fired at the chain to break free. The boat slipped loose just as the barge exploded—flames erupting into the night sky.

Days later, at IBAMA headquarters, Jane listened as Hugo described the work. She had always championed nonviolence. But after witnessing the destruction from the sky, something shifted.

She turned to Hugo, eyes resolute. "Take them down," she said. "Destroy every barge, every mine. Make arrests. The more, the better."

A Conversation with Jane

After filming wrapped, I sat with Jane on the porch of the Xipaya lodge. By now, I could read her rhythms—when she was alert, tired, amused, or contemplative. At that moment, she seemed reflective, turning over the meaning of the journey we had all shared.

"I wonder if you'd indulge a conversation of deeper waters," she said. "Why do you think I'm here, Dax? Not here in the Amazon—that much is obvious, I've not lost my mind. I mean here on this Earth. I've been chosen to do this work, and my life is no longer my own. Why do you think that is?"

"Wow," I said, pausing. "That's a big question."

But I understood. After days in the forest with the Xipaya—immersed in a world that strips life down to its essential truths—I had found myself reflecting deeply on purpose. And I began to suspect that Jane's question wasn't really about her. It was a gentle prompt for me to consider my own place in all of this. She was always a few steps ahead.

"Well," I said, meeting her gaze, "there are billions of animals without a voice in what happens to them—or their home. You're their voice. A living reminder of our responsibility to stand up for the voiceless. And beyond that, you've dedicated your life to something greater than yourself. You've become a servant of the planet: a messenger. I don't think there's a higher calling than that."

Jane has given her entire life in service of others. She speaks at schools and summits, rallying youth, diplomats, and scientists. Even now, at ninety, she spends nearly three hundred days a year on the road. That's sixty-four years of research and activism on behalf of the Earth.

In *The Five Love Languages*, Gary Chapman writes about acts of service as a way of expressing love. Jane's life has been one monumental act of service—for animals, for the Earth, for all of us. That's why so many people cry when they meet her. It feels like meeting the Pope, the Dalai Lama, a Chief Rabbi—someone who has transcended self and become something more.

"I think that's why people become emotional around you," I said, recalling the tearful reactions we'd witnessed during the trip.

"They're not crying for me," she said. "They're crying for the Earth. It's their grief, their longing, their hope—for the planet, for the animals, for what we've lost and what we still might save."

I believe she's right. Those tears come from an inner knowing—that to live as a human on this planet is to participate in its destruction. We take, we build, we consume. From early hunting tribes to industrial civilization, the story has been one of disruption—deforestation, pollution, extraction, extinction. From diamonds to rare metals, from cell phones to cattle ranches, we've strip-mined the Earth under the guise of progress. And if we don't change our course, nature will move on—without us.

Later, Jane and I walked into the forest, wandering under the afternoon canopy. We sat on a twisted log that Jane joked was "perfect for a jaguar finale—fangs and claws." We spoke of spirit, mystics, and whether the ghost of the forest had been watching us all along.

"You know," she said, "there's a difference between intellect and intelligence. We humans are intellectual. But animals—they're intelligent. An animal wouldn't destroy its own home."

It struck a chord. Our intellect builds towers, but our intelligence seems lost. Animals live within the bounds of their ecosystem. We don't. We override it, define our own rules, and trap ourselves in cycles of creation and destruction. And with each generation, we rewrite the rules and call it freedom. But real freedom, I think, looks more like balance.

I shared a thought from Genesis—the story of humans being cast out of the Garden, separated from the animal kingdom. When we leaned into intellect and left intelligence behind, we entered into suffering. To return to harmony, to Eden, we must reconcile what we've done.

Jane nodded slowly. "Yes," she said. "And sometimes, in the quiet places—deep in the forest, beside a river, in the eyes of an animal—you

In the stillness of the forest, every word from Jane Goodall feels like a seed planted in the soul.
Credit: Richard Ladkani

can still hear them...echoes from Eden. Reminders of what we once were. And what we could be again, if we choose wisely."

I thought back to Jane's "Damascus moment," the time when she saw chimpanzees locked in medical labs and knew she could no longer stay silent. She had gone into that fight a field scientist and emerged as a global activist. She freed thousands of chimps and sparked a movement.

"It was the chimpanzees who taught me there are no hard lines between us and the rest of the animal kingdom," she said. "They have personalities, emotions, intellect. Once you acknowledge that, everything changes. It becomes an ethical issue—how we treat sentient beings who can feel pain, joy, fear."

That shift—from witness to warrior—became Jane's true calling. Once she knew her voice could make change, she could never go back. That's the essence of activism. You don't do it because it's easy. You do it because if you don't, suffering will continue.

That's why she's loved by so many. Not because she's perfect, but because she never stops trying to make the world better.

The following day, we boarded the Greenpeace plane and headed for Santarém. Jane, Juma, Hugo, Richie, and I flew over the Amazon again. Hugo pointed out illegal gold mining zones, the same sites he and his IBAMA team had raided. But this time, after days with the Xipaya, the devastation hit harder. The scars in the forest felt personal.

The rivers below were splattered with mercury and cyanide. They glowed a sick, leaden gray. Once home to billions of living creatures, they now looked like wounds.

Jane stared out the window, her face quiet.

We all felt it.

Godmother

Back in Santarém, we stayed at Posada Alter do Chão. After a week in hammocks and jungle air, the comforts of air-conditioning and a real mattress were welcome. Still, I'd been changed—those nights on the sandbar had reshaped something in me.

At dinner, Hugo surprised us with beaded necklaces and a Kuripe—an Amazonian pipe used to administer Rapéh, a shamanic snuff made from ground tobacco and forest herbs. Some variations are mixed with psychotropic plants, but what Hugo prepared was gentle, purifying. The first dose entered the left nostril—symbolizing the death of negative energy—followed by the right: a rebirth of clarity and calm.

We sat on the terrace as twilight dissolved into starlight, sharing stories—Jane's jaguar quip, Juma's blessing, the helicopter ride with Hugo. The burnt-orange sky deepened to indigo. Stars multiplied above us, then spilled across the river like mirrored constellations.

Maybe it was the Rapéh. Or the quiet. But my thoughts wandered.

I thought of Kaarimã—of the jungle as cathedral. Every tree, every inch of soil alive with purpose. Lichens, mosses, fungi, ants, frogs, monkeys, birds—a symphony of interdependence. Nothing in the Amazon exists alone.

And neither do we.

What became clear to me on this journey is that the forest doesn't just need saving. It offers salvation. Its wisdom is written in leaf veins and river currents. Its warnings are clear. But so are its blessings—if we choose to listen.

The next morning, Jane invited us to her room for farewell hugs. The air carried that quiet sadness that comes at the end of something meaningful. But there was also a quiet excitement—a sense that it was also the start of something new—as we set out to complete the film *YANUNI* and launch a new partnership with Juma to support youth leadership and environmental stewardship in Indigenous communities through the Jane Goodall Institute's Roots & Shoots program.

Jane Goodall, godmother to Yanuni.
Credit: Richard Ladkani

Juma arrived with baby Yanuni nestled against her chest. Jane's face softened as soon as she saw them. She crouched slightly, her eyes full of emotion.

"I just loved witnessing Yanuni's ceremony," she said, her voice trembling. "To see her welcomed into the river, into the forest...it was one of the most beautiful things I've experienced."

Juma stepped forward, her eyes locked on Jane's. "We've thought about this, my husband and I," she said in a voice both strong and reverent. "And we would be honored—truly honored—if you would be Yanuni's godmother."

Time seemed to pause.

Jane's eyes welled with tears. She looked at Juma, then at the tiny life pressed close to her, and brought a hand to her heart. "That's...one of the greatest honors of my life," she whispered.

She reached out, placing her hand gently on Yanuni's forehead. "I promise to watch over her from near or far. And I'll always carry her spirit with me."

Juma and Jane each said quiet blessings over the child—one in Xipaya, one in English—two worlds meeting over a new soul. It was a moment of deep grace, the kind that doesn't need fanfare to carry eternal weight.

Then Jane added, her voice catching slightly, "And now I'm certain—she will grow to be as extraordinary as her mother."

A few hours later at the São Paulo airport, Jane, Susana, and I pulled our bags from the hotel van and headed into the quiet terminal. Jane, red roller in hand, eyed my monstrous duffel and gave me a wink. I knew I'd never live that down.

We checked in, passed through security, and walked toward the gate in silence.

"Dax, I'm beginning to feel a bit of separation anxiety," Jane said, reading my thoughts aloud.

"Me too," I replied. "But at least you've still got Susana and Mr. H."

She looked down at the little monkey tucked under her arm.

"You know the funny thing about Mr. H?" she said. "He's not a chimpanzee. He has a tail—chimps don't." She dangled the stuffed monkey by its tail and handed him to me. "All those years ago, Gary thought he was giving me a chimp. I took his hand and made him feel the tail. And he said, 'Never mind. Take this monkey with you, and know that I'm with you in spirit.' So now, Mr. H symbolizes the indomitable spirit of people."

I gave Mr. H a final squeeze, adding mine to the millions before me, and handed him back to Jane.

"We've done something important here, Dax," she said. "And we did it together. That will ripple outward like waves across the water—good things will happen."

And with that, she disappeared through the terminal in a red blur. I stood there for a moment, her words echoing in my chest. I knew she was right.

The next day, I received an email from Jane:

Dear Dax,

Finally back after an exhausting and long trip home. What a profound trip with you to the Amazon. Much more to do. I hope you got home safe.

Love, Jane and Mr. H.

The feeling was mutual. It was hard to say goodbye to Jane and Susana after such a powerful journey. But I knew deep in my heart that this wouldn't be our last.

There's still so much more to do.

Along the Upper Pitt River in British Columbia.
Credit: Alan Katowitz

EPILOGUE

Since embarking on this journey and pledging my support for the projects in this book, I've witnessed firsthand the extraordinary dedication of changemakers around the world. While the stories I've shared reflect the time of my visits, the work has not stopped. Conservation is a living, breathing process—one of constant action, resilience, and growth.

These projects have seen remarkable progress, and I'm honored to share some updates with you, though I'm certain that by the time this book reaches your hands, even more milestones will have been achieved.

In the Peruvian Amazon, Junglekeepers has expanded its protected area to 100,000 acres. This success ensures that the scarlet macaws, jaguars, and countless other species can continue to thrive. Paul and his team remain tireless stewards of this ancient forest, safeguarding its future. And JJ was included in the TIME100 Most Influential Climate Leaders in Business for 2024.

In the Congo, Strong Roots and the Forest Health Alliance have secured an additional ten forest concessions in the Kahuzi-Itombwe Corridor. At the time of this writing, I'm pleased to see that more than a million hectares are under the protection of the community-managed forest concessions, vital for endangered lowland gorillas and local communities, despite the ongoing threats posed by oil exploration. This race to ensure that protection outpaces destruction continues to demand all our effort.

In Haiti, KANPE has acquired land for a third model forest, planting fifteen thousand seedlings in its first year. These forests are not just reforestation efforts but symbols of hope, resilience, and regeneration for the people of Baille Tourible.

In British Columbia's Pitt River Valley, fresh water once again flows through what became known as the Red Slough. (They're going to need a new name—the water is now blue.) This project, one of the largest salmon habitat restorations in western Canada, marks a major success for the Katzie First Nation and the region's wildlife. The sight of young salmon returning to these waters is a testament to what can be achieved when we prioritize nature.

At Kenauk, the institute continues to lead groundbreaking research and inspire young environmental advocates. The Research Pavilion, funded in part by Age of Union, now hosts studies that aim to preserve the biodiversity of this extraordinary corridor for generations.

In New York, before a sold-out audience on closing night of the Tribeca Film Festival, Leonardo DiCaprio introduced *YANUNI*. Juma Xipaia sat beside us. "Juma's resilience and clarity in this film underscore the urgency of protecting the Amazon—a story we can no longer ignore," DiCaprio said. "The Amazon may feel distant, but its fate is deeply tied to us here at home. It regulates our climate, holds more biodiversity than anywhere on Earth, and sustains life far beyond its borders. Yet it survives only because of people like Juma, who refuse to let it disappear."

Watching Juma that night, I was reminded that the Amazon doesn't stand because of outside intervention; it stands because of Indigenous resistance. Juma and others like her don't protect these forests only for their own people. They protect them for the world. Because we all depend on them. These leaders are the line between balance and collapse. We owe them more than admiration—we owe them our attention, our alliance, and our action.

What I've learned through this experience is that conservation is about listening. Too often, organizations arrive with preconceived solutions, overshadowing the knowledge of those on the ground. But the answers—the real, actionable solutions—come from the changemakers themselves, the ones who dedicate their lives to protecting these ecosystems.

Paul Rosolie once told me I was one of the only donors willing to fund the actual conservationists, to pay their salaries. Without those people patrolling the forests, the work ceases to exist. You can't protect the land without ensuring that the people fighting for it have the resources to continue. These changemakers can't sacrifice forever; they need relief, respect, and recognition.

Wild animals need us now, more than ever, in this moment and in this decade. They face relentless pressures brought on by human activities—habitat loss from urban sprawl and deforestation, the grim toll of poaching and overfishing, the exploitation of the pet trade, and the fragmented ecosystems left in the wake of unchecked expansionism. This century is a tipping point. It is our responsibility to conserve significant wild spaces that offer refuge to these species, ensuring that they endure through this unprecedented period of human dominance. Scientists predict that by the year 2100, the human population will begin to decline, becoming more centralized in urban hubs. This offers a glimmer of hope for wild animal populations to recover, for forests and grasslands to regenerate, and for ecosystems to heal. But our wildlife cannot wait that long. What we do now, and in the coming decades, will determine whether species like the jaguar, orangutan, and leatherback turtle make it. Our actions today—protecting critical habitats, curbing destructive practices, and fostering coexistence—are the bridge to their survival and a healthier, more balanced planet for generations to come.

As you close this book, my hope is that the stories have inspired you not just to admire the beauty of these places, but also to take action. Conservation is not the work of a few; it's the responsibility of us all. Whether it's changing your habits, supporting a local initiative, or directly engaging with one of these incredible projects, your contributions matter.

Visit these places if you can. Donate to their causes. Share their stories.

Most importantly, awaken the changemaker within yourself. Every step, no matter how small, ripples outward in ways we can't always see.

The natural world has an extraordinary capacity for healing when given the chance. From the salmon that return to the rivers to the trees that grow taller over centuries, nature teaches us about resilience and regeneration. It is a gift worth fighting for.

Visiting all these magical places and tracking the projects I've been involved with, especially their successes, has proven to me that this isn't a time to give up. There are systems that we can put in place to allow nature the opportunity to show its resilience. In Paul Rosolie's case, he's asking the world one thing: do not cut or burn down the trees. And in his region, those efforts are working. Loggers are being converted to conservationists, locals and Indigenous communities are learning to live more harmoniously with nature, and supporters around the world are coming to the rainforest's defense. I urge you to join them.

These experiences have not only deepened my understanding of conservation but also strengthened my optimism. I see hope in the seedlings planted in Haiti, the wildlife corridors protected in the Congo, and the oceans being protected by Sea Shepherd. Change is possible when we act, and this book is the result of that evolution—a bridge between thought and action, between envisioning change and living it. It's my way of sharing what I've learned, in the hopes that it will ignite the changemaker in you, just as my travels across the globe have ignited the changemaker in me.

Echoes from Eden is my love letter to the forests, the seas, the deserts, and all their inhabitants. Their success is a testament to the power of collective action. Together, we can protect the wild places that remain and the wildlife that inhabits them, ensuring they thrive for generations to come.

With gratitude and hope,
Dax

ACKNOWLEDGMENTS

With appreciation for the individuals and organizations whose efforts have shaped and strengthened this work:

Dr. Jane Goodall, whose legacy and spirit continue to illuminate the path forward in conservation. Your friendship and fierce commitment to protecting the wild are both a gift and a responsibility we carry forward.

Susana Name and Mary Lewis of the Jane Goodall Institute.

Paul Rosolie, Juan Julio Durand, Dina Tsouluhas, and Roy Riquelme of Junglekeepers.

Dr. Kerry Bowman, Dominique Bikaba, and Matt Brunette, for your tireless leadership in the Congo and beyond.

Captain Paul Watson, Lamya Essemlali, and Sea Shepherd captains Alex Cornelissen, Thomas Le Coz, and Peter Hammarstedt.

Régine Chassagne and Dominique Anglade, co-founders of KANPE, for your leadership and commitment to environmental and social renewal in Haiti.

Ann Lee Young of CORE, for your courageous work on the ground.

Re:wild's Dr. Russell Mittermeier (and Mick!), Dr. Wes Sechrest, and Leonardo DiCaprio, for your leadership, vision, and tireless efforts to protect biodiversity around the world.

Suzan Lakhan Baptiste, Kyle Mitchell, Adrian Wilson, and Nature Seekers, for your unwavering commitment to protecting the leatherback turtles of Trinidad.

BC Parks Foundation's Andrew Day, Pitt River Lodge's Daniel and Lee Gerak, and Ian Hamilton, for your ground-level dedication to restoration and protection.

Rick Bailey and the Katzie First Nation, for your stewardship of British Columbia's natural habitats.

Juma Xipaia, Hugo Loss, the Xipaya, and countless other Indigenous leaders and communities around the world who welcomed us and shared their fight: Thank you for your stewardship.

Chanee, for your fearless work in Borneo and unwavering commitment to the Kalaweit sanctuary.

To the filmmakers and conservation storytellers who helped bring this mission to a broader audience: Richard and Anita Ladkani, Soleil Moon Frye, Trevor Frost, Melissa Lesh, and Harry Turner.

To Air Canada, for supporting our travel efforts and for sharing Age of Union's environmental films with audiences onboard their flights.

To our broader creative and operational support team: Mariette Raina, Will Allen, Olivier Jobin, Loïc Romer, Michael Proracki, Sylvain Brochu, Sarah El Gharib, Louis-Etienne Dionne, Daphne Rustow, Cassie Hoffman, Kelly Nunes, Jay Venkateswaran, and Justin Kingsley.

To our trusted allies and strategic advisors at NKPR, led by Natasha Koifman.

To Eric Hendrikx, whose storytelling craft and cultural insight were essential to bringing this book to life with clarity, purpose, and urgency.

To Erich Krauss, Lance Freimuth, Pam Mourouzis, Justin-Aaron Velasco, Susan Lloyd, and the rest of our team at Victory Belt Publishing.

To Tzeporah Berman, Irvyne Lafortune Jean-Baptiste, and Odinave Dominique, for your powerful advocacy and environmental leadership.

And with deep appreciation for our Age of Union collaborators, partners, and supporters: Liane Nowell, Patrick Pichette, Doug Harpur, Denise Foster, Joel Bonin, Julien Poisson, Annie Ferland, and Olivier Perrotte Caron.

Finally, to the next generation of changemakers: May your work surpass ours—and may you always fight for the wild.

AGE OF UNION

PARTNERSHIPS AND PROJECTS

Age of Union is a global conservation alliance supporting grassroots leaders and Indigenous communities to protect Earth's most threatened species and ecosystems. From rainforests to coral reefs, our partners take bold action on the front lines of environmental crisis. *Echoes from Eden* shares their stories. If you're inspired by the work in these pages, we invite you to learn more, talk to others about their missions, and support their efforts. Together, we can protect the wild before it's too late.
www.ageofunion.com
www.youtube.com/@ageofunion

Captain Paul Watson Foundation (Global)

www.paulwatsonfoundation.org

The Captain Paul Watson Foundation leads a bold movement in ocean conservation through a strategy of aggressive nonviolence and direct intervention against illegal activities exploiting marine life. The foundation takes fearless, impactful action to protect the oceans, combining advocacy with hands-on resistance to environmental destruction. As a public charity, it supports education, awareness, and enforcement efforts, carrying forward Captain Paul Watson's legacy of confronting poachers and defending marine ecosystems with unwavering determination.

Forest Health Alliance (D.R. Congo)

www.forestandhealth.org

The Forest Health Alliance is working in the Congo Basin to protect endangered species such as lowland gorillas, chimpanzees, and elephants by establishing a vital wildlife corridor through reforestation and the creation of protected areas. Its efforts include monitoring the critically endangered eastern lowland gorilla, mapping the Itombwe Nature Reserve, and evaluating the region's carbon sink potential using weather stations. The project also supports sustainable agriculture, agroforestry, and alternative livelihoods to reduce deforestation while empowering local communities—particularly the Batwa, with a focus on women—to build climate resilience and protect their environment.

French Creek Estuary (Canada)

www.bcparksfoundation.ca/projects/parks-bank/french-creek-estuary

With the support of Age of Union, BC Parks Foundation and the Regional District of Nanaimo (RDN) jointly acquired 8.4 ha of land from a developer at French Creek in 2022. BCPF then leased our portion of the property to the RDN for long-term management. Combined with the adjacent 0.84-hectare Community Drive Community Park managed by the RDN, the 9.22-hectare French Creek Estuary Nature Preserve (FCENP) was created. Under the lease agreement, the RDN is responsible for managing the FCENP as a nature preserve where the protection of its ecological values takes precedence over recreation.

Juma Institute (Brazil)

www.institutojuma.org

With support from Age of Union, Juma Xipaia's initiative in the Xipaya territory centers on reviving and sharing ancestral knowledge to protect the forest and its wildlife while empowering a new generation of Indigenous leaders. Anchored by the creation of the Juma Institute headquarters in Kaarimã village, the project hosts educational programs, traditional medicine teachings, and cultural events. It fosters collaboration with local communities, nonprofits, universities, and government agencies to preserve cultural heritage and the environment. The initiative also empowers youth and women as environmental advocates and future leaders while strengthening territorial protection through an Indigenous-led ranger program that promotes sustainability, security, and inclusive governance.

Junglekeepers (Peru)

www.junglekeepers.org

Junglekeepers is protecting the Amazon rainforest through a comprehensive land management strategy that integrates community collaboration, technology, and long-term conservation. By securing threatened land concessions from the Peruvian government, expanding its ranger program to include more Indigenous and female rangers, and partnering with local communities along the Las Piedras River, Junglekeepers fosters sustainable practices like reforestation and eco-cooking. The initiative also builds alliances with regional NGOs, trains rangers and remote communities in drone and SMART technology for forest monitoring, and collaborates with universities to support research that informs effective conservation strategies.

Kalaweit (Indonesia)

www.kalaweit.org

Since 2021, Age of Union has committed $1.5 million over four years to its partnership with Kalaweit, aimed at protecting critical habitats and wildlife in Indonesia. The project emphasizes proactive conservation by expanding ranger patrols, establishing water units to fight forest fires—especially during El Niño years—and deploying an ultralight seaplane for aerial surveillance. It also supports reforestation through innovative aerial seeding and works closely with local communities to ensure sustainable, long-term forest protection.

KANPE (Haiti)

www.kanpe.org

Age of Union is supporting a community-driven reforestation and agroforestry initiative in Baille Tourible, Haiti, in partnership with local leadership and the organization KANPE. With a Haitian project director overseeing on-the-ground efforts and a Canadian team securing funding, the project aims to plant over twenty-five thousand fruit and forest seedlings annually for five years to combat soil erosion and desertification. It also promotes sustainable livelihoods through education, agricultural development, and economic empowerment, with a strong focus on women's leadership—recognizing their vital role in building climate resilience and community self-sufficiency.

Kenauk (Canada)

www.kenauk.com

In 2022, Age of Union pledged $3 million over three years to support the Kenauk Institute's mission to protect a vital ecological corridor and expand its research and education initiatives. The funding supports land conservation with the Nature Conservancy of Canada, development of research programs focused on climate change, and construction of a new Research Pavilion to host more projects and summer education programs. Through partnerships with universities and community stakeholders, the goal is to establish the world's largest temperate research forest—preserving the land for future generations while advancing natural science and youth education.

Nature Seekers (Trinidad)

www.natureseekers.org

The project at Matura Beach is dedicated to protecting and recovering the endangered leatherback turtle population through a combination of conservation, research, and community engagement. Key strategies include patrolling nesting sites to increase survival rates, collecting data to monitor turtle health, addressing climate change impacts with adaptive solutions, and implementing recovery strategies to boost hatchling production. The initiative also involves creating artificial hatcheries for vulnerable nests and promoting sustainable community activities—like beach cleanups—that support both local livelihoods and successful nesting conditions.

Pitt River Watershed (Canada)

www.bcparksfoundation.ca/projects/parks-bank/upper-pitt-river

Age of Union donated CA $7 million to the BC Parks Foundation to protect and restore the Pitt River Watershed, a 733-acre territory under intense development pressure. The initiative includes acquiring the land for conservation, conducting biodiversity surveys and monitoring to inform protection strategies, and restoring damaged ecosystems in collaboration with the Katzie First Nation and local stakeholders. Crucially, the project also ensures renewed access for Indigenous communities to engage in traditional practices on this now-protected land.

Re:wild (Madagascar)

www.rewild.org

Beginning in 2025, Age of Union is committing $1 million over five years to support Re:wild's mission to combat deforestation and species extinction in Madagascar. In partnership with local communities and organizations, the project will focus on forest regeneration, keystone species conservation, and fostering sustainable economic growth. The first year will prioritize managing key rainforest sites with partners like Centre ValBio and Madagascar Biodiversity Partnership, initiating the national identification of Key Biodiversity Areas, and launching the Madagascar Biodiversity Action Fund to support targeted species recovery efforts—protecting critically threatened animals such as lemurs, chameleons, tortoises, and small mammals.

Saint Lawrence River (Canada)

www.natureconservancy.ca

The project to preserve the Saint Lawrence River—from Montreal to its estuary—focuses on protecting key natural habitats through approximately thirty-five targeted conservation and restoration initiatives. These efforts include land acquisition for permanent protection, habitat rehabilitation, and managing invasive species. The project also promotes sustainable farming practices, strengthens land stewardship with municipalities and stakeholders, and engages local communities and First Nations to integrate traditional knowledge and raise awareness about the river's ecological importance.

Sea Shepherd (Global)

www.seashepherdglobal.org

The mission of the M/Y *Age of Union* vessel is to protect marine ecosystems and combat illegal, unreported, and unregulated (IUU) fishing through a multifaceted strategy. This includes exposing destructive fishing practices like mass dumping by super trawlers, collaborating with governments—particularly in West Africa—to strengthen enforcement and sustainable marine management, training law enforcement personnel through initiatives such as Women in Maritime Affairs (WIMA), and engaging local communities to support conservation and protect livelihoods dependent on healthy oceans.

ABOUT THE AUTHORS

DAX DASILVA is a visionary entrepreneur and environmental conservationist known for bridging the worlds of technology, activism, and ecological preservation. As the founder and CEO of Lightspeed Commerce Inc., he has built a global commerce and payments company that empowers businesses in over one hundred countries. Beyond the corporate world, Dasilva has dedicated himself to protecting the planet's last wild places through Age of Union Alliance, the nonprofit organization he founded to support high-impact conservation projects around the world.

His passion for environmental action began at sixteen when he joined the historic protests to protect Clayoquot Sound, an experience that shaped his belief in grassroots activism. In 2019, he published *Age of Union*, a call to action for a new era of environmental stewardship. Since then, he has traveled to the front lines of conservation, working with Indigenous leaders, rangers, and activists to defend threatened ecosystems.

Dasilva's commitment extends beyond funding—he believes in storytelling as a catalyst for change. Through Age of Union, he has produced several award-winning documentaries, including *The Corridor*, *CAUGHT*, and *Wildcat*, which won the 2023 Emmy Award for Outstanding Nature Documentary. His films shine a light on those fighting to protect biodiversity, ensuring their work reaches a global audience.

In 2023, Dr. Jane Goodall invited Dasilva to join the Jane Goodall Legacy Foundation's Council for Hope, reinforcing his belief that conservation must be led by the next generation. All proceeds from *Echoes from Eden* will support the Jane Goodall Legacy Foundation (JGLF), established in June 2017 by Dr. Jane Goodall, DBE. The intent of JGLF is to build, invest, and manage an endowment to support programs of the Jane Goodall Institute, including Jane Goodall's Roots & Shoots.

www.DaxDasilva.com

ERIC HENDRIKX is a writer, journalist, and conservationist with a background in anthropology, working at the intersection of culture, adventure, and the natural world. He is a regular contributor to *Men's Journal*, *Rolling Stone*, and *Robb Report*, where he covers environmental impact, unfiltered adventures, and human resilience in places few dare to go.

www.EricHendrikx.com

Also Available from Dax Dasilva

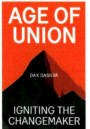

Age of Union is a compelling guide for igniting today's changemaker. Grounded in four pillars—leadership, culture, spirituality, and nature—the book advocates that the time for change is now and that our choices are the catalyst.

Dax Dasilva, a leading tech CEO, arts entrepreneur, and LGBTQ ambassador, shares his experience and presents observations to ignite a movement of unseparation, a united front across all people, cultures, and living things.

Helping entrepreneurs become leaders in their communities through Lightspeed's technology and elevating artists through his work at Never Apart are fundamental to Dasilva's philosophy. He fosters cultures of innovation, promotes diverse leadership, and values different viewpoints.

Here, he presents his model for the new changemaker, for the leader in all of us, to find purpose in collectively contributing to a better tomorrow and give rise to an age of union.